KT-549-545

9030 00001 8441 4

Bulletproof Web Design

Improving flexibility and protecting against worst-case scenarios with XHTML and CSS

Second Edition

Dan Cederholm

New Riders

Bulletproof Web Design: Improving flexibility and protecting against worst-case scenarios with XHTML and CSS, Second Edition
Dan Cederholm

New Riders
1249 Eighth Street
Berkeley, CA 94710
510/524-2178
510/524-2221 (fax)
Find us on the Web at www.newriders.com.
To report errors, please send a note to errata@peachpit.com.

New Riders is an imprint of Peachpit, a division of Pearson Education

Copyright © 2008 by Daniel Cederholm

Editor: Rebecca Gulick
Production Editor: Hilal Sala
Copy Editor: Liz Welch
Technical Reviewers: Ethan Marcotte and Virginia DeBolt
Compositor: David Van Ness
Illustrator: Stephen Dampier
Indexer: FireCrystal Communications
Cover Designers: Mimi Heft, Charlene Will, and Dan Cederholm
Interior Designers: Charlene Will and Maureen Forys

Notice of Rights

All rights reserved. No part of this book may be reproduced or transmitted in any form by any means, electronic, mechanical, photo-copying, recording, or otherwise, without the prior written permission of the publisher. For information on getting permission for reprints and excerpts, contact permissions@peachpit.com.

Notice of Liability

The information in this book is distributed on an "As Is" basis, without warranty. While every precaution has been taken in the prepa-ration of the book, neither the author nor Peachpit shall have any liability to any person or entity with respect to any loss or damage caused or alleged to be caused directly or indirectly by the instructions contained in this book or by the computer software and hard-ware products described in it.

Trademarks

Many of the designations used by manufacturers and sellers to distinguish their products are claimed as trademarks. Where those designations appear in this book, and Peachpit was aware of a trademark claim, the designations appear as requested by the owner of the trademark. All other product names and services identified throughout this book are used in editorial fashion only and for the benefit of such companies with no intention of infringement of the trademark. No such use, or the use of any trade name, is intended to convey endorsement or other affiliation with this book.

ISBN 13: 978-0-321-50902-4
ISBN 10: 0-321-50902-1

9 8 7 6 5 4 3

Printed and bound in the United States of America

LONDON BOROUGH OF WANDSWORTH

9030 00001 8441 4	
Askews & Holts	04-Aug-2011
006.74 CEDE	£28.99
	WWX0008086/0001

For Jack.

ACKNOWLEDGMENTS

To Michael Nolan for connecting me with New Riders as well as helping me solidify the concept of the book early on. Similarly, big thanks also go to Marjorie Baer for her guidance at the beginning of the project.

To Dave Roberts for stealing second.

To everyone at Peachpit who was involved in this book in some way, but especially Rebecca Gulick for steering the entire project, making the entire process as smooth as possible.

To Ethan Marcotte for being an excellent technical editor on the first edition. It was great to work with Ethan on this, and his comments and insight were invaluable. Thanks also to Virginia DeBolt for tech-editing the second edition.

To my colleagues who continue to provide inspiration, sharing their techniques and knowledge, on and off line. This book wouldn't have been written if it weren't for the previous work of the following (as well as many more who I'm forgetting to mention here): John Allsopp, Dan Benjamin, Holly Bergevin, Douglas Bowman, Andy Budd, Tantek Çelik, Joe Clark, Andy Clarke, Mike Davidson, Todd Dominey, Jason Fried, John Gallant, Patrick Griffiths, Jon Hicks, Molly Holzschlag, Shaun Inman, Ryan Irelan, Richard Ishida, Roger Johansson, Jeremy Keith, Ian Lloyd, Drew McLellan, Eric Meyer, Cameron Moll, Matt Mullenweg, Mark Newhouse, Dunstan Orchard, Veerle Pieters, D. Keith Robinson, Richard Rutter, Jason Santa Maria, Christopher Schmitt, Dave Shea, Ryan Sims, Greg Storey, Jeffrey Veen, Josh Williams, and Jeffrey Zeldman.

Special thanks to Jon Hicks for creating the original 3D CSS Box Model Illustration (www.hicksdesign.co.uk/3dboxmodel/), which inspired those found in the book.

To the readers and clients of SimpleBits, you've made it possible for me to work on things I love.

To the Greater Beverly Adult Dodgeball league, for providing a necessary escape every Tuesday evening at 7:30.

To my always amazingly supportive parents, my brother Matt and his family, and the rest of my extended family and friends.

And as always, to my partner in crime, Kerry, for being the rock star wife that she is.

Lastly, thank *you* for reading.

Contents

Introduction

I have a confession to make. There's no such thing as a *completely* bulletproof Web site. Now, before you close the book and put it back up on the shelf (hopefully sticking out a bit further than the others, thanks), allow me to explain.

Just as a police officer straps on a bulletproof vest for protection, so too can we take measures that *protect* our Web designs. This book will guide you through several strategies for bulletproofing Web sites: improving flexibility and preparing for worst-case scenarios.

THE BULLETPROOF CONCEPT

Out in the nonvirtual world, a bulletproof vest never guarantees complete, 100% protection, but rather being bulletproof is something that's constantly strived for. You're far better off wearing a bulletproof vest than if you weren't.

The same rule applies to Web design and the techniques described in this book. By increasing a page's flexibility and taking the necessary steps to ensure that it's readable in as many circumstances as possible, we're making a real difference in our work. It's an ongoing process, and one that becomes easier when utilizing Web standards such as semantic XHTML and CSS to construct compelling, yet adaptable, designs.

As the adoption of CSS-based layouts has steadily risen over the past several years, it's become increasingly important to learn how to utilize CSS *well*. The goal is to harness the benefits that make the technology powerful from a design standpoint: less code, increased accessibility, and easier maintenance, to name a few.

But just using CSS and XHTML doesn't necessarily mean things are automatically better. By embracing the flexibility that can be gained from separating the core content from the design, you'll be well on your way to creating better designs for all the Web's citizens. But what do I mean by *flexibility* exactly?

 **note**

I'm using the term *bulletproof* partly to describe flexibility—in other words, designs for the Web that can easily accommodate various text sizes and amounts of content, designs that expand or contract along with whatever is placed within them.

In addition, we can (and will) talk about flexibility from a editing, maintenance, or development view as well— improving the ease with which content is edited and code updated and maintained, while at the same time not hindering the design. This can be especially helpful and important for *internationalization* issues, where length of content can drastically vary between the various languages of the world.

And last, we'll also talk about flexibility from an environment standpoint. How will designs impact the integrity of a Web site's content and function? We'll make sure that what we create can adapt to a variety of scenarios, be it a Web browser, screen reader, or mobile device. Designing with flexibility in mind means better interpretation by a wider range of devices and software.

WHY IT'S IMPORTANT

Around the time that I began thinking about the topic for this book, I realized that there are two important pieces that make up great, compelling Web designs. One piece is the *visual component*—the piece that's obvious to anyone just looking at the finished page. This is a combination of the graphic design, colors, and typography the designer chose. Just visit the CSS Zen Garden (www.csszengarden.com), and it becomes obvious that compelling visual design is certainly possible and thriving when XHTML and CSS are used.

The second (but equally important) piece to building a great Web site is the *bulletproof implementation*. It's this piece that the book will focus on: you've wisely decided to use XHTML and CSS to build Web sites to reap all of the benefits that come along with them. And now you're ready to leverage those Web standards with some ingenuity to create visually compelling Web sites that are also as flexible, adaptable, and accessible as possible.

As the adoption of Web standards such as XHTML and CSS increases rapidly, it becomes more and more important to have resources that discuss *how* these standards can be utilized and implemented in the most optimal way.

THE BOOK'S STRUCTURE

Each chapter of the book describes a certain *bulletproof guideline*. We'll start by looking at an existing design from the Web, and we'll note why it isn't bulletproof. We'll then rebuild the example using XHTML and CSS, with the goal of improving its flexibility and decreasing its code.

Many of these examples are specific *components* of the page, which makes it easier to talk about how they might be bulletproofed in chunks. In the final chapter, "Putting It All Together," we'll round up all of the techniques from previous chapters to create a full-page template—reminding ourselves along the way why we've chosen the bulletproof techniques, and illustrating how they all can work together in one place.

The step-by-step nature of each chapter's examples should make it easy to follow along—even if you are new to using XHTML and CSS in your daily work. Along the way, I'll explain why these Web standards are beneficial, and specifically how each chapter's guideline can improve a Web site's *bulletproofness*.

THE CONTEXT OF THE BOOK'S EXAMPLES

All of the examples assume a basic page structure that surrounds them. In other words, what is shown in each chapter in terms of XHTML and CSS code happens within an assumed, existing HTML document in between the <body> and </body>.

For instance, the basic framework for the book's examples could be set up like this:

```
<!DOCTYPE html PUBLIC "-//W3C//DTD XHTML 1.0 Transitional//EN"
    "http://www.w3.org/TR/xhtml1/DTD/xhtml1-transitional.
dtd">
<html xmlns="http://www.w3.org/1999/xhtml" lang="en" xml:
lang="en">
<head>
  <title>Page Title</title>
  <meta http-equiv="Content-Type" content="text/html;
charset=utf-8" />
  <style type="text/css">
    ... example CSS goes here ...
  </style>
</head>

<body>
  ... example markup goes here ...
</body>
</html>
```

note

I'm using the XHTML 1.0 Transitional DOCTYPE here, but you could choose any XHTML DOCTYPE flavor you'd like. Wondering what the heck a DOCTYPE is? Not to worry, I'll talk more about them in the "How to validate" section of Chapter 6.

While the CSS is placed in the <head> of the page for convenience, it should eventually be hidden from old, tired browsers (Netscape Navigator 4.*x*, for example). This hiding is quite common, enabling designers to use advanced CSS for layout (as we do throughout the book), while offering older browsers that can't handle it a fully readable, CSS-free view of the document.

Hiding CSS from older browsers is commonly done by using the @import method for referencing external style sheets. For example, if we placed all of our styles into a file named screen.css, we could use the @import method to reference that external style sheet by its URL. Because older browsers (like Netscape 4.*x*) don't understand @import, the styles contained within screen. css will be hidden to them.

```
<head>
  <title>Page Title</title>
  <meta http-equiv="Content-Type" content="text/html;
charset=utf-8" />
  <style type="text/css">
    @import url("screen.css");
  </style>
</head>
```

COMMON TERMS USED THROUGHOUT THE BOOK

There are times throughout the book that I'll refer to various browser versions by their abbreviations. For instance, it's much easier to say IE5/Win than "Internet Explorer version 5 for Windows." That said, here's a little list of the shorthand browser version/platform conventions:

- IE5/Win = Internet Explorer version 5.0 and 5.5 for Windows

- IE6/Win = Internet Explorer version 6 for Windows

- IE7/Win = Internet Explorer version 7 for Windows

- IE5/Mac = Internet Explorer version 5 for Macintosh

When describing the common approaches found in the examples used for each chapter, I often refer to *nested tables* and *spacer GIF shims*. This describes the traditional techniques often used to build Web sites, in which tables are used to create pixel-perfect but inflexible beasts. Nesting tables inside one another made it easier to precisely align graphics and text, yet the result was a gigantic amount of code with accessibility problems galore.

The term *spacer GIF shim* refers to the use of a single transparent GIF image that's stretched to various dimensions in order to create gaps, columns, and divisions throughout a page. An *unbulletproof* Web site will have these littered throughout its markup, adding code and creating a maintenance nightmare.

But there are better ways of accomplishing the same visual goal using lean, meaningful markup and CSS. By embracing these Web standards, we can still create compelling designs that at the same time are flexible and ready for whatever situation is thrown at them. This is *Bulletproof Web Design*.

1

Flexible Text

Size text using keywords and percentages or ems to allow user control and maximum flexibility.

Few Web design topics are as storied and controversial as sizing text for the Web. Historically, it's been known to confuse beginners, fuel arguments, and divide nations. Well, perhaps that's exaggerating things a bit, but it truly can be a sticky subject for many.

While I'm in no position to rid the world of its war on text sizing, in this chapter I share two strategies for sizing text on the Web that are both flexible and easy to implement—and at the same time allow you to maintain as much design control as possible.

The allowance for flexibility in sizing text is one of the keys that drive the rest of the examples in this book—that by giving the *user* the ability to control the size of text on the page, we're increasing its readability for all the Web's citizens. The real challenge lies in enabling that flexibility, while still having the ingenuity to craft interesting design around it. And by the end of this book, you'll be well on your way to meeting that challenge, with a solid foundation of examples to guide you.

To understand how best to be flexible when sizing text, let's first look at a common example and why it's not flexible.

A Common Approach

To illustrate a common method for text sizing, let's take a look at eyeglasses.
com—surely its sight-impaired visitors would benefit from a Web site that
values readability and user control (Figure 1.1).

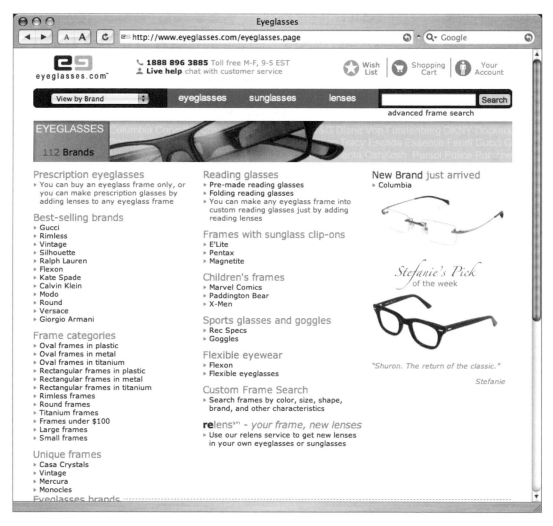

Figure 1.1 To demonstrate a common method for text sizing, we'll use the
Web site eyeglasses.com (shown here as it appeared in December 2004).

note 📖

It's important to point out that I'm not scorning the designers of eyeglasses.com. In fact, it's a very nicely designed site, built with structured markup and CSS for its design—precisely why I've chosen it. Bravo for that. I'm just in need of an excuse to talk about text sizing and the pros and cons associated with the most common method of all.

Eyeglasses.com makes good use of CSS for all of its design details and, like scores of other nicely designed sites on the Web, it uses the `font-size` property on the <body> element to declare a base size for the entire page in pixel units:

```
body {
    font-size: 11px;
}
```

By setting a size (11px in this case) for text on the <body> element, the designers ensure that the entire page (unless overridden by a subsequent rule) will display text at 11 pixels. The upside to using pixel units is that they stand the best chance of looking the same in size, regardless of what browser or device is reading the text. It's because of this consistent, predictable size that using pixel units has become a rather popular choice for designers. Those who desire pixel-perfect precision over the size at which type appears on a Web page choose pixel units over all other options. There is, however, one little problem.

WHY IT'S NOT BULLETPROOF

Sizing text with pixels gives the designer control over the size of type, yet poses a problem for users of the most popular Web browser out there (at the time of this writing): Internet Explorer for Windows (IE/Win).

Browsers typically provide the user with a means to control the size of text on the page, overriding the size that is specified by the designer. This is great, and extremely useful for someone who is visually impaired. To increase readability, a user with poor vision can choose a larger font size via a browser menu (Figure 1.2).

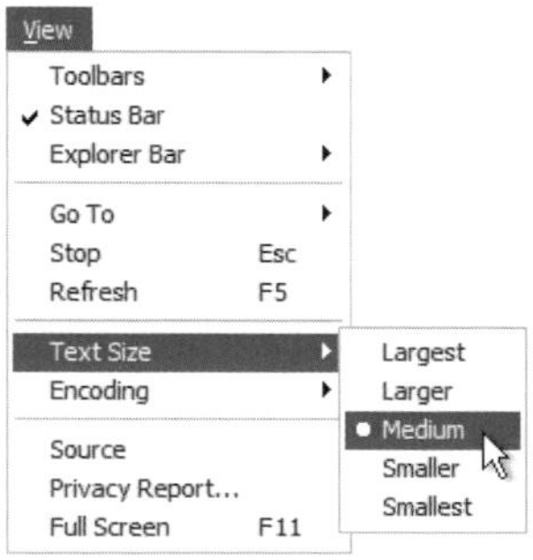

Figure 1.2 The Text Size menu in IE6/Win allows the user to adjust the size of text on the page in either direction.

Sounds perfect, doesn't it? But there's a catch. Internet Explorer users on Windows won't be able to override the size of text specified by the designer when pixel units are used. So while using pixel units gives the designer the greatest precision in determining font size, it also eliminates the possibility for IE/Win users to adjust that size if they so desire. Ouch. Users of other browsers can safely adjust font size no matter how the fonts are specified.

Internet Explorer 7 *does* introduce a new page zoom feature (Figure 1.3) that will magnify the entire page (not just the text). Clicking Ctrl+ (plus sign) or Ctrl– (minus sign) or the icon in the bottom of the browser window will scale the whole layout. The downside to zooming the full page, rather than just the text, is the probability that horizontal and vertical scrollbars will be necessary to fully view a zoomed-in page.

The ability to adjust text size is *essential* for people with poor vision, and those users who want to increase readability on Web pages that feature small text by default appreciate the option. As designers, it's our nature to want complete control over the appearance of an entire Web page. But in giving up just a *smidgeon* of that control related to text sizing, we're improving the experience and accessibility for everyone.

As for IE/Win's reluctance to resize text set with pixel units, perhaps the developers stuck to the idea that a pixel is a pixel—an infallible unit that should never change, even if users wish to supersede (which they should have every right to do). Regardless, all other browsers got it right, allowing text sized with pixel units to be overridden by user-defined controls.

Life would be simple if designers could choose to declare a font size in pixels and users could adjust however they wished, but because of the inability to scale that text in IE/Win, that's not optimal. So let's explore alternate methods for sizing text. Eventually, we'll settle on a strategy where we give up that exact precision that using pixel units offers but gain the important advantage of scalability in all browsers.

Weighing Our Options

In addition to pixel units, there are several other ways of sizing text using CSS, so let's take a look at our options next.

The possible values for the font-size property in CSS are broken down into four groups.

Figure 1.3 Internet Explorer 7 has introduced a zoom selection tool.

 **note**

Technically, a pixel is a relative unit of measurement, relative to the resolution of the device that is displaying or printing it. For example, a pixel's actual size differs depending on whether it's being displayed on a small computer screen or printed on a page with other elements. (For more on this, check out www.w3.org/TR/REC-CSS2/syndata.html#pixel-units.)

LENGTH UNITS

Length units can be either *relative* or *absolute* values. The following are relative-length units:

- em: relative to the font size of the parent element
- ex: relative to the height of the letter *x* of the specified font
- px: relative to the resolution of the device; the most common unit

Absolute-length units are primarily useful only for print or when the physical dimensions and properties of the browser and/or device are known:

- in: inches
- cm: centimeters
- mm: millimeters
- pt: points
- pc: picas

RELATIVE-SIZE KEYWORDS

Only two values are possible when using relative-size keywords:

- larger
- smaller

These values are relative to the current size of the parent element. The World Wide Web Consortium (W3C), an organization that sets Web standards, explains that, for example, if the parent element is set with a font size of medium, using the keyword larger will increase the current element's font size to large. (For more on this, check out www.w3.org/TR/CSS21/fonts. html#font-size-props.)

Think of these values in the same way you would the old-school <small> and <big> elements in HTML. They are essentially guidelines for size, taking into account sizes that may already be determined higher up the document tree.

PERCENTAGES

Using a percentage assigns a size that is relative to its containing (or parent) element. Specifying a setting of 120% would add 20% to whatever unit was previously specified (if any). I cover percentages (combining them with key-words) as part of our bulletproof approach that follows.

ABSOLUTE-SIZE KEYWORDS

Absolute-size keywords refer to a table of font sizes determined by the browser or device. The seven possible values are:

- `xx-small`
- `x-small`
- `small`
- `medium`
- `large`
- `x-large`
- `xx-large`

The W3C suggests to browser manufacturers a 1.5 scaling factor between each keyword, and recommends that scale remains constant no matter what physical size the text renders in. In English, that means `large` is one and a half times larger than `medium`, and similarly, `small` is one and a half times smaller than `medium`.

Their simple syntax is just one of the advantages of absolute-size keywords, which I cover more extensively in the next section of this chapter.

Now that we have a complete picture of all the possible values for the `font-size` property, we can move on and discuss a strategy that provides a flexible base for users and enables them to control text size.

A Bulletproof Approach

I'm going to share a strategy that's been successful for me in my own projects, combining absolute-size keywords with percentages. Using keyword values for the `font-size` property solves the problem I exposed earlier with eye-glasses.com (and millions of other sites). Unlike with pixels, users' browsers will be able to adjust the size of text on the page, regardless of what browser or device they are using. Let's take a look at how keywords work.

KEYWORDS EXPLAINED

As outlined earlier, we can choose from seven possible values when using keywords: xx-small, x-small, small, medium, large, x-large, and xx-large. Here's how one value would be used in a declaration for assigning the size of text on the <body> element:

```
body {
  font-size: small;
  }
```

The keyword sets the size of text in relation to the browser's current setting. In other words, if the user has adjusted his or her browser to display text larger or smaller than the default, then the keywords scale in relation to that base size. The scaling factor between each keyword value remains constant, no matter how large or small the base is.

For example, Figure 1.4 illustrates each keyword value, with a different scale depending on the browser's default text size. I'm using the Safari browser here to demonstrate.

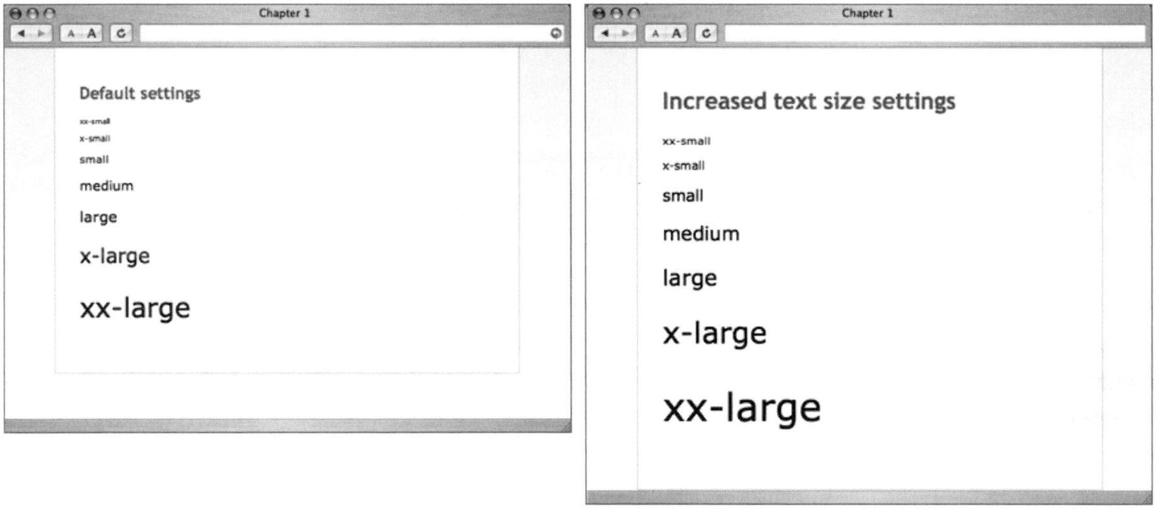

Figure 1.4 Here's a comparison of the keyword scale in Safari. The base text size has been bumped up a few notches on the right.

You'll notice that, while small will appear a different size depending on the base, the difference between the small value and the next size up or down remains a consistent scale.

LETTING GO OF "PIXEL PRECISION"

The largest obstacle to overcome for any designer using keywords (or any font size unit other than px) is that, depending on the browser, operating system, and settings, the same value may look slightly different when compared side by side.

For instance, the value small that I've just illustrated may look slightly different in size when compared in different browsers and/or operating systems, even if all are set at a default medium setting.

Whereas "a pixel is a pixel" could be assumed Web law, a keyword is more of a *guideline* for how large or small the browser or device should display text. If you can come to terms with a slight variation and embrace the flexibility that's gained when using keywords, then your designs (and users) will benefit.

TWO HURDLES TO JUMP OVER

Later on, I share some strategies for dealing with the slight variations in the way keyword values are displayed between browsers. First, though, I need to address two major discrepancies in the way Netscape 4 and IE5 for Windows handle those variations.

Netscape 4

Even at default medium settings, Netscape 4 has the unfortunate tendency to display text at the small end of the spectrum, too small to be legible on screen. Because of the danger of delivering unreadable text, it's better not to use keywords when using CSS to size text for Netscape 4. (For more on why, check out www.alistapart.com/articles/sizematters.) We're not going to worry too much about Netscape 4, however, since (like with all the examples provided in this book) we'll be hiding all styles from this ancient browser. One hurdle down.

IE5 Windows

The second hurdle is a little more complicated, because it's perhaps too premature to hide styles completely from IE5/Win—a browser whose user base is dwindling rapidly, yet still may be a necessary target depending on your particular site's statistics or project requirements. The discrepancy in IE5/Win is a bit more of an obvious mistake on the part of the browser's developers.

For reasons only known to Microsoft, IE5/Win displays keywords one full step larger than what other standards-compliant browsers display. For instance, if at default browser settings we declared

```
body {
  font-size: small;
  }
```

in IE5/Win, text would display at medium instead. Not good, and not what we intend. Figure 1.5 shows the difference between IE5 and IE6 using the small keyword.

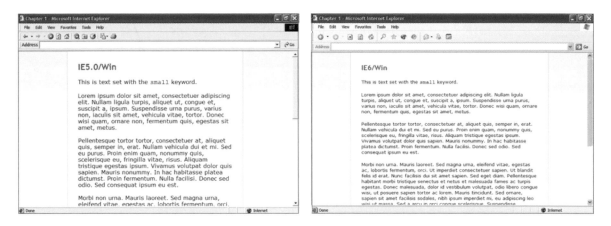

Figure 1.5 This comparison shows how the small keyword is rendered a step larger in IE5/Win than it is in IE6/Win (and other compliant browsers).

To skirt around this issue, and to get all browsers and devices on the same page in terms of a similar size, we'll take advantage of a CSS hack that enables us to declare separate rules for IE5/Win and other browsers. We'll be able to assign a keyword value specifically for IE5/Win that is one step below what we'll assign for everyone else. Consistency awaits.

The IE5/Win hack

In order to assign a font size in IE5/Win that is one step below our intended size, we use the famous Box Model Hack developed by Tantek Çelik (www. tantek.com/CSS/Examples/boxmodelhack.html), which tricks IE5/Win into thinking a CSS declaration has ended. Thanks to this mystical voodoo, we can assign a smaller value for IE5/Win first, and then override it with our intended size for compliant browsers.

The CSS that's necessary for declaring an intended size of small for the contents of the <body> element goes something like this:

```
body {
  font-size: x-small; /* for IE5/Win */
  voice-family: "\"}\"";
  voice-family: inherit;
  font-size: small; /* for compliant browsers */
  }
html>body { /* be nice to Opera */
  font-size: small;
  }
```

You'll notice that we're intending to set a base font-size using the keyword value small, yet we're declaring a step below our intended value for IE5/Win, which we then trick into thinking that the declaration has ended with this rule:

```
voice-family: "\"}\"";
```

Only IE5/Win recognizes this closing bracket, and it thinks that the declaration has ended. For all other compliant browsers, we override x-small with small. In turn, we'll now have a relatively consistent base text size to work from.

You'll also notice a second declaration in the preceding example, with a duplicate rule assigning font-size: small. This rule is referred to as the "be nice to Opera" rule, which prevents the Opera browser (and others) from potentially ignoring the rule that follows the hack. Whenever the Box Model Hack is used, this declaration should follow it; it essentially ensures that all compliant browsers are caught up and ready to go on to the next declaration in the style sheet.

THE SIMPLIFIED BOX MODEL HACK

Developed by Edwardson Tan, the Simplified Box Model Hack (or SBMH) achieves the same result (the ability to serve IE5/Win and all other browsers differing values) with a bit less code and perhaps an easier-to-understand syntax.

tips

For more on using keywords and the aforementioned workarounds, check out a detailed article by Todd Fahrner at *A List Apart* magazine (www.alistapart.com/articles/sizematters/).

If you don't mind text displaying a step larger in IE5/Win, then by all means skip this hurdle altogether. Don't jump over it—just sort of run around it, or knock it down, or something.

Using the SBMH this time, our previous example would look like this:

```
body {
  font-size: small;
}
* html body {
  font-size: x-small; /* for IE5/Win */
  f\ont-size: small; /* for other IE versions */
}
```

We start with a normal declaration for the <body> element, with our intended value small. Next, using the * html selector exploits a bug in IE, enabling us to serve the declaration to IE browsers only. IE5/Win ignores the backslash in the font-size property, so we're free to set x-small for IE5/Win and then override with small for other versions of IE.

We're accomplishing the same goal as we did with the original Box Model Hack, but this simplified syntax can sometimes be easier to grasp for those just learning the fix. (For more on SBMH, check out www.info.com.ph/~etan/w3pantheon/style/modifiedsbmh.html.)

You may be thinking that utilizing the Box Model Hack or SBMH is a bit messy, and a lot of trouble to go to just to correct a text-sizing issue. But if it's relative consistency you want, you have to pay the price.

Methods are available for strategically collecting all CSS hacks and workarounds and keeping them separate from your clean, compliant style sheets—and we'll be going over a few of those concepts in Chapter 9, "Putting It All Together."

Why It's Bulletproof

With the hurdles behind us, we're now left with a bulletproof base text size. Instead of declaring font-size in px, as eyeglasses.com and millions of other sites have done, we're using the keyword value small on the <body> element to set the default for the page. By using a keyword, we're ensuring that all browsers and devices (including IE/Win) will be able to override that value, if they so desire.

For people with poor vision, this is *essential*—and not just for people who are shopping for new eyeglasses, but also for those searching for recipes, purchasing goods online, reading an article, or any other task that's available on the Web. Although this small adjustment will be almost transparent to the everyday user, it will be a large improvement for those now able to take advantage of it.

A Flexible Base. Now What?

Thus far, we've explored how to set a single font-size for the entire page. Naturally, we'll want certain design elements to reflect *various* sizes throughout—headings, lists, subtitles, navigation, tables—each potentially having a different size than the default. But what is the best way to handle declaring additional sizes, whether smaller or larger than our base?

I'm recommending a method that's been successful for me, one that I believe is easy to grasp and that makes it easy to modify, add, or edit sizes throughout the life cycle of a Web site.

SET IT AND FORGET IT

The only absolute-size keyword value we'll set in the entire style sheet is the base on the <body> element, as we've been discussing throughout the chapter:

```
body {
    font-size: small;
    }
```

You'll notice that it's a close match (Figure 1.6). This will obviously vary slightly from browser to browser, and depends on how that software chose to render each keyword. But in general, using small as a base size is a bit like setting text at 12px (provided the user hasn't changed settings). Sometimes this helps designers get a handle on where to begin with keyword values.

Figure 1.6 Here's a comparison of text sized with the small keyword versus 12px. The result, at default medium settings, is very similar.

 **note**

To get things looking consistent, you may also opt to add the Box Model Hack for IE5/Win, discussed earlier.

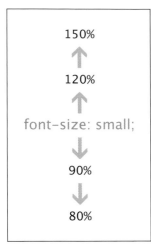

Figure 1.7 Percentages can work in either direction from a base keyword.

USE PERCENTAGES TO STRAY FROM THE BASE

From this base of small, we'll use percentages to modify the size in either direction. Using a percentage is a simple way of visualizing what size type you'd like a certain element to be. Figure 1.7 illustrates how a percentage could increase or decrease the font size from a base keyword.

For instance, if we wanted all <h1> elements to be quite a bit larger than the default size of small, we'd simply declare it:

```
body {
    font-size: small;
    }
h1 {
    font-size: 150%;
    }
```

Since <h1> elements are always contained within the <body> element, we can be sure that the size will be 150% of small (Figure 1.8).

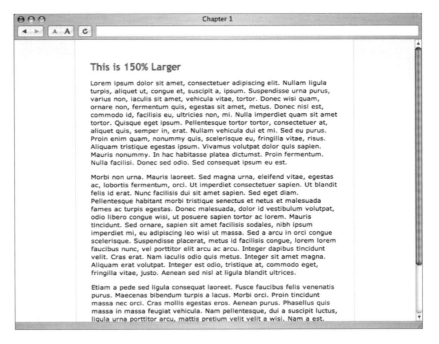

Figure 1.8 The <h1> element is set at 150% of the base keyword small.

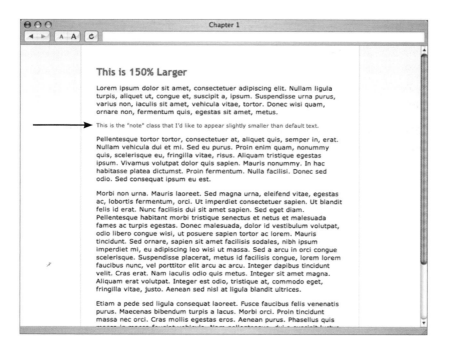

Figure 1.9 The note class is set at 85% of the base keyword small (and gray in color).

Similarly, you may also want to make certain paragraphs of text smaller than the default, in this case, smaller than small. In Figure 1.9, I've created a note class and attached it to a short paragraph:

```
<p class="note">This is the "note" class that I'd like to
appear slightly smaller than default text.</p>
```

I intend to set this paragraph slightly smaller in size to the default, so I'll add a declaration that uses a percentage below 100 to bring it down:

```
.note {
  font-size: 85%;
  }
```

You can begin to see that we could assign percentages for any element we'd like throughout the page, whether it be smaller or larger than the base we've set for the <body>.

For example, a simplified style sheet where certain elements are sized with percentages might look something like this:

```
body {
  font-size: small;
  }
h1 {
  font-size: 150%;
  }
h2 {
  font-size: 130%;
  }
h3 {
  font-size: 120%;
  }
ul li {
  font-size: 90%;
  }
.note {
  font-size: 85%;
  }
```

We have declared descending values for three levels of headings, made unordered list items slightly smaller, and included a note class that we could assign to any element we'd like to be smaller than the default. This is a rudimentary example, but should illustrate the two-step concept: **set a base keyword**, and then **use a percentage to increase or decrease other elements**. Change your base, and the rest will follow.

A nice advantage to using the base-plus-percentage model is that, should you decide to change the default, you need only change the single declaration on the <body> element. Everything else that's been assigned a percentage is working off that top-level element's size, so changing from small to large will, in turn, affect other elements proportionally. That can certainly come in handy, even if you decide at some point that you'd rather specify a base size using an alternate unit.

For that same reason, it makes it easy for those users who like to create their own user style sheets that override the site's defaults. A single rule that modifies your base size will in turn affect the entire page, proportionally.

Working with Keywords and Percentages

To better harness the advantages of working with keywords in combination with percentages, you should keep a few things in mind. The following should help with the adjusting of percentages, and I mention a caveat regarding the results from nesting percentages.

SETTING AN IN-BETWEEN KEYWORD BASE

One useful trick when setting your base text size is to adjust the keyword value slightly using an all-encompassing <div>. Often when building CSS-based layouts, we may use a containing <div>for various design-related reasons (see Chapter 8, "Fluid & Elastic Layouts"), but you can also take advantage of that element to set a percentage on the base keyword that will affect the entire page.

For example, let's imagine that you were working with a markup structure like this:

```
<body>
<div id="container">
  <h1>This is a Title</h1>
  <p>This is body text at default base size.</p>
</div>
</body>
```

We could set a base keyword value, as we have done previously in this chapter, as well as a larger percentage for <h1> elements:

```
body {
  font-size: small;
  }
h1 {
  font-size: 150%;
  }
```

But if we thought that the value small was a little large for our liking (when viewed with default browser settings), we could knock it down a bit by using a percentage on the #container that also encompasses every bit of text on the page:

```
body {
  font-size: small;
  }
h1 {
  font-size: 150%;
  }
#container {
  font-size: 95%;
  }
```

As Figure 1.10 illustrates, we've shaved a slight amount of size off the default, which affects the size of the page title as well.

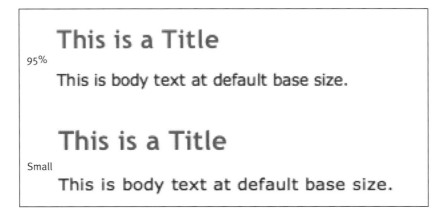

Figure 1.10 Here's a comparison of using the base keyword small versus shaving off a bit of that base by setting a container to 95%.

On the top, we've added the rule to render font-size of the #container at 95%, while on the bottom we see the page rendered using just the keyword value small. The difference here is very slight.

It's a useful way to give yourself a bit more precision in sizing text when your goal is something *in between* two keyword values. Using an existing <div> that wraps the rest of the page, you can go up or down from the keyword, creating a custom base size.

It's best not to get too caught up in extreme detail here, however, because slight variation is always a possibility among different browser-platform combinations. The important thing is that users will still have control over the size using their built-in browser controls.

BE CAREFUL WHEN NESTING PERCENTAGES

You have to be cautious when nesting percentages, as with the previous example where we set a base keyword of small for the entire page and then knocked that down to 95% of small using the container <div>. When you set a percentage on elements inside #container, things can get a little confusing.

For example, earlier we declared that all <h1> elements should be set at 150%. And since <h1> elements are lower in the document tree—inside and beneath #container in the cascade—then what we're really saying is not 150% of the initial small value, but rather 150% of 95% of small. Figure 1.11 illustrates how the nesting of elements in the document tree relates to the percentage values as well.

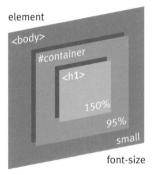

Figure 1.11 Here's how percentages are calculated along with their elements when nested.

Confused? Perhaps replacing the small keyword with a numerical value will help.

If our base on the <body> element equaled the number 10 (rather than small), then anything inside #container would equal 9.5 (or 95% of 10). <h1> headings live inside #container, and we've assigned a font-size of 150% for those elements. Now, 150% of our original base of 10 would equal 15, but since <h1>'s parent element is #container, the math would instead be as follows: 150% of 9.5 equals 14.25. This gets increasingly more complex the more levels down you choose to nest percentages. Confusing math aside, the moral of the story here is to be aware of any parent percentages that are already assigned when declaring new ones. Personally, I rarely nest more than a level or two when building a page, but understanding how the cascade affects percentages can avoid confusion when sizes aren't looking quite the way you thought they would.

> ✓ **tip**

An additional caveat when nesting percentages below 100%: Should the user decrease text size using the browser's controls, there is a danger of text becoming so small that it's illegible.

In other words, if you're designing with default settings in mind and have used a percentage that makes text very small but still readable at a medium browser setting, it's possible it will become unreadable when the user chooses a smaller-than-medium setting.

Test in a variety of browser and text-size scenarios to be sure text is always readable, regardless of the keyword-percentage combo that you might specify. This is good advice no matter what method you use to size text.

Also worth a visit is a comprehensive test of various browser, platform, and font-sizing methods from Owen Briggs (www.thenoodleincident.com/tutorials/box_lesson/font/method.html). Owen took 264 screen shots to reproduce varying test scenarios, making the results comparable from a single source (Figure 1.12).

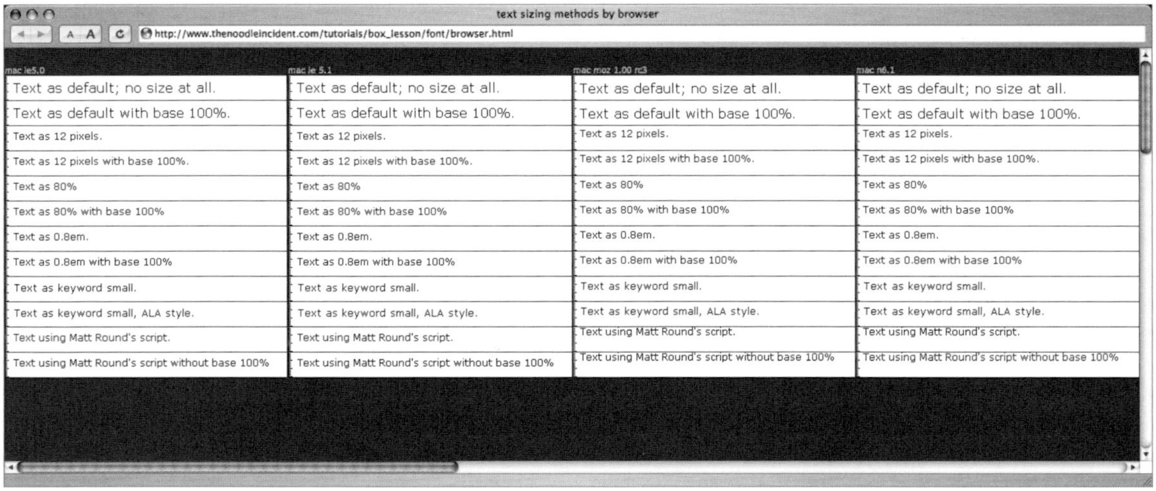

Figure 1.12 Owen Briggs's tests on text sizing are a valuable resource, featuring 264 screen shots of almost every combination possible.

EXPERIMENT WITH PERCENTAGE VALUES FOR CONSISTENCY

Experimenting with percentage values can lead to more consistent sizing across various browsers and platforms. Assuming users are viewing the page with default browser text size settings (all bets are off should they increase or decrease from the default), it's useful to experiment when assigning percentage values—especially those at small sizes.

If we use the previously mentioned note class as an example, we can compare setting the font-size for the class at both 85% and 90%. Some browsers will only recognize percentages in powers of 10 (70, 80, 90, etc.), whereas others recognize more specific values ending in 5 (75, 85, 95, etc.).

For example, in Figures 1.13 and 1.14, we can see Safari on the left and IE6/Win on the right. There is no noticeable difference between 85% (top) and 90% (bottom) in IE6/Win, yet there is a small increase on the Safari side between the two values. For this particular case, I'd most likely opt to use 90%, where the sizing between the two popular browsers is more closely matched.

I'm splitting hairs here, but I encourage you to experiment when assigning various font-size percentages. A change of 5% can mean that little extra difference across browsers and may lead you to consistency.

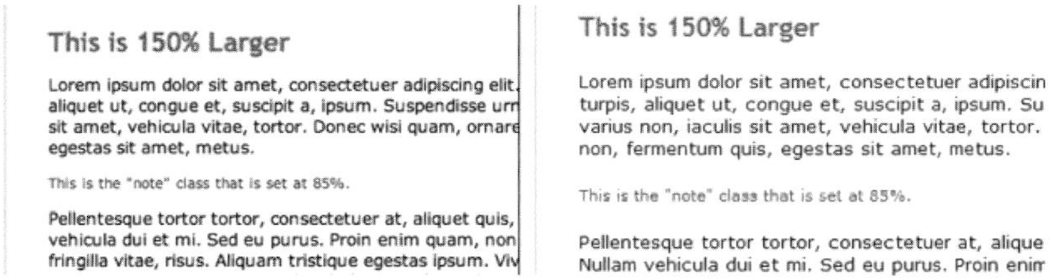

Figure 1.13 This shows the note class compared in Safari and IE6/Win at 85%.

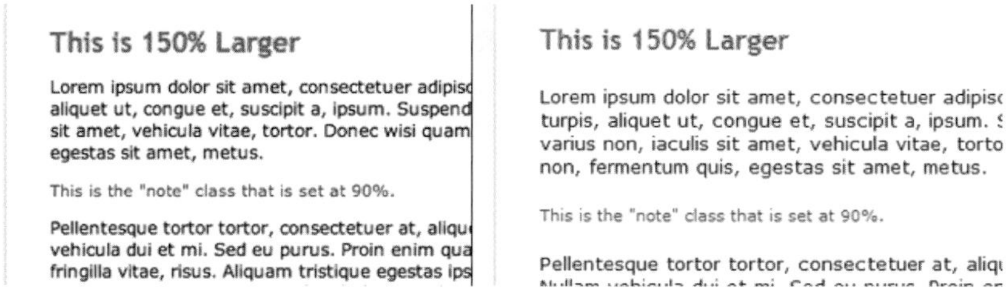

Figure 1.14 Here the note class is compared in Safari and IE6/Win at 90%.

Flexible Text Using Ems

An alternative to keywords—sizing text using em units—offers the same advantage for IE/Win that keywords do: it allows users to resize text. While ems are also relative units, they also offer a bit more precision and control, and when working from a consistent default base size, they can offer familiarity to designers who are used to thinking in pixels.

Let's reacquaint ourselves with what *em* actually means. Robert Bringhurst, author of the highly recommended bible on typography, *The Elements of Typographic Style*, writes:

> The em is a sliding measure. One em is a distance equal to the type size. In 6 point type, an em is 6 points; in 12 point type an em is 12 points and in 60 point type an em is 60 points. Thus a one em space is proportionately the same in any size.

Applying that to the Web world, if the current `font-size` is the default `medium` setting (16px in most browsers), 1em would equal 16px. If the default is set smaller at 11px, 1em would equal 11px. The advantage to using ems for font size, line height, and spacing between elements is that as text size is adjusted, those measurements will adjust *proportionately*.

Richard Rutter explains a crafty method for normalizing a base font size using ems (`http://clagnut.com/blog/348/`), where the units match (more or less) to pixel equivalents. The technique assumes a default browser text size set at `medium`, which is most often 16px.

Richard's method begins by knocking down the base `font-size` of the page to 62.5% on the <body> element:

```
body { font-size: 62.5%; }
```

This magic percentage essentially takes the default medium text down from 16px to 10px. The reasoning, Richard explains, is that having a base of 10px means you'll have a nice round number to deal with and you can *think* in pixels while actually setting type in ems.

For example, after you apply 62.5% to the <body>, 1em would appear as 10px, 1.2em as 12px, .9em as 9px, 1.8em as 18px, and so on. If we were specifying different values for various elements on the page, we might do something like this:

```
body { font-size: 62.5% } /* gives us a base of 10px */
h1 { font-size: 2em; } /* 20px */
h2 { font-size: 1.8em; } /* 18px */
p { font-size: 1.2em; } /* 12px */
#sidebar { font-size: 1em; } /* 10px */
```

For designers who are used to setting type in pixels yet want to allow all users the ability to resize the text, using this em-based method can be rather handy. Like the keyword/percentage model shown earlier in this chapter, ems can get a bit tricky when nesting occurs (particular when the nesting is more than one level).

Let's say, for instance, that we wanted all <abbr> elements within paragraphs to be 24px instead of the 12px we're specifying:

```
p abbr  { font-size: 2.4em; }
```

This code would render <abbr> elements that appear within a paragraph at 28.8px (since <abbr> is a child of <p> and we're essentially saying 2.4 times the parent's size, which in this case is 12px). <abbr> elements within paragraphs inherit the paragraph's font-size as a base. To adjust for that, we follow a simple formula from Richard's article:

```
child pixels ÷ parent pixels = child ems
```

This means that, for our example of 24px as the goal and 12px as the parent base of the paragraph, the formula is as follows:

24 ÷ 12 = 2

So to achieve <abbr> elements within paragraphs that render at 24px, we'd do the following:

```
p {font-size: 1.2em; } /* 12px */
p abbr { font-size: 2em; } /* 24px */
```

You can see the math isn't terribly baffling when we're nesting one-level deep, but things do get a bit more confusing when going any further beyond that. Under most circumstances, nesting is kept to a level of one or two, and the math required to keep a firm grasp on things is often manageable—but keep in mind the added complexity when choosing em-based or keyword/percentage methods if you foresee a lot of font sizing within *deeply* nested elements.

Summary

If there's one thing you should take away from this chapter, it's the importance of **allowing the user to control the size of text on any given page**. I've shared strategies that have been successful for me, using keywords and percentages, as well as an alternative method using ems. But every Web site is different; each has its own requirements and circumstances. Ideally, you can enable that flexibility in your own projects as well.

Here are some important points to remember:

- IE/Win users cannot resize text set with pixels.

- Keywords offer a simple, easy-to-grasp method of sizing text that permits user resizing.

- Percentages can make future updates or user-defined style sheets a quick and easy way to modify an entire site's text size with one CSS rule.

- Using the keyword/percentage combination can still allow a certain level of precision when targeted at default browser settings.

- Using Richard Rutter's em-based approach can offer a smoother transition from pixels to relative sizing.

- Deep nesting of elements requires a little math (or even a lot) in order to keep things consistent.

And here's some good news: this initial chapter is probably the least interesting of the entire book but very necessary in order to set a solid—no, *flexible*—foundation for the examples that follow. What we'll be able to do next is assume that the user can scale the size of text on the page any way he or she desires. With that knowledge in hand, we'll get creative with CSS, rebuilding traditional design components with flexibility in mind. And off we go.

2

Scalable Navigation

Provide site navigation that scales to any text size or content amount.

The navigation of a Web site can often be the anchor for its design. It's a page component that is as central and important as any. Traditionally, a Web designer might crack open a favorite image editor and lovingly craft some buttons, tabs, or text to be stuffed inside a few nested `<table>` elements. Additionally, JavaScript might be used to trigger rollover effects that swap a second set of images. In the end, the result might look great—but what lurks beneath the surface may not be so desirable, as we'll see by investigating a common approach to building Web site navigation.

Let's take a close look at an example based on the traditional approach to designing stylish, image-based tabs. After we analyze the shortcomings of this particular method, we then wipe the slate clean and construct a similar—but bulletproof—design using lean, valid markup; three tiny images; and CSS.

A Common Approach

I've decided to use the main navigation tabs found at LanceArmstrong.com as an example for two reasons (Figure 2.1). First of all, I'm a fan of Lance Armstrong, but more important, the design lends itself to being rebuilt using CSS in a way that will improve its flexibility. The goal here is to use CSS in a creative way that eliminates large chunks of code and results in a site that is easily maintained and scales gracefully.

Let's zoom in and examine the design elements involved in creating the tabs.

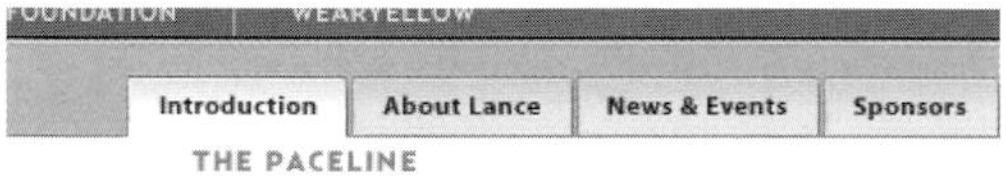

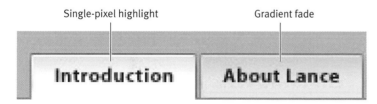

Figure 2.1 The nicely designed tab navigation of LanceArmstrong.com illustrates the selected and unselected states each tab may be in.

STRONG TABS

There's a subtle detail in these tabs that make them a bit more interesting than just the average border-and-background variety. For each on and off state, the tab itself has a light gradient that repeats at the top of the tab, horizontally, and fades vertically into a solid background color: white for the on state and light yellow for the off state. A single-pixel highlight at the top of the tab that is lighter in shade than the rest adds a slight dimension, as if the light source were coming from the top of the page, down (Figure 2.2).

Single-pixel highlight   Gradient fade

Introduction   **About Lance**

Figure 2.2 This is a close-up of the design details for each tab state. Notice a subtle highlight at the top of each tab, with the gradient fade used to simulate dimension and light.

Before we go any further, I'd like to point out that the tabs look, well, cool. Given that good design is subjective (you may have a different opinion), we should be able to at least agree that someone spent a good amount of time making the navigation for LanceArmstrong.com attractive and functional. Mission accomplished—and that's why I selected this example.

On LanceArmstrong.com, each tab set is a single image, with selected and unselected states, depending on what page you are viewing. This image also includes the site's logo. Figure 2.3 shows one of the four possible images, viewed all by itself.

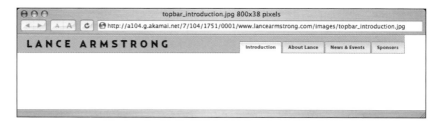

Figure 2.3 The entire tab set and logo are contained within a single, large image. The site includes at least three others like this one, highlighting each section.

COMMON ROLLOVERS

The navigation for LanceArmstrong.com does not currently feature any rollover effects, but by including some additional JavaScript and preloading a second set of images, it wouldn't be impossible, although it would require even more code. We add rollover effects to the tab set when we re-create the design in the "A Bulletproof Approach" section a bit further on. But instead of adding more code, images, and JavaScript, we accomplish the rollover with just a few lines of CSS.

So, on the surface, we have a set of navigational tabs that are specially designed to fit the rest of the site's look and feel. Clicking each tab takes you to the main sections of the site, and each tab has a corresponding text label. Good. Now, let's look under the hood, kick the tires, and eventually walk through an alternate way of handling a similar design.

Why It's Not Bulletproof

So what's wrong here? We're not looking to scorn the designers of LanceArmstrong.com—the method used here mirrors those used on millions of sites all over the Web. We're simply using this site as a guide, primarily because I think it's visually compelling, but also because re-creating such a site using CSS and valid, accessible markup will be simple. That said, let's outline the characteristics that make this site vulnerable.

MOUNTAINS OF CODE

Certainly a characteristic that plagues sites that use JavaScript and image-based navigation is the large amount of code that's required to lay them out and make them dynamic (in other words, switch states on rollover). Commonly, each tab is sliced out as its own image, with the current version using a series of nested tables, spacer GIF shims (transparent images used only for providing space between page elements), and other nonessential markup to achieve its pixel-precise layout. The result is a whole heck of a lot of code—and that means potentially slow download times and increased file size.

For LanceArmstrong.com in particular, all four tabs are contained within a single graphic, with an image map applied to make each tab portion of the graphic clickable. This requires less code than if each tab were a *separate* image and then positioned in table cells with spacer GIF shims. But the problems that follow are shared by both methods.

INACCESSIBILITY ISSUES

Another unfortunate side effect of using so much code is that it chokes the text browsers and assistive software used by visitors with disabilities. And because the entire navigation is one single image (looking back at Figure 2.3), most developers fail to specify alt attributes for each clickable area when using image maps. So, users browsing with screen readers, or those who turn off images to save download time (a common practice for users with slow connections), will have a tough time navigating the site.

note 📖

An exception to this scalability limitation is the "page zoom" feature found in the IE7 and Opera browsers that essentially magnifies the entire document.

SCALABILITY ISSUES

This is a big one. Because the tabs are *images*, there's no way for visually impaired users to bump up the text size in their browsers to increase readability. Image-based navigation just won't budge when it needs to.

LACK OF FLEXIBILITY

If, in the future, the editors of LanceArmstrong.com wished to change any of the tab wording, or perhaps replace "About Lance" with "Why Lance Rules," they would have a challenge ahead of them. Editing, removing, or swapping the wording on any of these image-based tabs requires the slicing out of new images, potentially altering the dimensions specified in the markup by way of the image map and thus creating a lot of work for all those involved.

And because the tab set is one single image, it means the update of at least four images to make a single change (one for each tab state)—certainly a potential headache down the road.

As you can see, there's plenty of room for improvement here, and depending on your priorities, any one of the downsides mentioned earlier could be reason enough to investigate an alternate method. So let's do just that.

A Bulletproof Approach

With the disadvantages of the traditional techniques for designing image-based navigation behind us, let's take the tab design from LanceArmstrong.com and rebuild it employing a clean and lean standards-based method using CSS. The goal here is to address the previously outlined downsides to the traditional approach.

As with any ideal project, we first need to decide how to make the markup as meaningful and accessible as possible. For navigation, it makes perfect sense to structure a list of links as, you guessed it, a list:

```
<ul id="nav">
  <li id="t-intro"><a href="/">Introduction</a></li>
  <li id="t-about"><a href="about.html">About Lance</a></li>
  <li id="t-news"><a href="news.html">News &amp; Events</a></li>
  <li id="t-sponsors"><a href="sponsors.html">Sponsors</a></li>
</ul>
```

A simple, unordered list is all we need to create our bulletproof set of tabs. The simple markup will ensure easy readability across all browsers, devices, and assistive software—not to mention it's lightweight and compact. Compare the amount of code used here with the traditional, nested-table approach, and the difference between the two becomes rather obvious.

Notice the unique `id` given to each list item. This will come in handy later on when we want to signify which page we're on by giving the tab a *selected* state.

SANS STYLE

Unstyled, an unordered list normally appears as a vertical list, with a bullet to the left of each item (Figure 2.4). A device or text browser that does not support CSS could render this navigation list without any problems.

TWO TINY IMAGES

You recall that the common approach uses a separate image for each entire tab set—actually there are four images, one for each area of the site where a specific tab is selected. To simplify things, we plan to get by with just two small images that we'll tile horizontally within each tab. Because they'll tile, we won't worry about widths and heights of each item—an important topic we return to a bit later in the chapter, in the section called "Why It's Bulletproof."

If you take a look at the original tabs again, you'll notice that the gradient fade starts at the top of the tab and then blends into a solid background color. Using our favorite image editor, Adobe Photoshop, we've created the two images (one for selected states and one for the unselected states) that re-create that gradient fade into a transparent background (Figure 2.5). We've chosen the color at the bottom of each image to be *knocked out* in favor of transparency. We'll be able to fill that empty transparency in using CSS later on.

- Introduction
- About Lance
- News & Events
- Sponsors

Figure 2.4 Here you see the untouched beauty of an unstyled, unordered list.

tip

Another advantage to using a list here is that many screen-reading applications will read aloud the number of items that are contained in the list that follows. This information provides the user with a clear cue as to what's on the horizon. For instance, users of the popular screen-reading application JAWS, from Freedom Scientific, would be able to skip to the next list or element on the page after hearing how many items are contained within. (For more on how JAWS navigates Web pages, see www. freedomscientific.com/ fs_products/Surfs_Up/ Navigating.htm.)

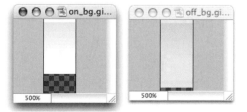

Figure 2.5 This is a close-up of the two images we'll use to tile the gradient fade behind each tab state. The color at the bottom of each image has been knocked out as transparent (the checkerboard area), to be filled in later by a color with CSS.

Notice that each image is only 10 pixels wide, and includes the one-pixel high-light along the top, followed by the gradient into a transparent background.

APPLYING STYLE

We have the ingredients. Now we just need to take our unordered list and two tiling images and apply some CSS to pull the whole thing together.

Our first step is to add CSS rules that will make the navigation list horizontal, rather than its default vertical presentation:

```
#nav {
  margin: 0;
  padding: 10px 0 0 46px;
  list-style: none;
  background: #FFCB2D;
  }
#nav li {
  float: left;
  margin: 0 1px 0 0;
  padding: 0;
  font-family: "Lucida Grande", sans-serif;
  font-size: 80%;
  }
```

We're using the float property to stretch the navigation horizontally, and at this point we've also declared the yellow background color that the tab set will sit on top of. It's important to include that yellow background, since it will be integral to ensuring that the whole system (yellow container and tabs) is scalable. We've also gone ahead and zeroed out default margins and padding (but giving a one-pixel right margin to space out each tab), as well as set a typeface and font-size that is 80% of the page's default. Using what we've learned in Chapter 1, "Flexible Text," we've used the small keyword on the <body> element to set the base size for the page. Now we'll sleep well at night, knowing that IE/Win users will be able to adjust the tab text size at will.

Figure 2.6 shows what our navigation system looks like so far.

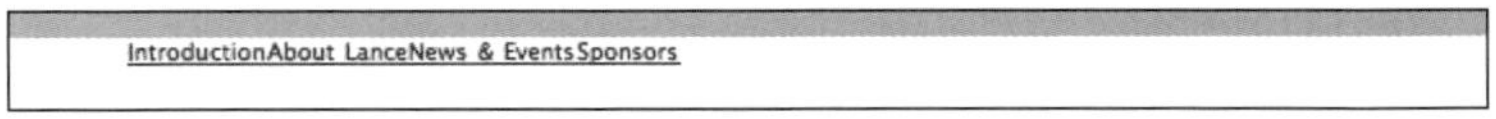

IntroductionAbout LanceNews & Events Sponsors

Figure 2.6 The initial navigation design looks quite disheveled.

Hmm. I know, not even close. But with a few more declarations, we'll be doing victory laps around the Champs-Elysées.

FLOAT TO FIX

The first issue we need to tackle is that because we're floating the <li> elements, they're taken out of the natural flow of the document and won't fill up the outer <ul>, which defines our background color. In other words, because we float the inner elements, the outer <ul> doesn't know how tall to be.

To fix this, let's also float the entire <ul> along with everything else. This allows the <li> items to fill up the space, stretching the yellow background behind it. Due to the fact that floating an element "shrink-wraps" its contents (expanding only as wide or tall as needed), we'll also add a specific width on the <ul>, imagining (for this example) that it lives inside a fixed-width layout of similar size (Figure 2.7).

> IntroductionAbout LanceNews & Events Sponsors

Figure 2.7 By floating the <ul> element along with each list item, we stretch the background behind it.

```
#nav {
  float: left;
  width: 720px;
  margin: 0;
  padding: 10px 0 0 46px;
  list-style: none;
  background: #FFCB2D;
  }
#nav li {
  float: left;
  margin: 0 1px 0 0;
  padding: 0;
  font-family: "Lucida Grande", sans-serif;
  font-size: 80%;
  }
```

note

While we've declared a width of 720px for the #nav, to indent the tabs we're also assigning left padding of 46px. Since padding is added to the width of the element, the navigation's total width equals 766px.

tip

Because we're floating #nav, we do have to make sure we clear any elements that follow. For instance, the next element that follows, be it another horizontal row or block of content, will need the clear: left; rule applied to ensure it'll sit *below* the navigation area.

Now, that's a little better. We can rest assured that whatever the dimensions, the yellow background will expand along with its contents, protecting this component of the design. This float-to-fix method is a handy way of avoiding the addition of extra wrapper <div>s that could be used to compensate for the background. It also means not having to set a height on the list—something we want to avoid to be as flexible as possible.

MAKING THE TABS TAKE SHAPE

Next, let's add some definition to the links themselves by adding padding, borders, and background color:

```
#nav a {
   float: left;
   display: block;
   margin: 0;
   padding: 4px 8px;
   color: #333;
   text-decoration: none;
   border: 1px solid #9B8748;
   border-bottom: none;
   background: #F9E9A9;
   }
```

We've chosen to use the display: block; rule here on the <a> elements to help make the entire tab clickable. Block-level elements will force each other to be on their own separate lines, so we use the float property to again make things horizontal.

We've also applied padding around each link, changed the color and text decoration, and added a border to all but the bottom of each side. It's important to apply padding to the <a> elements, since this ensures that the entire tab, not just the link text, will be clickable.

Amazingly, the tab appearance is starting to take shape as a result of the few extra CSS rules that we just added (Figure 2.8).

Figure 2.8 By adding padding to the <a> element, we make the entire button area clickable, making it easier for people to navigate the site.

ALIGNING THE BACKGROUND IMAGES

Our next step is to fold in the images we created earlier, assigning them as backgrounds that will tile within each tab:

```
#nav a {
  float: left;
  display: block;
  margin: 0;
  padding: 4px 8px;
  color: #333;
  text-decoration: none;
  border: 1px solid #9B8748;
  border-bottom: none;
  background: #F9E9A9 url(img/off_bg.gif) repeat-x top left;
  }
```

We've used the shorthand method for declaring a color and image in the same rule, allowing that specified color (#F9E9A9) to shine through the transparent areas of the image. This is the color at the bottom of the image that we removed in the image editor in favor of transparency.

We've also aligned the image to the top of the tab, and repeat-x is doing the horizontal tiling (Figure 2.9). Where the tiled image ends (including its transparent area) is where the specified background color will take over.

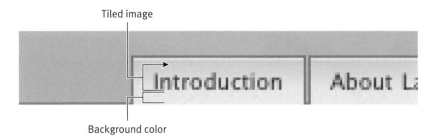

Tiled image

Background color

Figure 2.9 Tile the background image horizontally to add the highlight and gradient detail. Because the image is tiled, it means any width and/or height will not hinder the design.

Our remaining steps include adding a declaration for hovered and selected states (which we combine for this design). But first, let's add a solid border under the tabs that gets knocked out when a tab is selected, creating the illusion that the tab is part of the white page below it.

I've found that the simplest and most successful way of dealing with a border that at times you wish to overlap is to use a tiny tiled image that is the height you wish the border to be. This is where that third image comes into play; however, it's so tiny that it almost doesn't count (Figure 2.10).

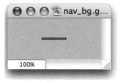

Figure 2.10 This one-pixel-tall image is used as the bottom border for the tabs, allowing the active tab to overlap it, blending the bottom of the tab with the rest of the white page.

This 1 x 37-pixel GIF image will tile horizontally along the bottom edge of our tab set. The width is arbitrary in this case, since we tile it horizontally, and for the life of me, I cannot remember why the odd width of 37 pixels was chosen for this particular image.

Figure 2.11 shows the stacking order of the navigation thus far, with the background color, one-pixel tiled border, and tab content coming together to complete the design.

tip

Giving background images that tile a substantial dimension improves rendering performance in Internet Explorer for Windows, which at times can be sluggish when you are using tiny images that repeat.

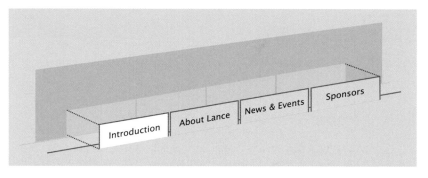

Figure 2.11 A 3D view of how the tiled background image is placed to create the bottom border of the navigation.

ADDING THE BOTTOM BORDER

So, to our previous #nav declaration, let's add the following call to the small background image:

```
#nav {
  float: left;
  width: 720px;
  margin: 0;
  padding: 10px 0 0 46px;
  list-style: none;
  background: #FFCB2D url(img/nav_bg.gif) repeat-x bottom
left;
  }
```

We're telling the image to tile horizontally while aligning it to the bottom. Because the image is only one pixel tall, the yellow background color we've also declared here (#FFCB2D) will shine through the remaining parts of the navigation bar (Figure 2.12).

Background color: #ffcb2d

Tiled 1px-tall image, aligned bottom

Figure 2.12 With the bottom border tiled as a background image, we're getting close to the finish line.

HOVERING SWAP

For hover and selected states, let's replicate the alternate gray tab color that's used on LanceArmstrong.com by just swapping out the beige background image we've set by default. All this takes is one simple declaration to handle both scenarios. Let's start by creating a hover style for the tabs:

```
#nav a:hover {
  color: #333;
  padding-bottom: 5px;
  border-color: #727377;
  background: #fff url(img/on_bg.gif) repeat-x top left;
  }
```

Notice that we've darkened the text and border colors and have referenced the gray background, which fades into white (#fff). We've also increased the bottom padding by one pixel (from 4 pixels to 5 pixels). This extra pixel will force the selected and hovered tabs to overlap the background border (which is also one pixel tall), giving it the appearance that it's connected to the rest of the page (Figure 2.13).

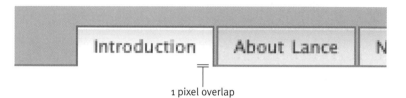

1 pixel overlap

Figure 2.13 By increasing the bottom padding from 4px to 5px on the hovered tab only, we'll cover up the bottom border, creating the illusion that the tab is in the foreground.

SELECTED STATE

How does the tab know when to stick on? That's where the descendant selector comes into play, which we'll add to the the hover declaration so they'll share the same styles.

`#nav a:hover, body#intro #t-intro a`

A descendant selector provides a way of targeting specific elements based on their parent elements. By specifying elements separated by spaces, we can narrow down a target based on the order in which these elements appear in the document tree. For more on selectors, see www.w3.org/TR/REC-CSS2/selector.html.

So, if we were to add an id to the <body> element of a page with a value of intro like so

`<body id="intro">`

then the declaration would read "on pages where there is a body id of #intro, also use the alternate background, darker colors, etc."—a handy way to let CSS handle the "you are here" effect common in most navigation designs. And in this particular case, we combined the tab's changed state for both hovering *and* selection into one CSS declaration.

Why It's Bulletproof

We just took a pleasing tab navigation design from a high-profile Web site, ripped it apart, and reconstructed a similar system with less code that is easily updatable, that is more accessible to a wider range of browsers, devices, and assistive software—and most notably—that is *flexible*, regardless of the size and amount of text placed within it.

Because of the steps we took to creatively align background images and assign colors, the entire tab set is *scalable*. If the user chooses to bump up the text size a few notches to increase readability, the entire design will scale along with it (Figure 2.14).

Figure 2.14 This tab design can be scaled up or down by adjusting the text size in the browser.

In a matter of minutes, we can also change the wording and/or add or remove tabs for instant updates, simply by editing the unordered list that's used to structure the navigation items (Figure 2.15). All that needs to change is the text within each list item in our markup:

```
<ul id="nav">
  <li id="t-intro"><a href="/">Home</a></li>
  <li id="t-about"><a href="about.html">Why Lance Rules
</a></li>
  <li id="t-news"><a hrefvnews.html">The Latest News</a></li>
  <li id="t-sponsors"><a href="sponsors.html">People Who
Like Lance</a></li>
  </ul>
```

Figure 2.15 It takes just a few seconds to change the text for each tab by updating our easy-to-read, unordered list.

A Variation Using Ems

For our reconstruction of the Lance Armstrong tabs, we specified padding around the link text in *pixel* units. This was partially necessary in order to increase the bottom padding by a single pixel to achieve the overlap of the one-pixel border on the bottom of the navigation bar. We needed to be exact by a single pixel.

If we remove the need for that one-pixel bottom border, we can then talk about using *ems* for padding around each tab's link text. Why ems? As we discussed in Chapter 1, the em is a *sliding measure*, which will vary depending on the current font size. So, by specifying padding in ems for each navigation link instead of pixels, we can ensure that the entire tab (not just the text) scales in proportion to the text if adjusted by the user.

Figure 2.16 shows a simplified version of our previous tab example, where we've removed the one-pixel border from the bottom of the navigation, and changed its background color to gray.

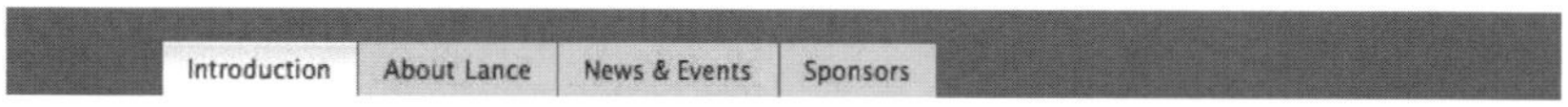

Figure 2.16 A simplified version of the navigation, sans bottom border.

```
#nav {
  float: left;
  width: 50em;
  margin: 0;
  padding: 1em 0 0 5em;
  list-style: none;
  background: #666;
  }
```

We've assigned a width this time of 50em, again assuming it will fit inside a layout of the same size (for more on em-based layouts, see Chapter 8, "Fluid & Elastic Layouts"). Padding around the tabs is also specified here in ems, with 1em on the top and 5em creating the indent on the left.

We'll now also change the #nav a declaration that styles each navigation item to use ems for padding as follows (additionally changing the background color to a light gray and removing the border around each tab):

```
#nav a {
  float: left;
  display: block;
  margin: 0;
  padding: .5em 1em;
  color: #333;
  text-decoration: none;
  background: #ccc;
}
```

You'll notice padding: .5em 1em, which translates to "half an em of padding on the top and bottom of the link, and 1 full em of padding on the left and right." Now, if we adjust the text size up or down, you'll see the tabs' text *and the spacing around them* scale in proportion to each other (Figure 2.17). Pretty nifty, eh? So instead of there always being a specific number of pixels surrounding the text that will remain the same regardless of the current font size, using ems we now have a *scalable* system that stays intact when bumped up or down.

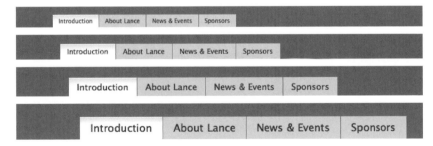

Figure 2.17 A tab variation based on ems, with text size adjusted to show proportions staying intact.

I mention this variation primarily to get you thinking about swapping ems for pixels in situations like padding, margins, line height, and so forth. It may not always be possible of course (e.g., our Lance Armstrong tabs), but depending on the requirements, adding ems to the mix can be beneficial in maintaining proportion throughout your designs—regardless of text size. Give *'em* a try.

Additional Examples

To take the concepts from this chapter a step further, be sure to dig into these additional examples that offer distinct designs that share the flexibility of the tabs we've just constructed.

MOZILLA.ORG

www.mozilla.org

A recent redesign of Mozilla.org introduced rounded tab navigation that scales along with whatever text size or textual content that's thrown at it (Figure 2.18).

Figure 2.18 Rounded corners can be easily achieved by using the Sliding Doors technique, as seen here at Mozilla.org.

The Mozilla team utilized a technique developed by Douglas Bowman called the Sliding Doors of CSS (www.alistapart.com/articles/slidingdoors/). Bowman devised a clever way of using two background images that spread apart as the contents inside them expand. By using two separate images, rounded corners and other non-box treatments can be aligned to the edges of tabs and other containers—all the while remaining flexible and accessible.

SLANTS

www.simplebits.com/bits/bulletproof_slants.html

The need for slant-separated yet flexible navigation arose for a client project, and the results required just a single background image that would reveal more or less of itself depending on the size of text contained within (Figure 2.19).

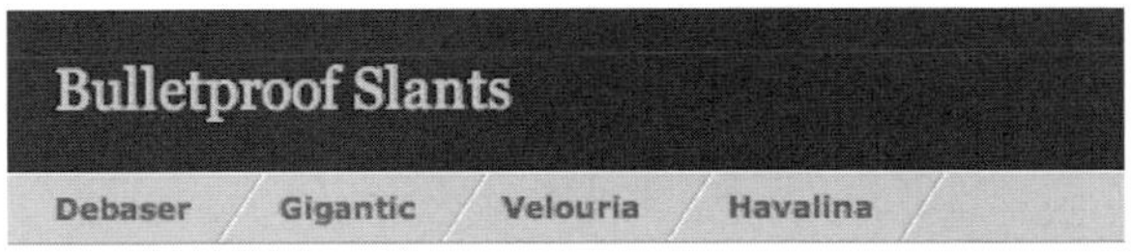

Bulletproof Slants

Debaser / Gigantic / Velouria / Havalina

Figure 2.19 By using a larger-than-necessary slant background image, the effect can remain intact no matter what text is placed in between.

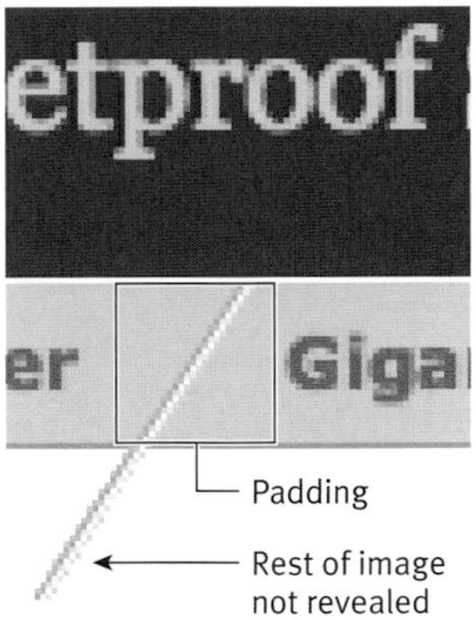

By aligning a single-slant image that is larger than necessary (at a default text size) as a background image, we ensured that more of that slanted image will expose itself as you increase the text size (Figure 2.20).

etproof

er | Giga

— Padding

← Rest of image not revealed

Figure 2.20 Here's a close-up of the slant, with only just enough of the image revealed.

ESPN.COM SEARCH

www.espn.com

The tabs used to toggle filters for a previous design of ESPN.com's Search were created using a method similar to this chapter's example. A larger image with a gradient fade was used as a background, where more of the image appeared as the user increased text size. Figure 2.21 shows the tabs at two different text sizes.

Figure 2.21 The tabs of a previous version of the ESPN Search would scale with varying text size and length.

To explain how this was achieved, we'll use the unselected tab state as an example, where there is a slight, one-pixel highlight on both the top and left sides of the background image. Because this highlight appears on these two sides only, we can get away with using a single image as a background, making it large enough to accommodate text at a large size.

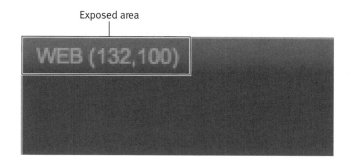

Figure 2.22 This shows a tab at default text size, with only the top-left portion of the background image revealed.

Figure 2.22 shows the tab at default text size, with only the top-left portion of the background image revealed, while Figure 2.23 shows the tab at a much larger text size, with a *larger* area of the background image revealed. By creatively positioning the image to the top left of the tab's <a> element, we can still show the highlight and gradient detail no matter what amount or size of text is placed inside.

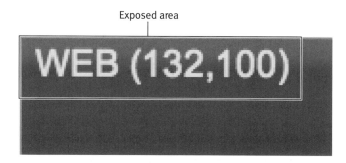

Figure 2.23 With an increased text size, more of the background image is revealed, yet the subtle highlight remains in the top and left of the tab.

Ensuring a flexible width was crucial to the design of these tabs, because the number of results would be displayed alongside each tab's label (the number in parentheses). Due the varying length of the results number, the tab needed room to "breathe," expanding or contracting as necessary while still maintaining the design.

Summary

Rebuilding a common method for image-based tabs has given us the opportunity to identify several downsides to using those techniques. At the same time, we've discovered advantages in using a simple unordered list, styled with creative CSS, not only allowing navigation designs to expand or contract with text size adjustments, but also permitting a *varying* amount of content to be placed within.

Here are a few points to remember when designing navigation:

■ Using image-based navigation means poor- or low-vision users cannot adjust its text size.

■ Simple markup (an unordered list) ensures greater accessibility to a wider range of browsers, devices, and software.

■ Text-based navigation is easily updated or edited, without the need to create new images each time a change is needed.

■ Creative placement of background images can add detail to a navigation's design without sacrificing its flexibility.

■ Try using ems for margins, padding, line height, and so forth to provide true scaling of your design (and not just text), regardless of font size.

■ There are times when using images for navigation is a requirement and unavoidable, whether for a company's typeface or because of limited screen real estate. This is not the end of the world by any means.

That last bullet point is an important one to stress. In the real world, requirements regarding typeface and/or width and height of the navigation may be decided by someone other than yourself. In those instances, run away very fast. No, not really—but you're now prepared to make a case for using something flexible in its place. There are no wrong answers—just some that may work better than others, taking into account each unique situation.

Now that we've established a flexible navigation concept, let's move on to other components frequently found on Web pages, reworking them as we go.

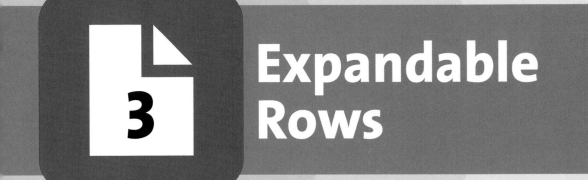

Expandable Rows

3

Resist specifying height and plan for vertical expansion of horizontal page components.

Horizontal page components such as site headers, login bars, breadcrumb trails, and search bars are no strangers to a typical Web site. These areas are often positioned near the top of the page and may contain a mixture of graphics (whether a background or otherwise) and text. In general, these areas are designed in such a way that prohibits *vertical expansion* — assuming that a larger text size or an increased amount of content would either never happen or wouldn't harm the design. While it's customary for areas that contain articles or long sections of text to accommodate any length or size of text and content, it's important — and not impossible — to treat other horizontal areas this way as well.

This chapter takes a look at a common approach to designing a login/promotional area that occupies the top portion of a typical Web page. We deconstruct the design and then rebuild it to accommodate any text size or amount of content.

A Common Approach

To help us get a handle on what it means to allow vertical expansion for these horizontal page components, let's use an example from the Web—a site we'll refer to as *The Best Store Ever* (its real identity has been hidden to protect the guilty). The Best Store Ever is your typical e-commerce site, selling a variety of semi-useful products to improve your home. We've fictionalized the site for this chapter, but its design is based on real-world techniques. To demonstrate a common approach to designing a horizontal login/promotion bar, we're going to zoom in on that area of The Best Store Ever's Web site (Figure 3.1). At the top of each page sits a colored row that contains login and local store information, followed by a second row that contains a promotional message that is regularly updated. Each row contains no more than one line of text.

Register row

Not registered? **Register** now!   Q Find a store

SPECIAL THIS WEEK: $2 shipping on all orders! ▶ LEARN MORE

Message row

Figure 3.1 This shows the top portion of our fictitious example site, The Best Store Ever.

These two rows (along with the entire layout) are constructed using a series of nested tables. Graphics (such as the rounded ends of each row) and text are placed within the table cells.

Figure 3.2 illustrates how the table cells of the top row might be structured; each cell is outlined in red. You can see how each section of the row is in its own separate table cell, including the rounded-corner graphics at each end. This is an *approximation* of the table structure, without venturing too deep into The Best Store Ever's code. But the important point here is that tables, spacer GIF shims, and small graphics have been combined to form the two rows seen here.

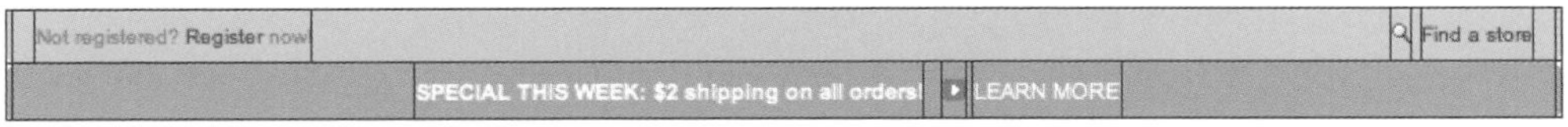

Figure 3.2 Each section of the row is in its own separate table cell.

Using tables and spacer GIFs to position graphics and text is a technique that's been honed over the years—it's the way most Web sites were built, and a lot of designers prided themselves on being able to replicate any possible design concept on the Web, right down to the last pixel. If you could design and *print* it, you could turn it into a Web page.

But we're all learning better ways of designing for the Web. And we're discovering methods that increase a site's readability and accessibility by using lean, semantic markup and CSS for design. A bit later we apply those methods to the two horizontal rows found at The Best Store Ever, but first, let's talk about why this design isn't bulletproof.

Why It's Not Bulletproof

We can make several improvements to the construction of these horizontal rows—improvements that will enhance this section's flexibility. Let's outline what's wrong so that we can gain a better understanding of what we'll need to bulletproof in this design.

NONESSENTIAL GRAPHICS

As we discovered earlier, the rows are built using a series of nested tables, with each section of the row surrounded by its own table cell. *Nonessential graphics*, such as the rounded ends, are placed in the markup alongside the text. These graphics will just get in the way of someone trying to access this site via a text browser or screen reader. Assigning the proper `alt` attribute values to the images would certainly help, although The Best Store Ever chose to omit those useful bits of information.

"Nonessential graphics" refers to graphics that don't apply any meaning to the content, or that don't provide any instruction or direction to the user. Rounded corners are a *design element*, and we'll be moving those to the style sheet later on.

THINKING IN FIXED HEIGHT

If we try bumping up the text size a few notches, you'll notice that the rows' design breaks down (Figure 3.3). Increasing the text size is always a good test for discovering how flexible design components are. Not only does it give you a sense for how well the readability fares at larger text sizes, but it can also reveal whether the design can handle a varying amount of content, regardless of its text size. In other words, if an editor later decides that he or she would like *two* lines of promotional text instead of the *one* that happened to be in the specification, then in a bulletproof world the row would *expand* without any adjustments. This saves time, money, and, well, that should be reason enough.

Corners won't expand

Figure 3.3 When text is increased, the static corner images won't expand with the rest of the design.

Looking again at Figure 3.3, we can see that the rounded-corner images that were created to cap off each row end have been designed for a fixed height. Anything tall stuffed inside will spill out, breaking the design. What I'm trying to convey in this chapter (and many others) is a shift in thought in terms of *height*. It is possible to compensate for larger text, more content, and whatever else is placed inside certain design components. We'll get to that in just a minute.

CODE BLOAT

As with most traditional methods of Web design, a large amount of code was needed to construct these rows. As you'll recall from Chapter 2, "Scalable Navigation," nesting tables adds a considerable amount to the markup. This code bloating will fill up servers, clog bandwidth, and wreak havoc with non-browser software and devices. Imagine trying to navigate through the sea of code using a text browser. Fortunately, there is a cleaner, flexible way to approach this same design requirement. Let's get to it.

A Bulletproof Approach

To bulletproof the design of the rows, we first have to settle on a markup structure. We then add color, positioning, and background images. In the end, we have a flexible end product, capable of accommodating any text size or amount of content. We begin with the markup, reducing that code bloat we mentioned earlier.

THE MARKUP STRUCTURE

To structure these two rows, we must look at the content within them. What elements would make best sense for this scenario? What elements would be the most meaningful? When writing markup from scratch, I like to answer these questions first, and then apply the best structure for the job. There may very well be more than one answer, but it's important to ask yourself these questions before you type your first character.

In this case, we'll need two containing elements, one for each row. For the top row, I see the two bits of text at each end as items of a list, while on the second row, there's just one paragraph of text.

That said, let's write out the complete markup structure we'll need to make this design happen:

```
<ul>
  <li>Not registered? <a href="/register/">Register</a>
now!</li>
  <li><a href="/find/">Find a store</a></li>
</ul>

<div>
  <p><strong>Special this week:</strong> $2 shipping on all
orders! <a href="/special/">LEARN MORE</a></p>
</div>
```

So, we have a list of two items for the top row, and a containing `<div>` wrapped around a single paragraph for the second. Nice and simple, very lean markup—and best of all we've already tossed out the code bloat associated with the nested-table approach.

In addition, we've achieved our goal of increased accessibility to the content. Regardless of the device or software reading it, these two rows of information will always be interpreted as a list followed by paragraph. And that's exactly what they are.

IDENTIFYING THE PIECES

Our next step is to uniquely identify all the elements that we need to assign styles to. Assigning a few ids will enable us to apply positioning, color, and images to turn this simple markup into the finished design.

```
<ul id="register">
  <li id="reg">Not registered? <a href="/register/
">Register</a> now!</li>
  <li id="find"><a href="/find/v>Find a store</a></li>
</ul>

<div id="message">
  <p><strong>Special this week:</strong> $2 shipping on all
orders! <a href="/special/">LEARN MORE</a></p>
</div>
```

We've just added unique ids to the list and each of its items, as well as the second row's containing <div>. These *style hooks* will be important in just a moment. You may be wondering why we couldn't just add the #message id to the <p> itself, eliminating the need for that extra <div> that surrounds it. But we'll need both elements to complete the design, and an extra containing element here and there is often necessary (and not a crime!) when creating flexible but rich designs. All in moderation.

SANS STYLE

Figure 3.4 is what our markup structure looks like in a browser, with just some basic font styling applied (The Best Store Ever uses the Arial typeface throughout).

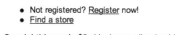

- Not registered? Register now!
- Find a store

Special this week: $2 shipping on all orders! LEARN MORE

Figure 3.4 This is an unstyled view of our bulletproof markup; it's easily read and understood by any device that happens to access it.

note

Before we start applying styles, we build these rows assuming a containing layout width of 768 pixels—the width of The Best Store Ever page. In other words, these rows sit inside a containing element (<div>, <table>, etc.) that already has a width specified.

A phone, PDA, or browser that doesn't support CSS would render the rows this way. The result is still very readable and easily understood by any device accessing it. Now it's time to start applying style.

On the <body> element we've also assigned a base font size using the keyword value of small.

```
body {
    font-family: Arial, sans-serif;
    font-size: small;
    }
```

tip

While The Best Store Ever intentionally specifies Arial as its primary font family, true typophiles might suggest using *Helvetica* (the popular, original typeface that Arial was based on) instead. Most Mac users will have Helvetica installed, and to give them (and others who are fortunate to have it) the arguably superior font experience, you could list Helvetica first, with Arial as the backup, like so: body { font-family: Helvetica, Arial, sans-serif; }.

The differences between Arial and Helvetica are often invisible to most, but type aficionados learn to spot the slight variations from a mile away. Learn more about the similarities from type designer Mark Simonson: http://www.ms-studio.com/articlesarialsid.html.

ADDING BACKGROUND

To begin adding style, let's first add the background color to each row. This step will help us define the dimensions.

```
#register {
    background: #BDDB62;
    }
#message {
    background: #92B91C;
    }
```

The results of adding the correct background color to each row are revealed in Figure 3.5.

Figure 3.5 Adding background colors first helps us visually define the rows as we add the rest of the pieces.

POSITIONING THE CONTENT

Next, let's position the content, placing the two list items of the top row at either end and the $2 shipping message in the center of the bottom row. Figure 3.6 shows the results of applying the following CSS:

Figure 3.6 We've positioned each list item on either end of the top row.

```
#register {
  margin: 0;
  padding: 0;
  list-style: none;
  background: #BDDB62;
  }
#reg {
  float: left;
  margin: 0;
  padding: 8px 14px;
  }
#find {
  float: right;
  margin: 0;
  padding: 8px 14px;
  }

#message {
  clear: both;
  text-align: center;
  background: #92B91C;
  }
```

From top to bottom, we've eliminated default margins and padding from the #register list. Also, we've prevented bullets from appearing by using the list-style: none; rule.

Next, we've used the *opposing floats* method for positioning the two list items at either end of the row. The first list item is floated left (#reg), while the second item is floated right (#find). Doing this enables us to align each item at an equal horizontal location yet at opposing ends of the row (Figure 3.7).

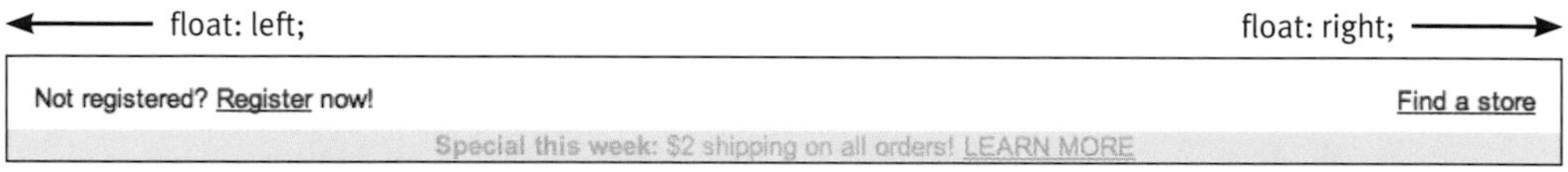

←——— float: left;   float: right; ———→

Not registered? <u>Register</u> now!   <u>Find a store</u>

Special this week: $2 shipping on all orders! LEARN MORE

Figure 3.7 The "opposing floats" method is a handy way of aligning content on either side of a container.

This method of floating elements *against* each other is a handy way of placing content at opposite ends of a containing element.

Looking again at the new styles we've added, in addition to floating each list element we've added some padding on all sides of each item. There will also be enough space to drop in the magnifying glass icon on the left of the "Find a store" link a bit later.

As for the bottom row, we've added a clear: both; rule, which clears the floats we've added to the row above it. And, to center the text, we're using the text-align: center; rule.

MISSING BACKGROUND

Where did the background color on the top row go? You may recall that we ran into a similar problem in Chapter 2. When we float inner elements (in this case the two <li>s), we're taking them out of the normal flow of the document. So, for the <ul> that wraps around them, it's as if the list items don't really exist. As a result, the <ul> doesn't know how tall and wide to stretch the background color behind itself.

To fix this problem, let's float the <ul> along with the list items (just as we did with the tabs in Chapter 2). In addition, we need to assign a width to make sure the row flows across the entire, intended width. It seems that most browsers have interpreted the CSS2.0 spec quite literally in that "a floated box must have an explicit width" (www.w3.org/TR/REC-CSS2/visuren.html#floats). If we don't specify a width here, the row will only be as wide as the contents force it to be (in this case, the two lines of text).

```css
#register {
  float: left;
  width: 100%;
  margin: 0;
  padding: 0;
  list-style: none;
  background: #BDDB62;
  }
#reg {
  float: left;
  margin: 0;
  padding: 8px 14px;
  }
#find {
  float: right;
  margin: 0;
  padding: 8px 14px;
  }

#message {
  clear: both;
  text-align: center;
  background: #92B91C;
  }
```

Figure 3.8 shows the rows so far, with the background color of the top row now restored.

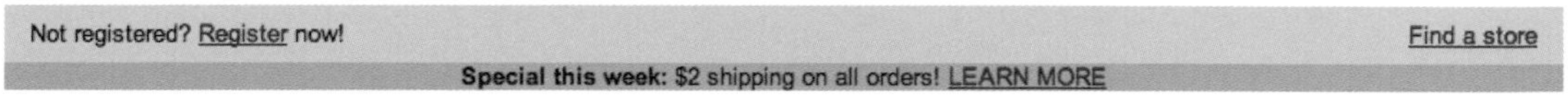

Figure 3.8 When floating items inside a container that is filling in the background, restore that background by floating the container as well.

Rounded corners

Figure 3.9 The rounded corner is really a few white pixels in a step pattern, attached to each corner of the row.

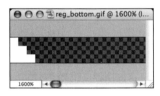

Figure 3.10 This is one end of the 768-pixel-wide GIF (zoomed at 1600%).

ADDING THE DETAILS

We're now left with adding the details that complete the design of these rows. Let's start with the top row and fill in the rounded corners that appear at the bottom edges of each end (Figure 3.9).

You'll notice that the *rounded* corner is nothing more than a few white pixels placed in a step pattern. When viewed at a normal distance (rather than zoomed, as it is in Figure 3.9), it creates the illusion that the row is rounded off at each end.

Chopping off pixels to create this rounded illusion is a great trick—and one that's easy to implement using a combination of the smallest image possible with a background color specified in the CSS.

We'll start by creating the image in Photoshop (or your favorite image editor). Because we're dealing with a fixed-width (768 pixels), we can create a single image that contains both the left and right corners. We can then reference this image as a background in our CSS.

Figure 3.10 shows a close-up view of the image we created. What you're seeing here is the left end of an image that is 768 pixels wide (the same width that our rows will be). For each end, we created this step pattern with the Pencil tool set to 1px using the color white (the same color as the page background). The rest of the image is transparent (shown by the checkerboard pattern in Photoshop). The white portions of this image will be laid on top of the background color that we've already specified in our CSS. This will create the illusion that the row's ends have been rounded off a few pixels.

Looking back at our declaration for #register (the containing <ul>), we add the following rule:

```
#register {
  float: left;
  width: 100%;
  margin: 0;
  padding: 0;
  list-style: none;
  background: #BDDB62 url(img/reg_bottom.gif) no-repeat
bottom left;
  }
```

We've just specified a background color and then set the image on top of it, set it to *not* repeat, and aligned it at the bottom and left. Transparent portions of the image will let the background color show through, while the white corners will obscure it. Aligning the image at the bottom ensures that no matter how tall the row needs to be (due to varying text sizes or amounts of content) the corners will always be in the right place (Figure 3.11).

Figure 3.11 A 3D view of the stacking order.

Figure 3.12 shows the results, with the rounded corners now showing at the bottom of the top row.

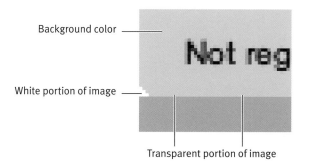

Figure 3.12 The background color and the white and transparent portions of the image work together to create the illusion of rounded corners.

FOUR ROUNDED CORNERS

For the second row, we need a way to apply rounded corners on both the top *and* bottom, all the while keeping the row vertically expandable. To accomplish this, we'll use two background images. One of them will be the same image we used for the bottom of the top row; the other (for the top edge) will be the same image again but turned upside-down. Because we need two background images, we also need two elements to assign them to. (Oh, how I wish we could assign more than one background image to a single element. One can dream.)

Lucky for us, we do have two elements to take advantage of. Notice that in the markup for the second row we have a containing <div> with a <p> inside for the content within:

```
<div id="message">
  <p><strong>Special this week:</strong> $2 shipping on all
orders! <a href="/special/">LEARN MORE</a></p>
</div>
```

Let's now assign each of our background images to each of these elements. The inverted version of our white corner graphic will be assigned to #message, while an identical image used in the top row will be assigned to the bottom of the <p>:

```
#message {
  clear: both;
  text-align: center;
  background: #92B91C url(img/mess_top.gif) no-repeat top
left;
  }
#message p {
  margin: 0;
  padding: 8px 14px;
  background: url(img/reg_bottom.gif) no-repeat bottom left;
  }
```

By assigning the top corners to #message (the outer <div>) and the bottom corners to the bottom edge of the <p> (Figure 3.13), we're ensuring that all four corners will stay positioned correctly no matter how large or small the text is within the paragraph. If we incorporate a larger text size or amount of text, the top corners will always be aligned top, and the bottom corners will always stay at the bottom of the paragraph (as we'll see in just a minute).

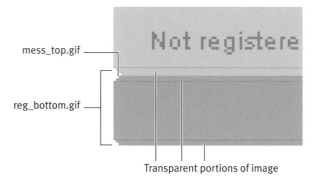

mess_top.gif

reg_bottom.gif

Transparent portions of image

Figure 3.13 For the bottom row, we use two images, letting the green background show through the transparent areas of the GIF.

Figure 3.14 shows the results of these declarations. As we did with the top row, we're using the transparent images that let the background color show through, with white corners masking only those four areas.

Not registered? Register now!	Find a store
Special this week: $2 shipping on all orders! LEARN MORE	

Figure 3.14 With backgrounds added, the rows are starting to take shape.

TEXT AND LINK DETAILS

We have just a few more styles to add to complete the design: link and text colors. We also need to add back in the arrow graphics that flank the "Find a store" and "LEARN MORE" links. Let's get to it.

First, let's define link and text colors for each row, adding the necessary rules to all of the styles we've declared thus far:

```
#register {
  float: left;
  width: 100%;
  margin: 0;
  padding: 0;
  list-style: none;
  color: #690;
  background: #BDDB62 url(img/reg_bottom.gif) no-repeat
bottom left;
  }
```

```css
#register a {
  text-decoration: none;
  color: #360;
  }
#reg {
  float: left;
  margin: 0;
  padding: 8px 14px;
  }
#find {
  float: right;
  margin: 0;
  padding: 8px 14px;
  }

#message {
  clear: both;
  font-weight: bold;
  font-size: 110%;
  color: #fff;
  text-align: center;
  background: #92B91C url(img/mess_top.gif) no-repeat top
left;
  }
#message p {
  margin: 0;
  padding: 8px 14px;
  background: url(img/reg_bottom.gif) no-repeat bottom left;
  }
#message strong {
  text-transform: uppercase;
  }
#message a {
  margin: 0 0 0 6px;
  padding: 2px 15px;
  text-decoration: none;
  font-weight: normal;
  color: #fff;
  }
```

We've set link colors for each of the items in the #register row, as well as default font-size and color for the text and link in the #message row (Figure 3.15).

Figure 3.15 The rows, with link and text color styles added. Notice the space allotted for the small icons that will sit to the left of "Find a store" and "LEARN MORE."

Previously, we had emphasized the "Special this week:" text using the <strong> element. We took advantage of that by using the text-transform property to change that portion of the message to uppercase, while keeping the text in the markup in *sentence case*. Why is that advantageous? For now, we want "SPECIAL THIS WEEK" and "LEARN MORE" to be set in uppercase—but that might not always be what we want. Let's imagine that down the road somewhere, a new design director steps in and wants those text bits in all *lowercase* instead. By using the text-transform property, we can easily make this change by updating the CSS *only*, leaving the markup untouched.

This is just another small example of preparing for alternate scenarios your typography might require in the future. **Keep the text in your markup presentation free**, and utilize text-transform to turn that text into upper- or lowercase as needed.

THE FINAL STEP

Our last step in bulletproofing the rows is to add the graphics that flank the "Find a store" and "LEARN MORE" links. We could add these images to the markup, but to make things easier to update later, and to keep nonessential images out of the document structure, we can easily add them as background images in the CSS.

First let's add the magnifying glass icon to the list in the top row, aligning it 0 50%, which will position it left and 50% from the top (centering it vertically):

```
#find {
  float: right;
  margin: 0;
  padding: 8px 14px;
  background: url(img/mag-glass.gif) no-repeat 0 50%;
  }
```

Figure 3.16 shows the results of adding the icon to the "Find a store" list item in the top row.

Background image

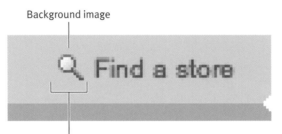

Padding on left of list item

Figure 3.16 The background image sits to the left of the list item, where padding was previously specified.

And finally, let's add the arrow graphic that sits just in front of the "LEARN MORE" link in the second row. Once again, we'll position it 0 50%, or all the way left and halfway down (to center vertically):

```
#message a {
  margin: 0 0 0 6px;
  padding: 2px 15px;
  text-decoration: none;
  font-weight: normal;
  color: #fff;
  background: url(img/arrow.gif) no-repeat 0 50%;
  }
```

Figure 3.17 shows the results of adding the arrow icon to the left of the "LEARN MORE" link by targeting the <a> element that lives within the message row.

Background image

Padding on left of list item

Figure 3.17 As we did with the top row, we added the arrow to the left of the "LEARN MORE" text, this time attaching it to the <*a*> element.

Figure 3.18 shows the final results with all the pieces in place. Visually, we're left with a set of rows almost identical to those found at The Best Store Ever, but the underlying markup structure, along with the measures we've taken to strategically place backgrounds and text, makes it *bulletproof*. Well, just about—we just need one last tweak for IE7.

Figure 3.18 This is the final, bulletproof version of the rows.

A FIX FOR IE7

If you take a look at the finished design in Internet Explorer 7, you'll notice an extra gap in the message row above the text (Figure 3.19). Hrmph. For reasons unknown, IE7 adds this extra space when other modern browsers (including its predecessor, IE6) do not. The easiest (and least disruptive) way to fix this particular issue is to again utilize the "float to fix" method described earlier in this chapter. We'd already floated the #reg <div> to "shrink-wrap" the opposing floats within it, and we'll now apply a float: left; on the #message <div> as well to fix this extra gap issue in IE7.

Figure 3.19 The finished example as viewed in Internet Explorer 7, showing the extra gap above the second row's content.

The revised declaration would be as follows:

```
#message {
  float: left;
  width: 100%;
  margin: 0;
  padding: 0;
  font-weight: bold;
  font-size: 110%;
  color: #fff;
  text-align: center;
  background: #92B91C url(img/ship_top.gif) no-repeat
top left;
  }
```

Just as before, we also added a `width: 100%`, necessary to force the row the entire width of the container (768px in this case). This floating-to-fix-a-float problem is quick, simple, and hack free for all browsers. For this example, it's probably the best choice in order to solve the IE7 issue—but there are other ways to clear floats and solve float problems. In the next chapter, we'll discuss another popular method for "self-clearing" floats that keeps containers independent and that does not reply on whatever comes *after* them in the flow of the document.

Why It's Bulletproof

After simplifying the markup and making creative use of small background images, we've successfully rebuilt the rows using bulletproof methods. Let's talk about *why*.

SEPARATION OF STRUCTURE AND DESIGN

We tossed out the tables and nonessential graphics and replaced the HTML with lean, structured XHTML. The meaningful markup stands a better chance of being understood properly by a wider range of devices and software— even in the absence of CSS.

Instead of coding the images that make up the design of the rows right in the markup, we moved them over to the style sheet instead. Making changes to this design later on down the road will be significantly easier, not to mention that the *amount* of code has been drastically reduced.

For example, going from two shades of green to red, blue, or any other color would be as simple as changing a few CSS rules. *Instant* design results.

NO MORE FIXED HEIGHTS

Rather than assuming these rows will always be *x* number of pixels tall, we creatively positioned background images, preserving the integrity of the design while allowing it to expand and contract as needed. This approach also allows us to freely use font-sizing methods (such as the one described in Chapter 1, "Flexible Text") without relying on a pixel dimension for the text contained within.

Figure 3.20 shows our reconstructed rows, now with a much larger text size applied to the content. Notice how the rounded corners and background of the design stay intact.

tip

Remember when we positioned the magnifying glass and arrow background images at 50% down from the top? Notice that, regardless of the text size, the image will always be centered vertically against the text.

| Not registered? **Register** now! | ⚲ Find a store |
| **SPECIAL THIS WEEK: $2 shipping on all orders!** ▸ LEARN MORE | |

Figure 3.20 With an increase in text size, the rows expand while the design is unhindered.

Let's imagine that an editor wants to write *two* promotional messages for the second row. We can easily add a second line without disturbing the design, which expands to fit the new message (Figure 3.21). This illustrates the biggest advantage of using bulletproof methods: the design accommodates even *unforeseen* requirements.

Not registered? **Register** now!	⚲ Find a store
SPECIAL THIS WEEK: $2 shipping on all orders! ▸ LEARN MORE	
FREE foam hammer with every purchase!	

Figure 3.21 Adding a second line to the `#message` row means zero work for the designer, since we built an unlimited amount of room into the design. Foam hammer?

If a client or manager says, "We only need room for one line of text here," and you go off and build it to spec, it's almost a given that they'll come back in a week saying, "Yes, we absolutely need room for *two* rows of text." With bulletproofing in mind, you've already built that ability into the design.

Make sure you tell them it took you another week to make that happen. Or even better, show them that you've already thought ahead about this, illustrating the benefits of using CSS to reduce maintenance headaches.

Another Example of Expanding

To illustrate another scenario where expandable rows are beneficial, I'm going to share the process involved in creating a flexible header for the TicTac template I designed for Blogger. Blogger is a popular weblog publishing tool owned by Google, and the application makes several predesigned templates available for new users when they set up their weblog. Making these templates bulletproof was extremely important so that the header could accommodate a site title of any length.

Figure 3.22 shows the header area of the template, with the wonderfully clever title of "Sample Blog" displayed in text. The graphic portions of the header are all referenced with CSS as background images. It was important to display the title of the site using *text*, so that Blogger users could apply the template without having to create any graphics on their own—truly, plug-and-play.

Figure 3.22 A sample of the TicTac Blogger template, where the importance of flexibility was key to the varying text contained within the header.

For one-line titles, at a certain font-size the header design works fine. But what if the weblog title is a bit longer (Figure 3.23)? If I had designed the header to be fixed-height, long titles (or those with larger text size) would run off the background, becoming unreadable and ugly.

Figure 3.23 When fixed heights are mixed with varying amounts of text, the result can be less than appealing.

So, integral to the design of a good, reusable template is the ability to accommodate all amounts of content. To make sure the Blogger template header could expand, I of course turned to CSS and the cunning placement of two background images.

THE MARKUP

Before I even thought about style and graphics, I set up the markup structure for the header. I needed the ability to reference two background images, and I also needed two elements in the markup to attach the images to:

```
<div id="blog-header">
  <h1>Sample Blog</h1>
</div>
```

As you can see, I chose to use an <h1> heading for the title of the weblog. If you'd rather save this element for other uses, you could use whatever you'd like here. The important thing is to have two elements at your disposal. So, a <div> wrapped around an <h1> gets the job done. The <div> could be seen as extraneous, but I think in this case, it's not harmful.

CREATING THE TWO IMAGES

To accomplish the expanding effect, I created two images. I made one image taller than I *thought* I would need it to be. Blogger users find that more or less of this image is revealed, depending on the length of their title. The second image I created caps off the bottom of the header. This image will always appear *below* whatever text the user places in the header.

Figure 3.24 shows the large image, with the pattern repeating across most of the height.

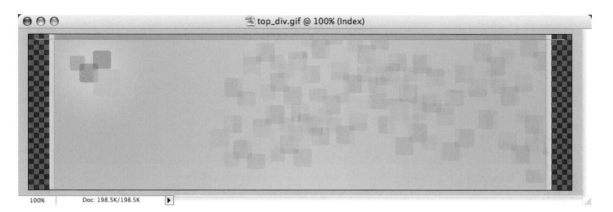

Figure 3.24 I gave the top image a much larger height than I originally needed.

Figure 3.25 shows the second image—the cap that will always be positioned *below* the title text. Notice how the entire top portion of this image is transparent. This allowed me to stack these images on top of each other, letting the top_div.gif image show through top_h1.gif.

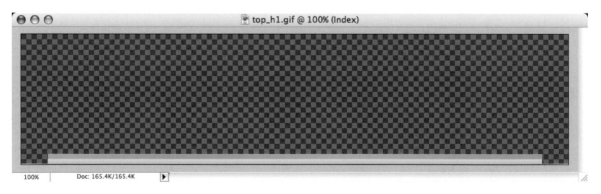

Figure 3.25 The top_h1.gif graphic contains the bottom cap for the header, with a transparent area above to let the other image show through.

APPLYING THE CSS

To pull all the pieces together, I used two rather simple CSS declarations. I first added the rules for the containing `<div>`:

```css
#blog-header {
  margin: 0;
  padding: 0;
  font-family: "Lucida Grande", "Trebuchet MS";
  background: #e0e0e0 url(img/top_div.gif) no-repeat
top left;
  }
```

As you can see, I added a default `font-family`, and I positioned top_div.gif at the top and left on a light gray background.

Next, I added the declaration for the heading element:

```css
#blog-header {
  margin: 0;
  padding: 0;
  font-family: "Lucida Grande", "Trebuchet MS";
  background: #e0e0e0 url(img/top_div.gif) no-repeat
top left;
  }
#blog-header h1 {
  margin: 0;
  padding: 45px 60px 50px 160px;
  font-size: 200%;
  color: #fff;
  background: url(img/top_h1.gif) no-repeat bottom left;
  }
```

With this CSS, I adjusted `font-size` and `padding` around the text, and positioned top_h1.gif at the *bottom* and left of the heading. Because `#blog-header` will only expand as tall as its contents make it, only just enough of its background will be revealed behind the heading text.

Figure 3.26 illustrates how all the pieces fit together.

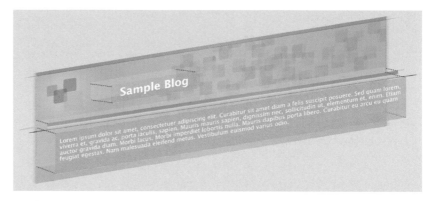

Figure 3.26 An illustration of how the pieces fit together, with the top portion of the header expanding only as tall at the title contents make it.

EXPAND-O-MATIC

To put the expanding header to the test, let's add a long site title and see what happens. As Figure 3.27 shows, with a larger title, more of top_div.gif is exposed, and top_h1.gif gets pushed down, always remaining below the title text.

Figure 3.27 Success means planning ahead for unknown amounts of content.

The opposite is true as well. If the text is one line, and the site owner prefers the title to be displayed in tiny text, the header will *contract* to fit. We now have a graphically rich header for the template, yet it's ready and waiting for the unexpected.

Summary

You may be familiar with the term *baker's dozen*. A smart baker will always add an extra muffin, cookie, or whatever to the batch. If one of the cookies burns or falls apart (or gets eaten by the baker), there's always an extra to make a *complete* dozen. In this way, the baker plans for the unpredictable. Why not bake an extra cookie or two when you've gone to all the trouble of mixing up an entire batch? Sometimes, the extra cookie is needed; sometimes it isn't.

All cookies aside (but still within reach, of course), when we build vertical expansion of horizontal components into our designs, it's as if we're making a baker's dozen of our own—we're planning for the unexpected and making room for text adjustments and varying amounts of content. In the end, we're saving time and giving the user (as well as site editors) better control and increasing accessibility.

Here are some points to remember when you're building horizontal design components:

- Taking nonessential graphics out of the markup and using background images within the CSS can help control code bloat.

- Use the "opposing floats" method for positioning content on opposite sides of a container.

- When the amount of content to be placed inside a design component is unknown, use two background images to let that component expand and contract.

- Plan for more space than you *think* you need. Make that extra chocolate chip cookie.

4

Creative Floating

Use floats to achieve grid-like results.

In previous chapters, we started each bulletproof approach by first deciding how the component we're dealing with should be structured—that is, what markup is most appropriate for the content being displayed? This, I believe, is an important step when building any Web site. With a goal of selecting elements that convey the most *meaning* to what they surround, you hope to be left with enough "style hooks" to apply a compelling design with CSS. But more important, choosing the best markup for the job means the content of the page has the best chance of being understood properly across the widest possible range of browsers and devices. It's the foundation and should convey a clear message, regardless of the design applied on top of it via CSS. Additionally, if we take time to consider optimal structure (meaningful XHTML) and design (CSS) *separately*, changing that design later on down the road becomes less like finding a needle in a haystack and more like changing the slipcover on a sofa.

Settling on an optimal structure doesn't have to limit the way it's displayed, however. As we'll explore in this chapter, the creative use of the float property can give us grid-like results—with a *fraction* of the code we'd need with the nested-tables approach. By paring down the markup to its barest essentials, we make it easier for browsers, software, and all devices to read our content—at the same time making it easier for other designers and developers to modify and edit these components.

We start this chapter off by rebuilding a box containing multiple pairings of an image, title, and description. This is a common layout requirement found on sites all over the Web, and one that we can handle elegantly using minimal markup and CSS.

A Common Approach

Often found on sites to display teasers to articles, products, files, and so forth, the image/title/description package should look familiar to you. A related image is usually aligned to one side against the title and quick description (Figure 4.1).

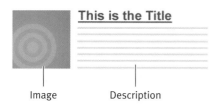

Figure 4.1 Image, title, and description "packages" like this one are found throughout the Web.

There might also be several of these pairings in a row, each pointing to an article, product, or other destination. Traditionally, one might use a `<table>` to structure all of this, using spacer GIFs to control white space and gutters in between the items (Figure 4.2).

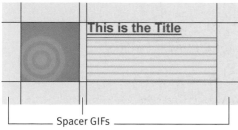

Figure 4.2 Tables and spacer GIFs may be used to space and position the items.

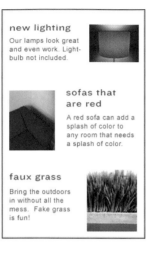

Figure 4.3 The Furniture Shack home page features a box of "teasers."

Some could argue that what we're dealing with here *is* tabular data (think spreadsheets, calendars, statistics), and I'm not here to debate the use of tables. What we *will* do is use a particular component from a popular real-world site as a guideline, which we'll then reconstruct using *far* less markup and CSS to achieve table-esque results. In the end, we'll toss out extraneous markup and unnecessary images to create something more flexible, accessible, and manageable from an editing viewpoint.

Figure 4.3 shows the component from Furniture Shack (a fictitious online merchant of fine home furnishings) that we'll reconstruct. As you can see, it's a bordered box containing three "teasers" to a variety of products available from the Furniture Shack stores.

Each "teaser" contains a product image, title, and short description. Both the style and layout fit the look of the company's stores and catalogs—so, well done there.

Under the hood, this box is built using a series of nested tables and spacer GIFs, and it's worth pointing out that the title text is served as an image. The code required to render this particular layout could easily fill a beautiful cherry-stained chest of drawers (with brushed-nickel knobs).

Why It's Not Bulletproof

For this particular example, the amount of code required could be reason enough for considering a better approach (Figure 4.4). Reducing the code will not only cut down on file size (which in turn will reduce required server space and speed up the downloading of pages), but it will also make the editing of the component from a production standpoint far easier. When we take the time to choose the best markup for the task at hand, the simplified results will be easier for servers *and* site editors to read and understand. Think of it as flexibility in terms of maintenance as well.

Because of the code bloat, the common approach also scores low in terms of accessibility to a wide range of software and devices. Accessing the rigid construction of nested tables and spacer GIF shims that are used to lay out the design with anything but a standard Web browser could certainly prove to be trying for any user. As we'll discover, deflating the code bloat and increasing the accessibility doesn't have to compromise the design.

```
spacer.gif" width="1" height="3" alt="" border="0"><br><a href="http://ww2.furnitureshackshack.com/cat/
themeindex.cfm?cid=thmgor&altsrc=shpcfurN7Crshop" onMouseOut="MM_swapImgRestore()"
onMouseOver="MM_swapImage('editoeg3','','http://a451.g.akamai.net/7/451/1713/0001/image2.styleinamerica.com/
fsimgs/images/bld-20050401-004/common/arr_right45_white.gif',1)">new lighting<img src="http://
a451.g.akamai.net/7/451/1713/0001/image2.furnitureshackshack.com/fsimgs/images/bld-20050401-004/common/
spacer.gif" width="3" height="1" alt="" border="0"><img src="http://a451.g.akamai.net/7/451/1713/0001/
image2.furnitureshackshack.com/fsimgs/images/bld-20050401-004/common/arr_right44_white.gif" width="4"
height="7" alt="" name="editoeg3" border="0"></a><br><img src="http://a451.g.akamai.net/7/451/1713/0001/
image2.furnitureshackshack.com/fsimgs/images/bld-20050401-004/common/spacer.gif" width="1" height="3" alt=""
border="0"><br><a href="http://ww2.furnitureshackshack.com/view.cfm?pg=body/orgguide"
onMouseOut="MM_swapImgRestore()" onMouseOver="MM_swapImage('editoeg4','','http://a451.g.akamai.net/7/451/
1713/0001/image2.styleinamerica.com/fsimgs/images/bld-20050401-004/common/arr_right45_white.gif',1)">Our
lamps look great and even work.  Lightbulb not included.<img src="http://a451.g.akamai.net/7/451/1713/0001/
image2.furnitureshackshack.com/fsimgs/images/bld-20050401-004/common/spacer.gif" width="3" height="1" alt=""
border="0"><img src="http://a451.g.akamai.net/7/451/1713/0001/image2.furnitureshackshack.com/fsimgs/images/
bld-20050401-004/common/arr_right44_white.gif" width="4" height="7" alt="" name="editoeg4" border="0"></
a><br><img src="http://a451.g.akamai.net/7/451/1713/0001/image2.furnitureshackshack.com/fsimgs/images/bld
-20050401-004/common/spacer.gif" width="1" height="2" alt="" border="0"><br></font></a></td>
                </tr>
            </table></div><div align="center">
<table border="0" cellpadding="0" cellspacing="0" width="199">
<tr>
<td colspan="2"><img src="http://a451.g.akamai.net/7/451/1713/0001/image2.furnitureshackshack.com/fsimgs/
images/bld-20050401-004/common/spacer.gif" width="1" height="24" alt="" border="0"></td>
</tr>
<tr>
<td valign="top" width="108"><table border="0" cellpadding="0" cellspacing="0"><tr><td><br><font
face="Verdana, Geneva, Arial, Helvetica" size="1" color="666666" class="text"><a href="http://
ww2.furnitureshackshack.com/cat/roomindex.cfm?cid=romliv" onMouseOut="MM_swapImgRestore()"
onMouseOver="MM_swapImage('edit5sss','','http://a451.g.akamai.net/7/451/1713/0001/image2.styleinamerica.com/
fsimgs/images/bld-20050401-004/common/arr_right45_white.gif',1)">sofas that are red<img src="http://
a451.g.akamai.net/7/451/1713/0001/image2.furnitureshackshack.com/fsimgs/images/bld-20050401-004/common/
spacer.gif" width="3" height="1" alt="" border="0"><img src="http://a451.g.akamai.net/7/451/1713/0001/
image2.furnitureshackshack.com/fsimgs/images/bld-20050401-004/common/arr_right44_white.gif" width="4"
height="7" alt="" name="edit5sss" border="0"></a><br><img src="http://a451.g.akamai.net/7/451/1713/0001/
image2.furnitureshackshack.com/fsimgs/images/bld-20050401-004/common/spacer.gif" width="1" height="5" alt=""
border="0"><br>
```

Figure 4.4 Avoid drowning in a sea of code.

A Bulletproof Approach

To simplify the structure of this box, we'll strip away the tables in favor of minimal markup. We'll then turn to our friend CSS to replicate the grid-like layout of the *teasers* (the image/title/description grouping), while still creating a compelling design.

As always, to get things started, let's decide how best to structure the box with markup.

THE ENDLESS CHOICES FOR MARKUP

In assessing what we need in terms of markup for this design, let's refamiliarize ourselves with our goal by sketching out what we need in the way of structure.

Figure 4.5 illustrates the basic framework we're dealing with. We'll need an outer container for the box to hold everything and create the border. Inside, the three teasers each contain an image floated to one side, alongside a title and short description.

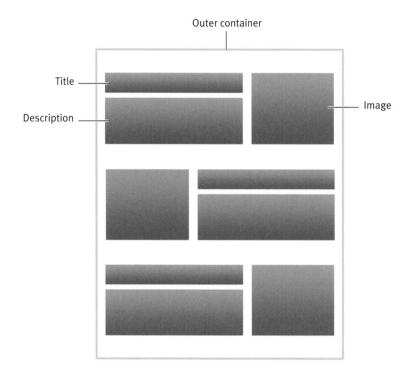

Figure 4.5 This wireframe of the structure will help us lay out our example.

Because I know what we'll be up against further on, I know we need an element that also *surrounds* each teaser. This element will group each image, title, and description together as a unit. And semantically, this makes sense as well, isolating each discrete chunk (or teaser) with a containing element.

With that said, we can weigh our options in terms of the markup we choose here. As in most things Web design, there are no *wrong* choices—only choices and *better* choices.

USING DEFINITION LISTS

Definition lists are underused in my opinion, especially for applications that aren't an obvious title and description pairing (as they are commonly used for). A definition list consists of an outer <dl> element, with any number of definition terms <dt> and descriptions <dd>:

```
<dl>
  <dt>This is the Term</dt>
  <dd>This is the description.</dd>
</dl>
```

In its specification for definition lists (www.w3.org/TR/html4/struct/lists.html#h-10.3), the W3C hints at other uses for these elements by suggesting that a) definition lists can contain multiple terms and/or definitions and b) definition lists can also be used for other applications, for example a dialogue that could be marked up like so:

```
<dl>
  <dt>Younger Cop</dt>
  <dd>And was there anything of value in the car?</dd>
  <dt>The Dude</dt>
  <dd>Oh, uh, yeah, uh... a tape deck, some Creedence tapes,
and there was a, uh... uh, my briefcase.</dd>
  <dt>Younger Cop</dt>
  <dd>[expectant pause] In the briefcase?</dd>
  <dt>The Dude</dt>
  <dd>Uh, uh, papers, um, just papers, uh, you know, uh, my
papers, business  papers.</dd>
  <dt>Younger Cop</dt>
  <dd>And what do you do, sir?</dd>
  <dt>The Dude</dt>
  <dd>I'm unemployed.</dd>
</dl>
```

It's b) that I (and other designers) have taken to heart, using definition lists for a variety of markup applications to provide a more meaningful and clearly organized structure.

So, with that in mind, I've chosen to use a *series* of definition lists to structure each image, title, and description.

THE MARKUP STRUCTURE

To make things more interesting (although I suppose furniture *can* be interesting), I'll be swapping out the Furniture Shack content for something of my own, featuring a few photos from a recent trip to Sweden. Each tease will consist of a definition list containing the title as the definition *term* and the image and description as... well, *descriptions* of that title. As mentioned earlier, we'll also need an outer containing element to set a width and the border that surrounds the entire component.

With all of that mapped out, our simple markup structure looks like this:

```
<div id="sweden">
  <dl>
    <dt>Stockholm</dt>
    <dd><img src="img/gamlastan.jpg" width="80" height="80"
alt="Gamla Stan" /></dd>
    <dd>This was taken in Gamla Stan (Old Town) in a large
square of amazing buildings.</dd>
  </dl>
  <dl>
    <dt>Gamla Uppsala</dt>
    <dd><img src="img/uppsala.jpg" width="80" height="80"
alt="Gamla Uppsala" /></dd>
    <dd>The first three Swedish kings are buried here, under
ancient burial mounds.</dd>
  </dl>
  <dl>
    <dt>Perpetual Sun</dt>
    <dd><img src="img/watch.jpg" width="80" height="80"
alt="Wristwatch" /></dd>
    <dd>During the summer months, the sun takes forever to
go down. This is a good thing.</dd>
  </dl>
</div>
```

We've given the outer container an id of sweden, and inside we have three definition lists, each containing a title, followed by an associated image and short description. At this point, you may be wondering why we chose to use three separate <dl>s as opposed to one big list. The reasoning here will be revealed a bit later.

SANS STYLE

Without any style applied to our markup, the structure is still apparent when viewed in a browser (Figure 4.6).

Typically, a browser will indent <dd> elements, making it easier to view the relationship between them and the <dt> elements that precede them. Because we've chosen lean, simple markup, any device or browsing software should have no problems whatsoever understanding what we're delivering here. But it doesn't exactly look the way we want it to yet. Let's start adding some style.

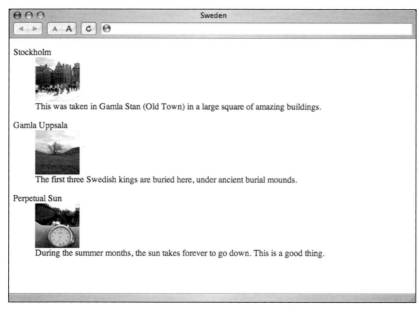

Figure 4.6 With CSS disabled, or not applied, the structure of the example is still readable and easily understood.

STYLING THE CONTAINER

To begin, let's add a declaration that will set a width and blue border around the entire list. We'll add these styles to the outer <div> previously marked with id="sweden".

```
#sweden {
  width: 300px;
  border: 2px solid #C8CDD2;
  }
```

By setting a width of 300px and a colored border around our entire box, we end up with the results shown in Figure 4.7.

note

A default font of Arial has been set on the entire page, with font-size set using the absolute-size keyword small.

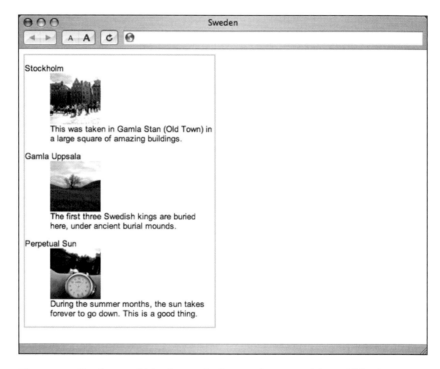

Figure 4.7 Setting a width of 300 pixels contains everything within the main <div>.

We could have assigned padding to this outer container as well, but since we're declaring a set width, we can avoid having to use the Box Model Hack (see Chapter 1, "Flexible Text") to prevent IE5/Win from calculating the wrong dimension. Instead, we'll assign margins to the definition lists that live *within* #sweden. (Would these lists be considered *Swedes*? Sorry...)

IDENTIFYING THE IMAGE

To make things easy to control later on, one step we need to take before going any further is to add a class to each <dd> element that holds the image. Because we'll float the image (and not the second <dd> that holds the description text), we need a way to uniquely identify that element in the markup so that we may later apply style to it with CSS:

```
<div id="sweden">
  <dl>
    <dt>Stockholm</dt>
    <dd class="img"><img src="img/gamlastan.jpg" width="80"
height="80" alt="Gamla Stan" /></dd>
    <dd>This was taken in Gamla Stan (Old Town) in a large
square of amazing buildings.</dd>
  </dl>
  <dl>
    <dt>Gamla Uppsala</dt>
    <dd class="img"><img src="img/uppsala.jpg" width="80"
height="80" alt="Gamla Uppsala" /></dd>
    <dd>The first three Swedish kings are buried here, under
ancient burial mounds.</dd>
  </dl>
  <dl>
    <dt>Perpetual Sun</dt>
    <dd class="img"><img src="img/watch.jpg" width="80"
height="80" alt="Wristwatch" /></dd>
    <dd>During the summer months, the sun takes forever to
go down. This is a good thing.</dd>
  </dl>
</div>
```

With each <dd> that contains the image flagged with a class="img", we're now prepared to move on.

APPLYING BASE STYLES

Let's now apply base styles for each tease, leaving only the positioning of the image to be done a bit later.

To evenly apply 20 pixels of space around the teasers as well as the inside of the box (Figure 4.8), we'll break up the margins between the containing

note

Unfortunately, IE5/Win incorrectly calculates the width of a box by subtracting any padding that is added to it. Other browsers correctly *add* padding to any specified width. There are ways around this, most commonly using the Box Model Hack described back in Chapter 1, "Flexible Text," where two different width values can be served to IE5/Win and all others. We can avoid hacks altogether in this case, however, by adding *margins* to the lists instead of padding to the containing <div>, which has a specified width attached to it.

<div> and the teasers themselves. First, let's apply 10 pixels of padding to the top and bottom of the containing <div id="sweden">. Then, we'll apply 10-pixel margins on the top and bottom of each <dl>, as well as 20-pixel margins on both the left and right of each <dl>. Applying left and right margins around the lists rather than *padding* to the sides of the <div> avoids the box model problem that plagues the IE5/Win browser.

```
#sweden {
  width: 300px;
  padding: 10px 0;
  border: 2px solid #C8CDD2;
}
#sweden dl {
  margin: 10px 20px;
  padding: 0;
}
```

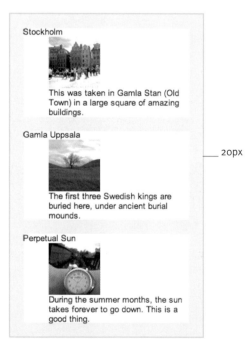
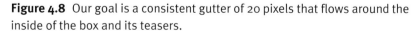

Figure 4.8 Our goal is a consistent gutter of 20 pixels that flows around the inside of the box and its teasers.

Figure 4.9 shows the results of adding the margins and padding. We've also zeroed out any default padding that may be attached to definition lists. And the box is already looking better.

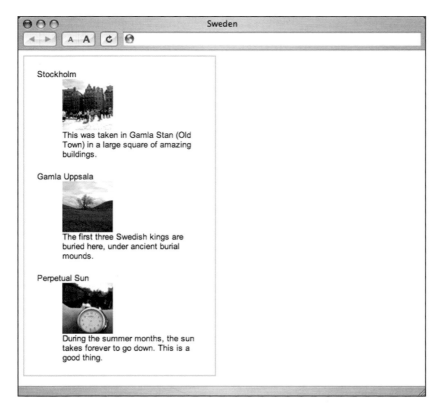

Figure 4.9 With margins and padding distributed among the elements, the box begins to take shape.

Next, let's introduce color and custom text treatment to the title of each tease by styling <dt> elements within our box:

```
#sweden {
  width: 300px;
  padding: 10px 0;
  border: 2px solid #C8CDD2;
  }
#sweden dl {
  margin: 10px 20px;
```

```
    padding: 0;
    }
#sweden dt {
    margin: 0;
    padding: 0;
    font-size: 130%;
    letter-spacing: 1px;
    color: #627081;
    }
```

note 📖

I'm using the Safari
browser throughout this
example, taking advantage
of Mac OS X's beautiful
antialiasing of text. You
could get similar results
using Windows XP with
ClearType enabled.
Users of other operating
systems would receive
mixed results.

Looking at Figure 4.10, you'll notice that we've increased the size of the title, added the lovely slate-blue shade, and increased space between letters by a fraction using the letter-spacing property, mimicking the style from the Furniture Shack example, where images were used in place of styled text.

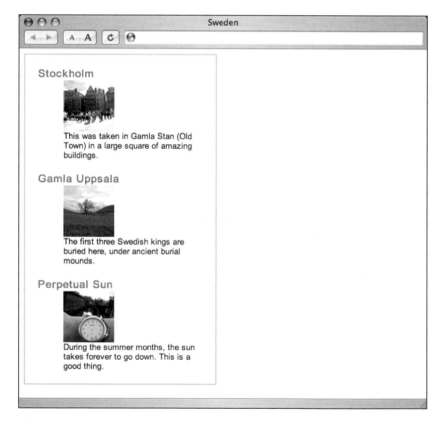

Figure 4.10 Simply text styling can do wonders for a component's design, and often eliminates the need for image-based type.

We'll also want to add a bit of style to the <dd> elements as well, matching the smaller, gray text from the Furniture Shack example:

```
#sweden {
  width: 300px;
  padding: 10px 0;
  border: 2px solid #C8CDD2;
  }
#sweden dl {
  margin: 10px 20px;
  padding: 0;
  }
#sweden dt {
  margin: 0;
  padding: 0;
  font-size: 130%;
  letter-spacing: 1px;
  color: #627081;
  }
#sweden dd {
  margin: 0;
  padding: 0;
  font-size: 85%;
  line-height: 1.5em;
  color: #666;
  }
```

Figure 4.11 shows the results, with the short description text now looking smaller and gray. We've also increased the line-height (the space between lines of text) to one and a half times the height of normal text. This lets the description breathe a bit more. Also important is the removal of the default indenting that's often applied to <dd> elements by the browser. We've overridden that by zeroing out margins and padding.

Figure 4.11 To match the Furniture Shack example, we've decreased the size of the description and made the text gray.

POSITIONING THE IMAGE

Our next challenge is to position the image to one side of both the title and description. For now, let's worry about lining things up on the *left* only. Later, we'll address how best to alternate the alignment as seen in the Furniture Shack example.

Because of the order in which things appear in the markup—title, image, then description—if we simply just float the image to the left we'll have the title always sitting *above* everything else (Figure 4.12). What we really want is the top of the image *and* title to be aligned at the same level.

Stockholm

This was taken in Gamla Stan (Old Town) in a large square of amazing buildings.

Figure 4.12 With the image coming after the title in the markup, just floating it to one side leaves the title above everything.

In the past, I've swapped the order of elements to make this work, putting the image in the <dt> element and using <dd> elements for both the title and description. Because the image appeared first, floating to either side would allow us to line it up just right. But semantically, it makes far more sense to have the title be the definition term, followed by an image and text that *describe* that title (as we've done in our markup structure for this example). It takes only a little more CSS magic to have the best of both worlds: optimal markup structure and the image to one side of both the title and description.

OPPOSING FLOATS

You may remember the "opposing floats" method explained in Chapter 3, "Expandable Rows." Essentially, we used the float property to place two elements on opposite ends of a container. We use the same method here, allowing us to align the image to the left of both the title *and* the short description while keeping the markup in an optimal order.

Remember that we've previously tagged <dd> elements that contain the image with a class="img"—which allows us to float images within those elements to one side while keeping the descriptions in place.

So, to begin let's float <dt> elements *right* and images *left*:

```
#sweden {
  width: 300px;
  padding: 10px 0;
  border: 2px solid #C8CDD2;
  }
#sweden dl {
  margin: 10px 20px;
  padding: 0;
  }
#sweden dt {
  float: right;
  margin: 0;
  padding: 0;
```

```
   font-size: 130%;
   letter-spacing: 1px;
   color: #627081;
   }
#sweden dd {
   margin: 0;
   padding: 0;
   font-size: 85%;
   line-height: 1.5em;
   color: #666;
   }
#sweden dd.img img {
   float: left;
   }
```

By using the opposing floats method, we can position the image to the left of both the title and description, regardless of the fact that the title comes *first* in the markup (Figure 4.13).

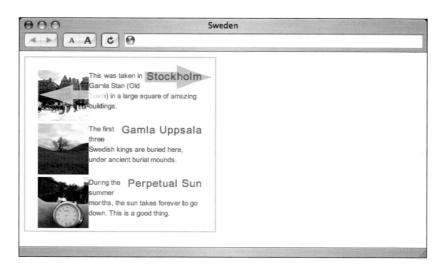

Figure 4.13 Here we see opposing floats at work, aligning the tops of the image and title.

Notice that, while we've successfully positioned the image, the description has slipped in between the image and title. To fix this, we need to apply a little math to set up a grid-like layout for each tease.

Quite simply, we just need to assign a width on the <dt> elements, forcing them to span across the top of each description on their own line. To calculate this width, let's start with the total width of the box (300 pixels), minus the margins around each definition list (20 pixels times 2), minus the width of the image (80 pixels). The result is 180 pixels (Figure 4.14).

By simply adding a width of 180px to the declaration for <dt> elements, we ensure that things start falling into their intended places:

```
#sweden dt {
  float: right;
  width: 180px;
  margin: 0;
  padding: 0;
  font-size: 130%;
  letter-spacing: 1px;
  color: #627081;
  }
```

Figure 4.15 shows where we are at this point, having successfully positioned the image, title, and description via opposing floats.

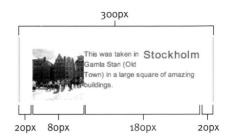

Figure 4.14 Determining the width for the <dt> elements involves a little calculation.

Figure 4.15 With the width assigned for <dt> elements, the items fall into place.

CLEAR THE WAY FOR ANY DESCRIPTION LENGTH

Thus far in the example, each description has been long enough to roughly meet the bottom of each image. Because of this length, we haven't yet had to worry about *clearing* the floats. To illustrate what could happen when the description is shortened, take a look at Figure 4.16. Not exactly bullet-proof, is it?

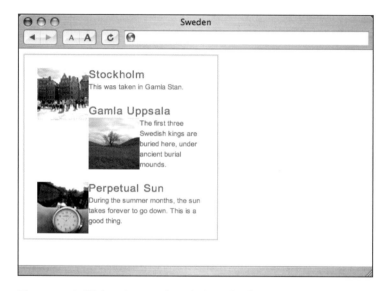

Figure 4.16 With a shorter description, the floated images can lead to undesired results.

When you are first learning how to use floats, understanding how they need to be properly *cleared* can be tricky. When an element is floated, it is taken out of the normal flow of the document and doesn't affect the vertical stacking of elements that follow it. Floated elements will always extend beyond the height of their containers. If the description happens to be long enough to meet or exceed the bottom of the floated image, then all is right with the world. But if the content next to the floated image is *shorter*, that's when you'll run into problems.

Figure 4.17 shows the outline of the definition list marked in red. You can see that the image is taller than the title and description combined in the first tease. And since the image is floated left, the next definition list in line will attempt to wrap around it. What we need is a way to clear the floated image before going on to the next tease. For example, in the old days one might add the following to clear any previously declared in the markup: `<br clear="all">`. This works, but is rather unnecessary when we're dealing with CSS-based designs, not to mention that the `clear` attribute is considered invalid in recent XHTML specifications (XHTML 1.0 Strict, XHTML 1.1). What we'd rather do is use CSS (and not markup) to clear floats, and we'll explore a few ways to do just that next.

Figure 4.17 The red box shows where the `<dl>` containing the float really ends.

SELF-CLEARING FLOATS

There are several ways to clear floats using CSS, and to get a handle on many of them (and why problems arise), I encourage you to start off by reading CSS guru Eric Meyer's article, "Containing Floats" (`www.complexspiral.com/publications/containing-floats/`).

I'm going to share three popular methods for *self-clearing* floats—that is, the process of applying CSS to a container that has floated elements inside it. By self-clearing the floats within, it **keeps the container independent**, regardless of what comes before or after it in the flow of the document. This is a key element of being bulletproof: if we keep "modules" (containers of various mini-layouts) independent, they stand a better chance of staying intact if moved around, changed, or edited later by either you or your client or boss. Self-clearing is essential for that modularization when you're using floats and requires no extra markup (such as `<br clear="all">`).

Let's look at three ways to do this, applying each method to our example:

- **The "Set a Float to Fix a Float" method** (described in Eric Meyer's article and used previously in this book). This technique often depends on what comes after the container on the page, but this cross-browser method is simple to implement.

- **The "Simple Clearing of Floats" method using the** `overflow` **property**. This is probably the simplest method to implement but has some possible side effects. It's described in detail at SitePoint: www.sitepoint.com/blogs/2005/02/26/simple-clearing-of-floats/.

■ **The "Easy Clearing" method using generated content** (described at http://positioniseverything.net/easyclearing.html). This method requires jumping through a few hoops for Internet Explorer, but once you grasp the idea, I think it's the most solid choice.

First, we'll use the "Set a Float to Fix a Float" method and apply that to our example.

Setting a float to fix a float

Essentially, a container will stretch to fit around floated elements within it—if the container is *also* floated. So, taking Eric Meyer's advice, we want to float each <dl> left in order to force each teaser below the floated image above it. In addition, we need to float the entire containing <div>, ensuring that the border will enclose all of the floated elements within it:

```
#sweden {
  float: left;
  width: 300px;
  padding: 10px 0;
  border: 2px solid #C8CDD2;
  }
#sweden dl {
  float: left;
  margin: 10px 20px;
  padding: 0;
  }
#sweden dt {
  float: right;
  width: 180px;
  margin: 0;
  padding: 0;
  font-size: 130%;
  letter-spacing: 1px;
  color: #627081;
  }
#sweden dd {
  margin: 0;
  padding: 0;
```

```
  font-size: 85%;
  line-height: 1.5em;
  color: #666;
  }
#sweden dd.img img {
  float: left;
  }
```

Adding the previous rules to our example, we have properly cleared floats, with each tease ending up below the other—regardless of description length (Figure 4.18).

Figure 4.18 Even with a short description, we have properly cleared floats.

Our next step is to add a quick fix for both IE/Win and IE/Mac.

A margin fix for IE/Win

When adding a left or right margin to a floated element, IE/Win can have the unfortunate tendency to *double* the margin on the same side as the float direction (i.e., right-hand margin for right floats, left margin for left floats, www.positioniseverything.net/explorer/doubled-margin.html).

We of course appreciate the free pixels, but we'd like IE/Win to display the margins *correctly*. In this example, the bug affects the 20-pixel margin on the left and right of each <dl> that we've previously assigned. In IE/Win, 20 pixels become 40 pixels (Figure 4.19).

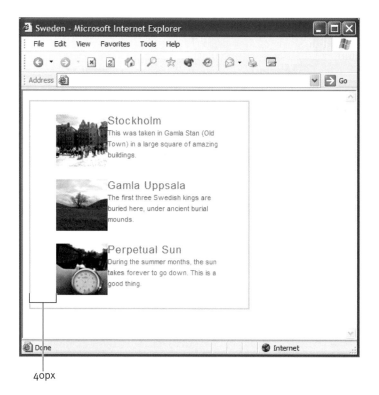

40px

Figure 4.19 IE/Win doubles the margin from 20 pixels to 40 pixels on the floated <dl> elements.

Luckily, there's an easy fix, described in an article on the "Position Is Everything" Web site (www.positioniseverything.net/explorer/ doubled-margin.html). The article explains that adding the rule display: inline; to the floated element mysteriously triggers IE/Win to correctly apply margins. Fortunately, this rule also has no ill effects on other browsers, so simply slide this little rule in and we're ready to move on. We've labeled the fix with a comment so that others might understand why we added it. You could even go a step further and quarantine this browser-specific fix to a separate part of the style sheet or even a separate file altogether. I'll go more in-depth on the subject of hack management in Chapter 9, "Putting It All Together."

```
#sweden dl {
  float: left;
  margin: 10px 20px;
  padding: 0;
  display: inline; /* fixes IE/Win double margin bug */
}
```

A width fix for IE/Mac

To cure IE/Mac's affliction of stretching floated elements *wider* than the specified width of their container, we need to add a width to each <dl> element if we want to play nice with IE/Mac fans.

Specifying a width here is rather harmless, since we're already locking this box down to a fixed width. We're more concerned with leaving room to breathe vertically, which we still allow for, even with this fix:

```
#sweden dl {
  float: left;
  width: 260px;
  margin: 10px 20px;
  padding: 0;
  display: inline; /* fixes IE/Win double margin bug */
}
```

With the clearing of our floats solved for all major browsers, we're now ready to put the finishing touches on our example.

THE FINISHING TOUCHES

To put the final polish on this example, let's adjust the spacing between images and text, and later allow for floating the image both to the left *and* right.

To adjust the spacing between the images and text, we'll just have to add a right margin to the image, then subtract that amount from the width we've defined for the <dt> elements. While we're at it, let's also add a little framed border around each image. We can fold these additions into the master style sheet for this example, where you can see that the CSS remains rather compact:

note

I've come up with a width of 260 pixels by taking our total width for the box of 300 pixels and then subtracting the 20-pixel margin from each side.

```
#sweden {
  float: left;
  width: 300px;
  padding: 10px 0;
  border: 2px solid #C8CDD2;
  }
#sweden dl {
  float: left;
  width: 260px;
  margin: 10px 20px;
  padding: 0;
  display: inline; /* fixes IE/Win double margin bug */
  }
#sweden dt {
  float: right;
  width: 162px;
  margin: 0;
  padding: 0;
  font-size: 130%;
  letter-spacing: 1px;
  color: #627081;
  }
#sweden dd {
  margin: 0;
  padding: 0;
  font-size: 85%;
  line-height: 1.5em;
  color: #666;
  }
#sweden dd.img img {
  float: left;
  margin: 0 8px 0 0;
  padding: 4px;
  border: 1px solid #D9E0E6;
  border-bottom-color: #C8CDD2;
  border-right-color: #C8CDD2;
  background: #fff;
  }
```

Figure 4.20 shows the results of the new styles added. We've added an 8-pixel margin to the right of each floated image, as well as 4 pixels of padding and a 1-pixel border around the image itself to create a frame. Since we've added this extra width, we have to add all that up, then subtract that total from the width we previously set on <dt> elements. The math goes like this: 8-pixel right margin + 4-pixel padding on both sides + 1-pixel border on both sides = 18 pixels. So, as you can see, we've dropped the width for <dt> elements down to 162 pixels to accommodate the extra space that the image will now take up.

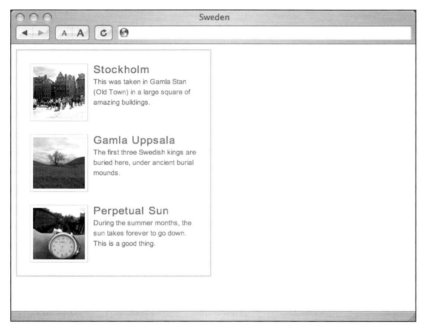

Figure 4.20 We've achieved proper spacing between images and text.

For the border around the image, we've chosen to make the right and bottom edges a slightly darker shade than the top and left. This creates a subtle three-dimensional effect on the photo, as if it's lying on top of the box (Figure 4.21).

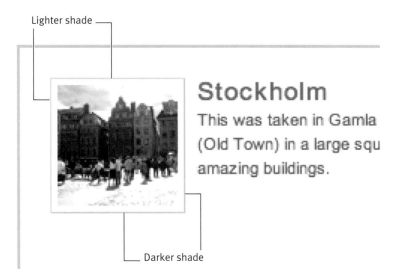

Lighter shade

Stockholm

This was taken in Gamla
(Old Town) in a large squ
amazing buildings.

Darker shade

Figure 4.21 A simple trick for creating dimension is to use darker right and bottom borders.

TOGGLING THE FLOAT DIRECTION

Another aspect of the original Furniture Shack example that we'll want to replicate is that the side to which each image floats swaps back and forth. One tease will have the image aligned left, while another will have it aligned right. We want to build in the ability to change this at will, with a simple class="alt" added to the <dl> when a swap is desired.

First, we tag the <dl> that we'd like to change float direction on. We've chosen the second teaser:

```
<div id="sweden">
  <dl>
    <dt>Stockholm</dt>
    <dd class="img"><img src="img/gamlastan.jpg" width="80"
height="80" alt="Gamla Stan" /></dd>
    <dd>This was taken in Gamla Stan (Old Town) in a large
square of amazing buildings.</dd>
  </dl>
  <dl class="alt">
    <dt>Gamla Uppsala</dt>
```

```
    <dd class="img"><img src="img/uppsala.jpg" width="80"
height="80" alt="Gamla Uppsala" /></dd>
    <dd>The first three Swedish kings are buried here, under
ancient burial mounds.</dd>
  </dl>
  <dl>
    <dt>Perpetual Sun</dt>
    <dd class="img"><img src="img/watch.jpg" width="80"
height="80" alt="Wristwatch" /></dd>
    <dd>During the summer months, the sun takes forever to
go down. This is a good thing.</dd>
  </dl>
</div>
```

Having added the alt class to the second tease, we can now include a few rules at the end of our style sheet that will override the default, which currently aligns the image to the left. The alt style will reverse the direction, floating the image on the *right*. This class could be swapped in and out at will, giving site editors easy control over the layout of the box.

The following CSS should be placed after the previous declarations we've already written:

```
/* reverse float */

#sweden .alt dt {
  float: left;
  }
#sweden .alt dd.img img {
  float: right;
  margin: 0 0 0 8px;
  }
```

Here we're telling the browser that it should do the following:

- For <dt> elements within a <dl> marked with the alt class, float those *left* (instead of the default right).

- Float images within the alt class *right* (instead of the default left).

- Change the 8-pixel margin that was to the right of the image over to the left instead.

Figure 4.22 shows the results of adding these two little declarations to the style sheet. Because the second tease is marked with the alt class, its image is aligned to the right. The idea here is that we can add or remove a simple class at any time to assign the float direction for a particular image.

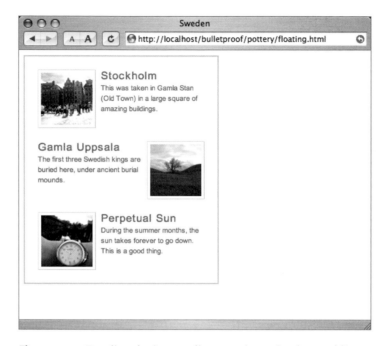

Figure 4.22 Toggling the image alignment is as simple as adding or removing the alt class.

THE GRID EFFECT

If we were dealing with longer descriptions (or if the user increased the text size), we'd find that the description text would wrap down around the image. That's the nature of a float: it will take up as much space as it needs to but will let content flow around it (Figure 4.23).

Stockholm
This was taken in Gamla Stan (Old Town) in a large square of amazing buildings. This is another line of text in the description. If long enough, it will eventually wrap around the image that is floating beside it.

Gamla Uppsala
The first three Swedish kings are buried here, under ancient burial mounds.

Perpetual Sun
During the summer months, the sun takes forever to go

Figure 4.23 Longer descriptions will wrap around the floated image.

This could be the intended effect, but if a more column-like grid is what you're after, applying a margin to the description will keep the text and images away from each other.

The width of the margin that we'll add to the description should equal the width of the image, plus padding, borders, and margin already specified between the image and description (Figure 4.24).

Stockholm
This was taken in Gamla Stan (Old Town) in a large square of amazing buildings. This is another line of text in the description. If long enough, it will eventually wrap around the image that is floating beside it.

← 98px →

Figure 4.24 Adding the image width, margin, padding, and border together comes to 98 pixels.

So by adding a left margin of 98px to all <dd> elements and then overriding that value to 0 for <dd class="img"> elements (since we don't want the *image* to have a margin, yet it resides inside a <dd>), we'll in a sense be creating *columns* on either side.

To reverse the margins for the `alt` class when the image is floated right instead of left, we need to add another rule to our "reverse float" section at the end of the style sheet:

```
#sweden {
  float: left;
  width: 300px;
  padding: 10px 0;
  border: 2px solid #C8CDD2;
  }
#sweden dl {
  float: left;
  width: 260px;
  margin: 10px 20px;
  padding: 0;
  display: inline; /* fixes IE/Win double margin bug */
  }
#sweden dt {
  float: right;
  width: 162px;
  margin: 0;
  padding: 0;
  font-size: 130%;
  letter-spacing: 1px;
  color: #627081;
  }
#sweden dd {
  margin: 0 0 0 98px;
  padding: 0;
  font-size: 85%;
  line-height: 1.5em;
  color: #666;
  }
#sweden dl dd.img {
  margin: 0;
  }
#sweden dd.img img {
  float: left;
  margin: 0 8px 0 0;
  padding: 4px;
```

```
  border: 1px solid #D9E0E6;
  border-bottom-color: #C8CDD2;
  border-right-color: #C8CDD2;
  background: #fff;
  }

/* reverse float */

#sweden .alt dt {
  float: left;
  }
#sweden .alt dd {
  margin: 0 98px 0 0;
  }
#sweden .alt dd.img img {
  float: right;
  margin: 0 0 0 8px;
  }
```

Notice that we've added a declaration that resets the margin value to 0 for <dd> elements that are flagged with class="img". This will override the *right* margin set in the "reverse float" section further down the style sheet. It will also save us from repeating the override after the #sweden .alt dd declaration assigns a right margin that we again don't want showing up on <dd> elements that contain our floated image.

Figure 4.25 shows the results of the previous additions to the style sheet. You can see that with the text size significantly increased, and/or with longer descriptions, the text and image both stick to their respective "columns," as if we'd used a table here for layout.

AN ALTERNATE BACKGROUND

As a final touch to this example, let's trade in the solid-blue border that surrounds the box for a background image that fades to white. We'll create the image in Photoshop, at a width of 304 pixels (300 pixels + a 2-pixel border on both sides).

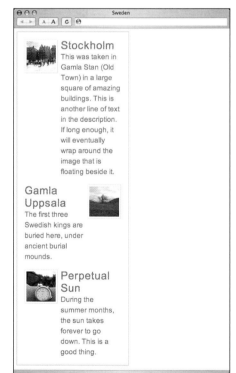

Figure 4.25 With a margin applied to the description, it's as if the text is held within columns.

Figure 4.26 shows the completed image, which we created by filling a bordered box with a lighter shade of blue and then using the Gradient tool (Figure 4.27) to fade white to transparent from bottom to top.

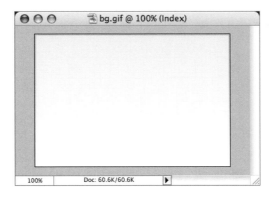

Figure 4.26 We created a blue background by using the Gradient tool.

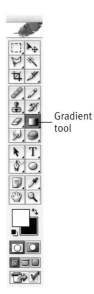

Gradient tool

Figure 4.27 You'll find the Gradient tool in the Tools palette in Photoshop.

To reference this image in our style sheet, we just adjust the declaration for the main containing `<div>`:

```
#sweden {
  float: left;
  width: 304px;
  padding: 10px 0;
  background: url(img/bg.gif) no-repeat top left;
  }
```

We've adjusted the width of the container from 300 pixels to 304 pixels to account for the loss of the 2- pixel border (which is now part of the background image), and we've aligned the fade top and left. Because it fades to white (the background color of the page) and is aligned at the top, we need not worry about what's contained *in* the box; it will accommodate any height, with its contents just spilling out of the fade. Another plus is that I happen to think it just looks cool (Figure 4.28).

If we zoom in on the top image, you can see that the padded frame remains white on top of the blue background (Figure 4.29). You may remember that we assigned a `background: #fff;` in addition to 4px of padding on the floated images to accomplish this. If we hadn't specified a background color here, then the blue fade would show through the image's frame.

Figure 4.28 Here is our completed, bulletproof example.

White background

4px padding

Figure 4.29 Combining padding and a background color creates a frame around the image.

MORE FLOAT-CLEARING FUN

We've just finished the example using the "float to fix a float" method that's been used previously in the book. We floated each <dl> in order to clear the opposing floats that were contained within.

This is a simple concept to grasp—and an easy method to implement cross-browser. But it's somewhat reliant on a few things: we must set a width on the container (so that the floated containers stack vertically and so that IE/Mac won't expand anything wider than its container, as previously described in this chapter), and we must anticipate what comes before or after the container of floats (since we could run into issues with the floated *container* needing to be cleared as well, thus starting a vicious, never-ending cycle).

So while floating a container to clear floats within it can work in certain circumstances, there are other methods that are consistent regardless of the scenario. Let's take a look at a few more options.

Simple clearing of floats using the overflow property

Applying the overflow property on a container will self-clear any floats within it (see Alex Walker's article at SitePoint: www.sitepoint.com/blogs/2005/02/26/simple-clearing-of-floats/). The approach is simple and easy to implement, although it's not obvious that it will work under most circumstances. But it does.

Using our example, if we removed the floats from each <dl> and replaced them with overflow: auto, we'd be achieving the same goal.

Here's the original declaration:

```
#sweden dl {
  float: left;
  width: 260px;
  margin: 10px 20px;
  padding: 0;
  display: inline; /* fixes IE/Win double margin bug */
  }
```

And here it is with the overflow trick to clear floats instead:

```
#sweden dl {
  overflow: auto;
  width: 260px;
```

```
  margin: 10px 20px;
  padding: 0;
  }
```

You'll also notice that we removed the display: inline; rule, as it's no longer needed in this case. That rule fixed the previously mentioned double float margin bug in IE, and since the <dl> is no longer floated to fix the floats within it, we can toss that hack.

Now in most circumstances, the overflow trick will likely work out fine—but there are situations where it could become problematic. We've used the value auto, which could trigger scrollbars around the element, should its contents be wider than its specified width (260px). So that's one possible scenario. You could also specify overlow: hidden; instead of overflow: auto;. The hidden value will (you guessed it) hide its contents should they exceed the container's width.

If you're positive that neither of those scenarios will happen, then perhaps overflow is worth a shot. As for me, I'm more likely to want a solution that I don't have to worry about in the future—and that's just what we'll get with the next method.

EASY CLEARING USING GENERATED CONTENT

The most robust, reliable solution for self-clearing I've found is documented in an article at Position Is Everything: "How to Clear Floats Without Structural Markup" (http://positioniseverything.net/easyclearing.html). The idea is rather clever: it uses the :after pseudo-element in CSS (www. w3.org/TR/CSS21/selector.html#before-and-after) to insert a period after the container of floats. The clear: both rule is also added to clear all floats, and then the period is hidden. Let's take a look at the declaration in action:

```
#sweden dl {
  width: 260px;
  margin: 10px 20px;
  padding: 0;
  }
#sweden dl:after {
  content: ".";
  display: block;
  height: 0;
```

```
clear: both;
visibility: hidden;
}
```

For the main #sweden dl declaration, we don't need to add float or overflow as we did for the previous methods. It's the next declaration that does the float-clearing magic, so let's break it down and figure out exactly what is happening here.

We're essentially saying, "Put a period after each definition list (content: "."; will do that), clear all floats the precede them (clear: both;), and then make sure the period is hidden (height: 0; and visibility: hidden;)." Pretty crafty, eh?

By using the :after pseudo-element to self-clear any floats, we've done so without having to float the container, and we don't have to worry that overflow may cause issues down the road.

If only this worked in *cough* Internet Explorer. Yes, that's right, IE *doesn't* support the :after pseudo-element (ditto for :before). But not to worry— fortunately, there are additional rules we can target to IE that self-clear floats just as confidently.

Autoclearing in IE5 and 6

Conveniently, IE/Win will do its own "autoclearing" on containers as long as a dimension is applied to it. This isn't correct behavior, of course, but we'll use this spec deviation to our advantage. Historically called the "Holly Hack"(named after Holly Bergevin, the hack's author), it involves setting a height: 1%;, targeted specifically to IE and IE only, that forces the container to expand around its contents (even floated elements). If the height of the container's contents exceeds 1% (which it almost always will), that's OK—it will expand as needed, thus ignoring the height rule. Again, this isn't correct behavior in terms of the spec, but it's an inconsistency that actually helps us solve this autoclearing problem (among others).

The hack uses the * html selector (which precedes the declaration) and is read only by IE/Win versions 5 and 6 (we'll tackle IE7 in just a moment):

```
* html #sweden dl { height: 1%; }
```

That one declaration will autoclear any floats in each definition list, and by using the * html hack, you will target IE5 and 6 *only*. Other modern browsers will ignore it.

So, by offering the :after declaration for modern browsers that recognize it (Mozilla, Firefox, Safari, etc.), as well as the Holly Hack (for IE5 and 6), we have a majority of the browser market share covered with solutions that self-clear in a solid, reliable way. Ideally, we'd keep the Holly Hack (and any other IE-specific CSS) quarantined in its own style sheet (we'll talk more about why later in Chapter 9).

Solving the IE7 problem

IE7 was released with significantly better standards support—*a lot* was fixed, and we thank the developers for that. But support for *everything* that browsers like Firefox, Safari, and Opera have provided for years didn't materialize—which makes a few things a little tricky. This easy-clearing method is one of them.

IE7 fixed the height: 1%; bug. Where IE6 would expand a container to shrink wrap its contents—even when that exceeded a dimension specified with CSS—IE7 will now *correctly* honor that dimension. This is now proper behavior, so we can't blame the IE7 developers for fixing this. And like other, more standards-aware browsers, IE7 also now ignores declarations that begin with the * html selector, which is also proper behavior.

The problem, though, is that IE7 *still* doesn't support the :after pseudo-element. And so by fixing the height: 1% bug and not supporting :after, the IE7 developers ensured that we're stuck in terms of getting the browser to autoclear floats using one of these methods.

To address this issue, enter this bit of code:

```
*:first-child+html #sweden dl { min-height: 1px; }
```

Setting a min-height on a container in IE7 also expands a container in the same fashion that adding a height in IE6 does. That wacky-looking selector that precedes #sweden dl (*:first-child+html) is the piece that targets IE7 and IE7 *only*.

Hooray! Now we have the three pieces in place that will self-clear things in the most popular browsers. Let's take a look at all of them together in one place:

```
#sweden dl:after { /* for browsers that support :after */
  content: ".";
  display: block;
  height: 0;
```

 tip

If you're curious, height: 1%; is actually triggering something in IE called hasLayout. You can read a thorough (but lengthy) article titled "On Having Layout" (www.satzansatz.de/cssd/onhavinglayout.html) if you're interested in understanding the inner workings. Tread softly and pour yourself an extra large coffee prior to diving into this article.

```
  clear: both;
  visibility: hidden;
  }
* html #sweden dl { height: 1%; } /* for IE5+6 */
*:first-child+html #sweden dl { min-height: 1px; } /* for
IE7 */
```

Again, ideally the patches that target IE specifically would be placed in a separate style sheet, kept separate so as to avoid tainting the clean code (more
about that in Chapter 9). But with these three declarations, we have a solid,
reliable way of self-clearing floats. The code may seem a bit verbose at first,
but once you start using these rules consistently, you'll find that they become
indispensable for creating flexibility without concern that your floats will fall
apart in the future.

Combining selectors to save code

You can also combine selectors that share this self-clearing code by building a single declaration instead of repeating them for each container. For
instance, suppose you are also self-clearing floats found in the header of the
document:

```
#header:after,
#sweden dl:after { /* for browsers that support :after */
  content: ".";
  display: block;
  height: 0;
  clear: both;
  visibility: hidden;
  }

* html #header,
* html #sweden dl { height: 1%; } /* for IE5+6 */

*:first-child+html #header,
*:first-child+html #sweden dl { min-height: 1px; } /* for
IE7 */
```

As you're constructing your layout, you simply add elements to these three
declarations as necessary, thus saving you from repeating the code for each.

Choosing what works for you

Now that we've looked at three methods for self-clearing, I'd like to point out that (as with almost everything in web design) there's no *one* way that is correct 100% of the time. After experimenting with them all, you'll find that one method might work better than the others for you, depending on the situation.

I like the easy clearing method because of its robustness in just about any scenario, but I'll often throw `overflow: hidden;` on a container when *initially* building a layout, which is quick and easy to remember while proto-typing. Later, I'll do a quick search for that rule and build the three declarations that make up the easy clearing method.

Whatever method you choose, the important thing to remember is that **self-clearing can be a powerful tool** that maintains the flexibility that floats can bring to layout while keeping components of the page independent.

Why It's Bulletproof

After all of the CSS sorcery we've applied to this example, we may have long forgotten why we went down this path to rebuild this box of image, title, and descriptions. But in choosing a lean, semantic markup structure over the lines and lines of code that it takes to create this using tables and spacer GIFs, we're left with a compact and flexible unit—flexible in part because of its ease in updating, adding, or removing the content. The simplicity of the code also makes it easier for browsers, software, and even site editors to read.

You could also chalk this up as a big win for database-driven sites, where a uniform and more predictable markup structure could be reused more easily. Instead of worrying about whether the image comes before the title and description in the markup (when dealing with tables), the structure remains consistent and easily repeated in dynamic templates.

In choosing to use CSS to structure our grid-like layout, we've removed presentational code and graphic titles from the component, and in turn have gained flexibility in image placement and title/description size, style, and content.

Summary

By working through the construction of this example, my hope is that it will help make a case for creatively using floats to achieve grid-like effects. By understanding how to clear floats, you gain access to a wide range of possibilities without having to add extra markup. There are certainly times when using a <table> is appropriate (for tabular data), but even using compact and meaningful markup doesn't mean the design has to suffer. We can serve markup that a wider range of devices and software can easily understand, and use CSS to do the rest.

Here are a few points to consider:

- Choose optimal markup from the start. You can always adjust as needed, but try to get by with the most compact, most meaningful structure when you are just beginning.

- Consider the "opposing floats" method for aligning items on either side of each other, regardless of where they appear in the markup. In our example, the title came before the image, but we wanted both to line up vertically. Opposing floats to the rescue!

- Be aware of clearing floats: test various amounts of content and text sizes to ensure your intended layout doesn't break down.

- Experiment with the different methods of self-clearing floats to maintain flexibility and components with independence.

5 Indestructible Boxes

Plan for the unknown when constructing styled boxes.

Although the very nature of CSS tends to be rather boxy, that doesn't mean designs have to be constrained to square dimensions. The CSS box model defines rectangular boxes that are generated for elements within a document's structure (www.w3.org/TR/REC-CSS2/box.html)—in other words, a rectangular box is the standard method for organizing elements when using CSS. The result can lead to square, boxy designs being the norm.

This is nothing new, of course. Even prior to the widespread use of CSS layouts, table-based designs were constrained to a box design as well, with each table cell rectangular in shape by default.

This chapter describes a method for creating *rounded-corner* boxes using background images in CSS. We rebuild an existing design from the Web, making it flexible and thus preparing for the worst-case scenario in terms of what *could* be placed inside the box. Later, we discuss an alternate method for creating a rounded-corner box that is flexible in every direction but that requires extra markup. Finally, we look at some simple examples for modifying the boring box.

A Common Approach

As with the previous examples we've deconstructed thus far, we first take a traditional approach to building a rounded-cornered box and rebuild it using CSS. For this example, I've decided to use the box design found in the "Your Account" section of the popular DVD subscription site Netflix (Figure 5.1).

The rounded box is a common component on the Netflix site (and on many others), and rounded-off corners give that extra level of detail that would otherwise be just, well, *boxy* (Figure 5.2).

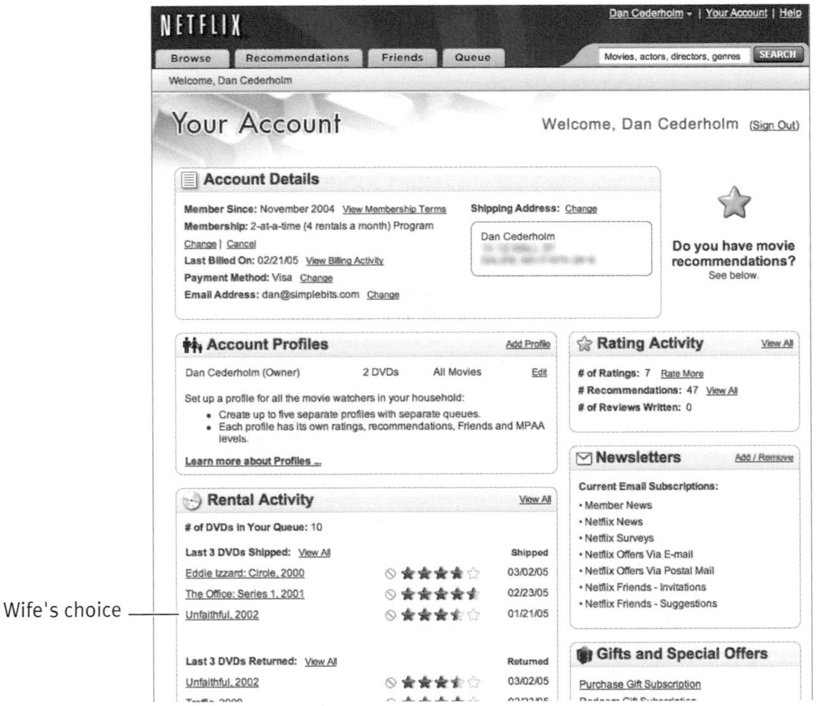

Wife's choice

Figure 5.1 The "My Account" page on Netflix.com (from April 2005).

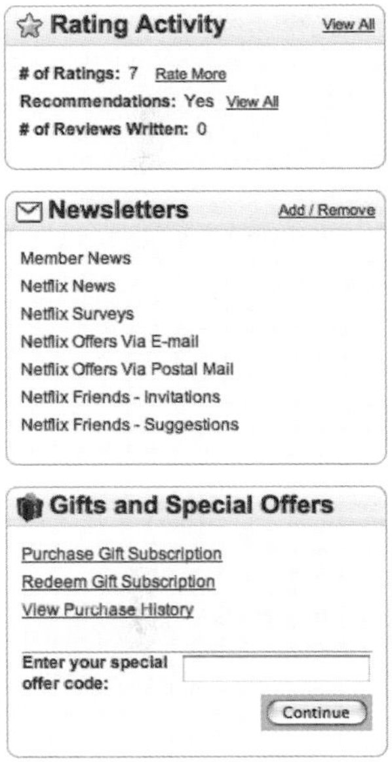

Figure 5.2 The rounded boxes found on the Netflix site are common on many sites.

Figure 5.3 With the box content removed, we can more easily inspect the design details.

You can probably guess what I'm going to say next regarding *how* these boxes are actually constructed on the Netflix site. That's right: using nested tables with GIF images referenced in the markup.

This section focuses on rebuilding one of these boxes, so let's zoom in and inspect the design details, noting what we need in a "materials checklist" for later. I've stripped away the content in Figure 5.3, so that you can clearly see, graphically, how the box is put together.

If we focus on the top portion of the box, we'll notice each end is rounded at the top, followed by a gradient fade down to a solid line as a background for the box's heading (Figure 5.4).

Similarly, the bottom of the box has rounded corners on both ends, but without a gradient fade (Figure 5.5).

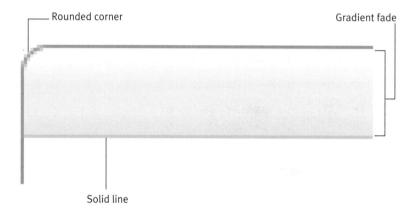

Figure 5.4 A close-up of the background that sits behind the box's heading reveals a gradient fade down to a solid border.

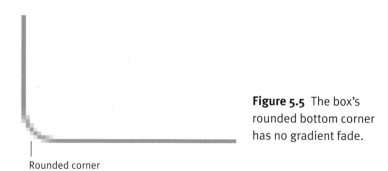

Figure 5.5 The box's rounded bottom corner has no gradient fade.

Why It's Not Bulletproof

For many of the reasons found in the previous chapters' examples, these rounded boxes have certain problems. First, there exists a mound of presentational markup, due to the use of nested tables. We know now that this issue can be easily addressed by turning to CSS to handle the design of the boxes, while meaningful markup can be used to *structure* them.

Second, the box design is unable to accommodate a large text size or heading length over a certain number of characters. Figure 5.6 shows our example box with the text size increased a few notches.

You'll notice that while the box *is* able to grow vertically in the content area, the heading's background image was designed for a certain line length at a specific font size. If the line wraps, or if the user increases the text size, the design breaks down.

The image that sits behind the box's title is set as a background image on the `<td>` element. In the markup, this might have been achieved like so:

```
<td background="/images/box_top.gif">
```

By default, a background image specified this way will tile within the cell, and in this case that tiling becomes visible when the text expands the table cell past the point of the original image height.

Again, this isn't a Web design crime, but it's certainly something worth addressing.

Figure 5.6 With text size increased, the heading's background image is repeated, but the image was built for only one line of text.

A Bulletproof Approach

To cure the box's plague of inflexibility and excess code, let's rebuild the style of this box using a fraction of the markup and taking advantage of CSS to control the design elements that make the box unique.

To begin, we need to develop a strategy for making two areas of the box vertically flexible. The gradient fade behind the box's heading will have to be able to expand *down* as more or larger text is placed within the heading. In addition, the rest of the box below the heading needs to be able to expand or contract vertically, depending on how much content it contains, with the rounded-corner bottom always sitting below everything else (Figure 5.7).

note

While this particular example calls for a fixed-width box that can expand only vertically, it is possible to create a rounded box that expands horizontally as well. We'll be exploring that later on in the chapter.

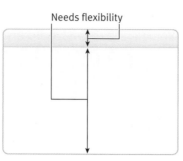

Needs flexibility

Figure 5.7 These two areas of the box will need to be vertically flexible.

To accomplish this, we need to employ some crafty use of background images and CSS. But first, let's come up with a compact markup structure.

THE MARKUP STRUCTURE

In deciding how best to structure the rounded box, we must keep in mind the following requirements: fixed width, a heading on top, variable amounts of content below. That said, I think it makes the most sense to wrap each box in a containing `<div>`, followed by a heading element for the box title, and then any content below. For this example, I'll simplify the contents of the box to include just a list of three links (since we're really just focusing on the box's rounded style here).

Because this particular box style is used repeatedly throughout a single page, we should come up with styles we can reuse—meaning we'll want to use a `class` (for multiple occurrences) rather than an `id` (used once per document) to label the `<div>` that sets up the box style, as shown here:

```
<div class="box">
  <h3>Gifts and Special Offers</h3>
  <ul>
    <li><a href="/purchase/">Purchase Gift Subscription</
a></li>
    <li><a href="/redeem/">Redeem Gift Subscription</a></li>
    <li><a href="/view/">View Purchase History</a></li>
  </ul>
</div>
```

There you have it. Pretty darn simple, isn't it? Just a simple `<div>` labeled with a `class="box"`, with a heading level 3 and an unordered list of three links contained inside. As far as lean markup goes, this is optimal.

The outer `<div>` element will help us give the fixed width we need to the box, as well as provide a contextual flag that will allow us to uniquely style the heading and content within the box.

AN IMAGE STRATEGY

The trickiest and most important step to rebuilding this example involves separating the graphic elements from the design so that they will accommodate varying amounts of content and text sizes. We need to build in a height that is larger than we *think* we need for both the heading area and the main body of the box.

For instance, looking at the heading area of the box first, we must create an image that will accommodate large or multiple lines of text. Since we'll reference the image as a background for the `<h3>` in our markup (with more or less of this image appearing behind whatever text is used), this image will also contain the rounded corners for the top of the box.

Figure 5.8 shows the image I've created (h3-bg.gif); as you can see, I've made it tall enough for several lines of heading text. Notice that I've left out the darker bottom border that separates the heading from the body of the box. We'll use CSS to create this one-pixel line that flanks the bottom of the heading. Doing so will enable us to align this image at the top, creating the rounded corners for the top of the box and leaving a variable area for the heading text, followed by a one-pixel border created by CSS.

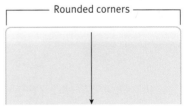

Rounded corners

Gradient fade to solid

Figure 5.8 The background that will be used behind the box's heading is tall enough to accommodate several lines of text.

The second image we'll need creates the rounded corners on the bottom of the box, as well as the one-pixel borders on each side. Just as we did with the heading image, we'll want to build in extra vertical space to account for varying lengths of content that might be placed within the box.

tip

This technique is inspired by Douglas Bowman's ingenious "Sliding Doors" method (mentioned in Chapter 2, "Scalable Navigation") of using two images that are large enough to accommodate varying amounts of content, and then using CSS to piece them together showing only what's needed as dictated by the size or amount of content they're surrounding. It needs to be said that it does have its breaking point—when the size or amount of content exceeds the dimensions of the images that you've created. Ideally, you'll settle on a happy medium: images that are large enough to accommodate varying content amounts but aren't so gigantic that they'll take too long to download for people on slow dial-up connections.

Figure 5.9 The background image that will sit behind the box's content includes sufficient height to accommodate a large amount of content.

tip

I'm using a class here to declare the box styles, because we'll be applying these styles to multiple boxes on the page. A class is used for multiple instances on a page, whereas an id is used only once.

Figure 5.9 shows the finished image (div-bottom.gif); as you can see, I've given it a substantial height, thus planning ahead for whatever happens to fill it later on.

With the images created, we're ready to use CSS as the glue that holds the design and content puzzle together.

APPLYING STYLES

Now that we've structured the markup optimally and have strategically created images that will allow for expansion, we're ready to put all the pieces together by applying the CSS.

Our example has a base font-size of small and a default font-family of Arial. To begin, let's give the box (and therefore its contents) a width.

```
.box {
  width: 273px;
  }
```

As far as referencing the two images we've created, we first want to attach div-bottom.gif as the background of the entire <div>. The reason is that the rounded corners cap off the box at the very bottom—below whatever content is inside.

```
.box {
  width: 273px;
  background: url(img/div-bottom.gif) no-repeat bottom left;
  }
```

So, by aligning the image at the bottom, we ensure that those rounded corners appear in the right spot: under everything else in the box.

Figure 5.10 shows our results thus far, with the width and single background image applied.

Gifts and Special Offers

- Purchase Gift Subscription
- Redeem Gift Subscription
- View Purchase History

Figure 5.10 With the background image aligned at the bottom, the upper portion of the image is hidden until it's needed to accommodate increased content.

Our next step is to fold in the background image for the heading, aligning it to the top to create the top-left and -right rounded corners.

```
.box {
  width: 273px;
  background: url(img/div-bottom.gif) no-repeat bottom left;
  }
.box h3 {
  background: url(img/h3-bg.gif) no-repeat top left;
  }
```

Figure 5.11 shows the addition of the background image behind the text of the <h3>, completing the rounded border around the box. Next, we'll want to add back in that one-pixel border that rides along the bottom of the heading, in addition to margins, padding, and font adjustments.

```
.box {
  width: 273px;
  background: url(img/div-bottom.gif) no-repeat bottom left;
  }
.box h3 {
  margin: 0;
  padding: 6px 8px 4px 10px;
  font-size: 130%;
  color: #333;
  border-bottom: 1px solid #E0CFAB;
  background: url(img/h3-bg.gif) no-repeat top left;
  }
```

Gifts and Special Offers

- Purchase Gift Subscription
- Redeem Gift Subscription
- View Purchase History

Figure 5.11 The background image behind the heading completes the rounded corners on all four sides.

By giving the <h3> elements within the box some padding and adjusting the size and color we leave room for the background image, which we've aligned top and left. The border-bottom will sit below the heading's text, while the image behind it will show only the part of itself that's needed (Figure 5.12).

Gifts and Special Offers

- Purchase Gift Subscription
- Redeem Gift Subscription
- View Purchase History

Figure 5.12 The heading's background and border work together to allow the heading's text to expand and contract, revealing more of the image as necessary.

Our last task is to provide some padding around the unordered list that sits inside the box by removing the default bullets from each list item.

```
.box {
  width: 273px;
  background: url(img/div-bottom.gif) no-repeat bottom left;
  }
.box h3 {
  margin: 0;
  padding: 6px 8px 4px 10px;
  font-size: 130%;
  color: #333;
  border-bottom: 1px solid #E0CFAB;
  background: url(img/h3-bg.gif) no-repeat top left;
  }
.box ul {
  margin: 0;
  padding: 14px 10px 14px 10px;
  list-style: none;
  }
.box ul li {
  margin: 0 0 6px;
  padding: 0;
  }
```

Gifts and Special Offers

Purchase Gift Subscription
Redeem Gift Subscription
View Purchase History

Figure 5.13 Here is our finished, bulletproof box.

By turning off default margins and bullets (via the list-style property) and giving the unordered list some padding, we're left with the finished box design (Figure 5.13). That was rather painless, was it not?

With the box design completed, let's now talk a bit about why this particular method is bulletproof. Later, we look at a few other techniques for achieving cornered boxes using CSS.

Why It's Bulletproof

If we combine all the code snippets needed to complete this box design, we're still left with an amount of code that is staggeringly less than what the nested-tables approach requires. And because we took the time to think about what made sense in terms of markup structure, we can rest assured that these boxes will mean increased accessibility and readability in a wide range of browsers and devices. Less code—more *meaningful* code—equals faster, more accessible, and readable content using anything from a phone to a desktop browser to access it.

Just as beneficial as the code trimming is the fact that this box design is truly *flexible*. Because of our cunning strategy for our background images, increasing the text size or including multiple lines of text cannot break the design.

Figure 5.14 shows the box at a few different text sizes, and its indestructible and bulletproof nature is revealed. Varying amounts of content are not a problem for this particular design. You can see that, as the box's content is increased, more of each background image is revealed. Because the bottom corners are aligned `bottom` on the `<div>` that wraps the whole box, that image will always shift down to reveal more of itself at the top. Similarly, because the top corners of the heading background are aligned `top`, more of that image's lower portion is revealed as the size or amount of text is increased.

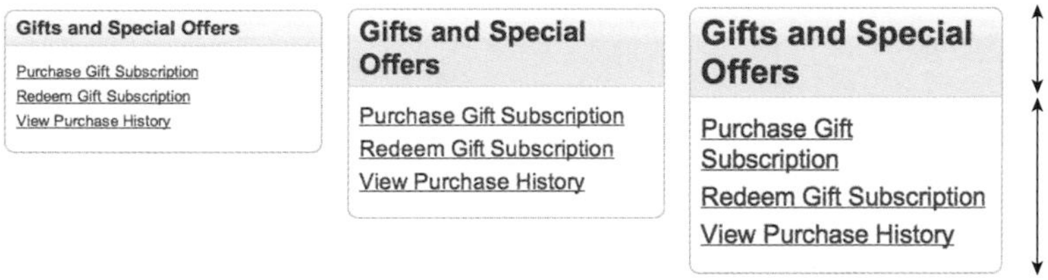

Figure 5.14 The box's heading and content area can stretch vertically with increased text size.

Other Rounded-Corner Techniques

While the previous approach was a good example of a *fixed*-width box featuring rounded corners using CSS, things get a bit more complicated when a *fluid*-width box is desired. By fluid width, I mean the box is flexible horizontally as well as vertically.

Why is it more complicated? Because it requires the placement of four separate images—one for each rounded corner. Each corner needs to be separate in order for the box to be *stretchable* in every direction. And four images means four markup elements are required to reference each image as a background.

Some methods involve using *generated content* in the style sheet, using the :before and :after pseudo-elements to insert more than one background image on a *single* element. The problem with these methods is that at the time of this writing, Internet Explorer (IE) does not support generated content, therefore excluding a large portion of the browsing world from seeing the rounded corners.

So, what to do? Well, if a fixed width is predetermined, you can easily use the method described earlier in the chapter and use just two background images: one for top-left and -right rounded corners, and one for bottom-left and -right rounded corners. Having two markup elements available to reference those images is usually not a problem. If a fluid-width box is a requirement, then you'll have to add extra markup if you'd like IE users to see the same design.

HAPPILY ROUNDED

Here's how Ethan Marcotte, standards craftsman and technical editor for this very book, handles the challenge for the Browse Happy Web site (Figure 5.15, http://browsehappy.com).

Ethan uses a rounded box to indicate a standards-compliant browser that a user has "switched to," containing the name of the browser and its icon (Figure 5.16).

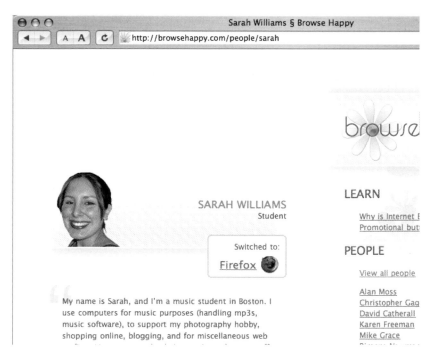

Figure 5.15 Browse Happy is a site designed to help people learn about standards-compliant alternatives to Internet Explorer.

Instead of assigning a fixed width for the box, Ethan allows the box to expand and contract horizontally as well as vertically when more (or larger) text is placed within it, using a variation on the aforementioned "Sliding Doors" technique (Figure 5.17).

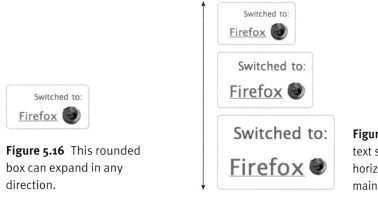

Figure 5.16 This rounded box can expand in any direction.

Figure 5.17 With increased text size, the box will grow horizontally and vertically while maintaining its rounded shape.

Let's build another example, based on the techniques that Ethan has employed to achieve a truly flexible box, capable of anything and everything that is thrown at it.

The markup structure

note

I've changed the markup slightly here, to keep the example simple since it's out of context. Originally, the rounded box was part of a definition list that also contained the name of the "switcher" and other information. This is a clever and smart way of leveraging definition lists—check the source of http://browsehappy.com for details.

As I mentioned earlier, in order to maintain a flexible-in-every-direction box, the unfortunate reality is that we need to add *extra* markup to the mix. This extra markup is necessary to reference the four corners of the box independently, so that it can expand in all four directions if needed.

Keeping in mind that we need a minimum of four elements in which to reference background images from, we create a markup structure as follows:

```
<div class="container">
  <p class="desc">This box is:</p>
  <p class="link"><em><a href="/browsers/firefox/
">Indestructible!</a></em></p>
</div>
```

A container `<div>` followed by a paragraph gives us the first two elements. For the complete four, we wrap the arrogant "Indestructible!" link with a second paragraph and (here's where the arguably extraneous markup comes in) an `<em>` element. I'm using `<em>` here because technically I could be intending to convey emphasis on the link as well. At the same time, I'm admittedly sneaking this element in here. It's something I try to avoid, but in this case, we'll need that fourth element in order to reference the necessary background images that create the corners (Figure 5.18).

Figure 5.18 We've structured the box's markup to give us four available elements to assign background images to.

Image strategy

Although we'll reference a background image four times (one for each corner), let's borrow the crafty solution used on the Browse Happy site, which requires only *two* GIF images. This approach will start to make sense as we look over the images themselves.

Shown in Figure 5.19, rounded-left.gif is a 9-pixel-wide GIF image that contains both the top *and* bottom rounded corners of the left edge. We created it at a much taller height than anticipated to account for larger amounts of content.

Shown in Figure 5.20, rounded-right.gif is a similar image; it handles the top and bottom rounded corners on the right, as well as the top, right, and bottom edges. This image is the same height as rounded-left.gif, and is also much wider than originally needed.

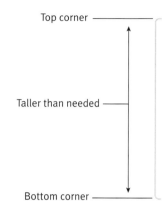

Figure 5.19 The rounded-left.gif image contains both the top- and bottom-left corners.

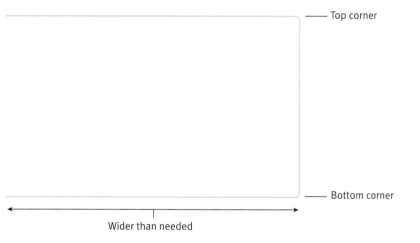

Figure 5.20 The rounded-right.gif image contains the top- and bottom-right corners. This image also fills in the top and bottom borders for the box.

It's time to position these images—and this is where the cleverness comes in. The rounded-left.gif image will be aligned `top` for the top-left corner (Figure 5.21), and then used again aligned `bottom` for the bottom-left corner.

As long as the box never gets taller than the image, then the unused, hidden corner is never revealed (which explains why we made the image sufficiently tall to begin with). The reverse is true for rounded-right.gif, which will also be used twice—for the top- and bottom-right corners.

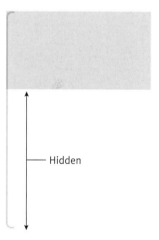

Figure 5.21 When aligned to the top, the image's lower corner will be revealed only if the box grows large enough for it to peek out.

Use your best judgment as to how tall and wide to make these images, depending on what type of content will be placed inside. Build in some breathing room for unexpected text sizes and content amounts.

Let's now move on to applying style to our markup and pull the whole design together.

Applying styles

Because we don't want to assign a fixed width to the box and yet we want the rounded corners to "cling" to the content within in it, let's float the container. Floating the container prevents the box from being as wide as the window (or other container above it). Instead, the width of the content inside the box dictates how wide the box will stretch.

```
.container {
  float: left;
  color: #666;
  }
```

In addition to floating the box left, we've added a base color for text within the box: a dark gray.

Next, let's strategically place the two background images across the four available elements in our markup. We first assign the top-right corner as the background for the main container, using the top half of rounded-right.gif by aligning the image to the top and right of the element.

```
.container {
  float: left;
  color: #666;
  background: url(img/rounded-right.gif) top right no-repeat;
  }
```

Notice that we're specifying the image to sit at the top and right of the element as a background.

Figure 5.22 shows the results, with the upper half of rounded-right.gif showing through as the background image for the entire container.

This box is:

Indestructible!   **Figure 5.22** Aligning the image to the top and right reveals the corner.

The next element in line is the first paragraph within the container, which we've identified with a class="desc" (for description). Let's assign the top-left corner by using the upper half of rounded-left.gif, aligning it top and left. We also zero out default margin and padding for the <p> element here. We'll add back in the appropriate padding a bit later.

```
.container {
  float: left;
  color: #666;
  background: url(img/rounded-right.gif) top right no-repeat;
  }
.desc {
  margin: 0;
  padding: 0;
  background: url(img/rounded-left.gif) top left no-repeat;
  }
```

Figure 5.23 shows the results of the second background image, which adds the top-left corner.

This box is:

Indestructible!   **Figure 5.23** Aligning this image to the top left reveals the corner.

Next, we add the bottom-left rounded corner by assigning the lower half of rounded-left.gif to the second paragraph that we've marked with a class="link". Where we previously used the upper portion of this image by aligning it top and left, we now align it bottom and left to reveal the bottom corner. We also add 9px of padding to three sides of the first paragraph to give it proper spacing against the sides of the box, as well as 9px of padding on the left side of the second paragraph. This is the same width as the image itself, which allows the corner to be seen behind the "Indestructible!" link.

```
.container {
  float: left;
  color: #666;
  background: url(img/rounded-right.gif) top right no-repeat;
  }
.desc {
  margin: 0;
```

```
  padding: 9px 9px 0 9px;
  background: url(img/rounded-left.gif) top left no-repeat;
  }
.link {
  margin: 0;
  padding: 0 0 0 9px;
  background: url(img/rounded-left.gif) bottom left no-
repeat;
  }
```

Figure 5.24 shows the progress thus far, with three of the four corners assigned to their correct positions. One more to go.

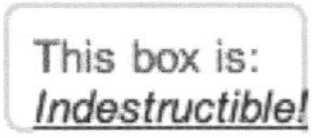

This box is:
Indestructible!

Figure 5.24 We added the third corner by reusing rounded-left.gif but aligning it to the bottom.

The final background image will be attached to the <em> element that is nested within the second paragraph. We'll assign the lower half of rounded-right.gif by aligning it `bottom` and `right`, in addition to including a bit more padding to properly space the text evenly within the box. Most browsers will italicize text wrapped with <em>, so we'll also want to override that back to normal.

```
.container {
  float: left;
  color: #666;
  background: url(img/rounded-right.gif) top right no-
repeat;
  }
.desc {
  margin: 0;
  padding: 9px 9px 0 9px;
  background: url(img/rounded-left.gif) top left no-repeat;
  }
.link {
  margin: 0;
  padding: 0 0 0 9px;
  background: url(img/rounded-left.gif) bottom left no-
repeat;
  }
```

```
.link em {
  display: block;
  padding: 0 9px 9px 0;
  font-style: normal;
  background: url(img/rounded-right.gif) bottom right no-
repeat;
  }
.container a {
  font-size: 130%;
  color: #e70;
  }
```

Normally, <em> is an *inline* element, which doesn't expand as wide as its parent container and therefore wouldn't work for holding the background image behind it. To fix that, we add the rule display: block; to turn the <em> into a *block-level* element, forcing the dimensions of whatever text is contained within to reach the edges of the box. In addition, we set links within the box to be larger than normal, and orange—because, well, that's what an indestructible link should be.

Figure 5.25 shows the completed box, with four rounded corners created by aligning two background images.

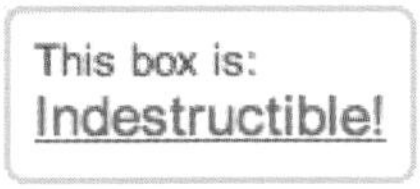

This box is:
Indestructible!

Figure 5.25 Here is our completed, "indestructible" box.

Indestructible nature

Just as in the Browse Happy example, notice that our rounded box will expand and contract in all directions, depending on text size or content amount. It is *truly* indestructible (Figure 5.26).

This box is:
Indestructible!

This box is:
Indestructible!

This box is not only rounded and bulletproof, but it could also be considered:
Indestructible!

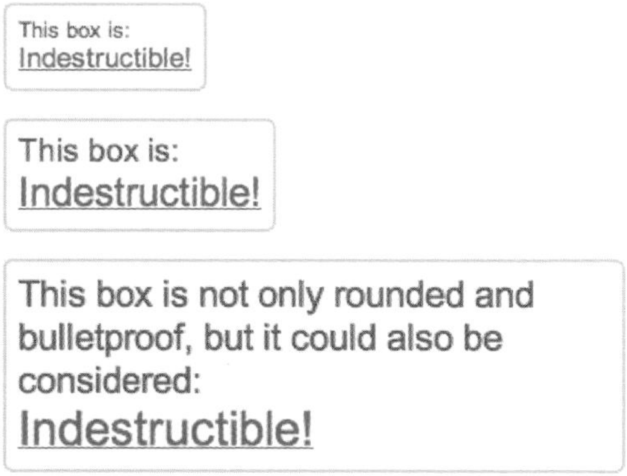

Figure 5.26 Regardless of content size or length, the box will grow and grow.

note 📖

Since version 1.3, Safari has supported multiple background images per the CSS3 draft (http://webkit.org/blog/15/multiple-backgrounds/), and both Safari and Firefox have proprietary border-radius properties that round corners with mixed results. These aren't exactly things we can *rely* on cross-browser—but people are experimenting nonetheless.

Box Hinting

After walking through the previous example, you can see how generating truly flexible, rounded boxes isn't exactly simple. We're stuck with a few limitations on how these decorated boxes are created. Yet there are glimpses of hope for the future. CSS3 (which will likely be implemented fully in most browsers by the time my great-grandchildren are graduating high school) contains concepts for multiple background images on a single element (yay!) and a border-radius property for automatically creating rounded corners of varying scale (yay!), among other tantalizing yet not fully supported features.

What we can do now is keep in mind techniques and treatments that *hint* at the boxy containing element or that modify it slightly. In other words, we can focus on methods that utilize a single background image and/or color that are decorative and yet maintain clean markup and flexibility should they expand or collapse.

Box hinting and modifying can be a bulletproofer's secret weapon—to be used when appropriate, of course. But a strategically placed background image can turn the boring box into a styled interface design. Let's take a look a few examples.

SINGLE ROUNDED CORNER

Let's imagine you have an ordered list containing small chunks of text. The simple markup might go something like this:

```
<ol>
  <li>Lorem ipsum dolor sit amet …</li>
  <li>Lorem ipsum dolor sit amet …<li>
  <li>Lorem ipsum dolor sit amet …</li>
  <li>Lorem ipsum dolor sit amet …</li>
</ol>
```

Each alternate row has a light green background color to offset the items (Figure 5.27), so we'll add a class to every other row so that we can change the style for those items using CSS:

```
<ol>
  <li class="alt">Lorem ipsum dolor sit amet …</li>
  <li>Lorem ipsum dolor sit amet …<li>
  <li class="alt">Lorem ipsum dolor sit amet …</li>
```

```
<li>Lorem ipsum dolor sit amet …</li>
</ol>
```

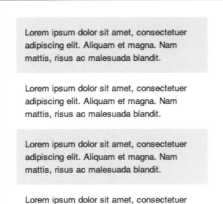

Figure 5.27 An ordered list with each alternate row having a background color (also called "zebra striping").

The CSS to build this little list looks like this:

```
ol {
  width: 22em;
  margin: 0;
  padding: 0;
  list-style: none;
  }
ol li {
  margin: 0;
  padding: 1em;
  }
ol li.alt {
  background: #e0eac5;
  }
```

I first noticed the following treatment on Jon Hicks's quintessential weblog, Hicksdesign (`http://hicksdesign.co.uk`), where Jon cleverly placed a single rounded background image (Figure 5.28) in the bottom-right corner of each alternate item's box. This *very subtle detail* tied in quite nicely with the rest of the site's design.

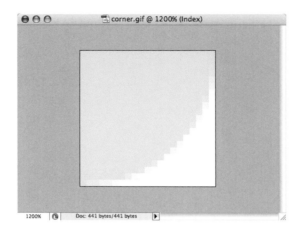

Figure 5.28 The GIF that creates the rounded bottom-right corner, zoomed.

By placing that image along with the green background color (just as Jon had done), we have a simple, completely flexible style that's easily achieved with no extra markup and elementary CSS (Figure 5.29).

So that alternate style for every other `<li>` becomes:

```
ol li.alt {
  background: #e0eac5 url(img/corner.gif) no-repeat bottom
right;
  }
```

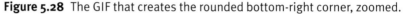

Figure 5.29 The ordered list with alternating background color and rounded bottom-right corner.

By positioning the background image to the bottom right of the box, we'll always maintain a consistent style no matter how big or small the box becomes—*in any direction* (Figure 5.30). This particular design doesn't rely on widths or heights, and that's the beauty of it.

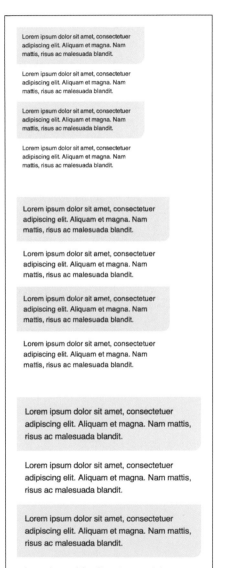

Figure 5.30 With text size adjusted, the rounded bottom-right corner stays in place, while the background color expands.

CORNER HINTING

A great example of box hinting can be found on Veerle's Blog (http://
veerle.duoh.com), the personal site of Belgian designer Veerle Pieters.

Figure 5.31 shows a portion of her comment form, where you'll see a rounded
corner that fades out from top left. It's a prime example of *hinting* at a
rounded container, while only requiring a single background image that does
not rely on the heading's size. The text on top of the image can stretch as far
right as it needs to, or it can wrap to multiple lines without disrupting the
treatment. Once again, we have a simple, bulletproof design element.

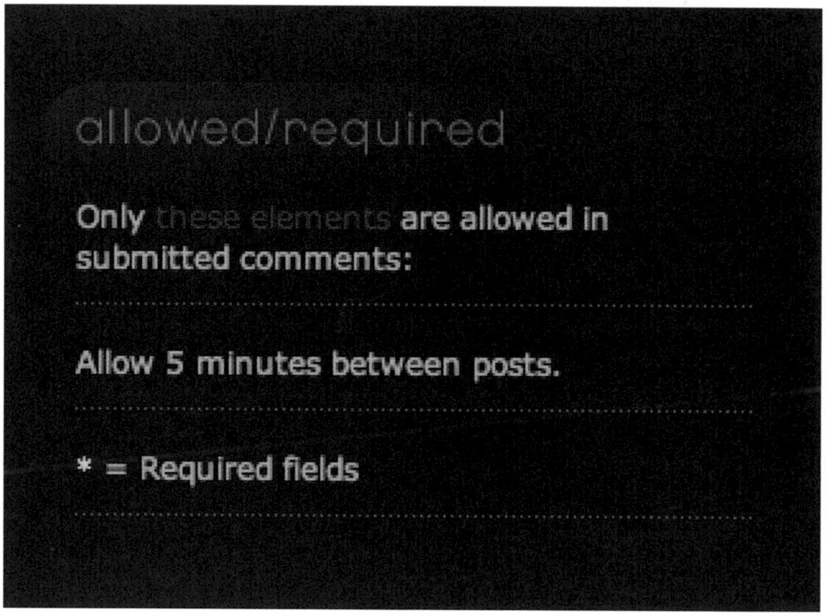

Figure 5.31 An example of box hinting from Veerle Pieters' blog.

A BULLETPROOF ARROW

We're not limited to only round corners, of course. Take Figure 5.32, for example: it's a boring green box, but with a single background image that creates an arrow point on one side. By creating a single background image that's much taller than needed (Figure 5.33), we can center it vertically and allow more or less of the diagonals in the arrow image to be shown or hidden depending on the box's size (Figure 5.34).

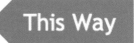

Figure 5.32 An otherwise boring green box, with a single background image that creates an arrow.

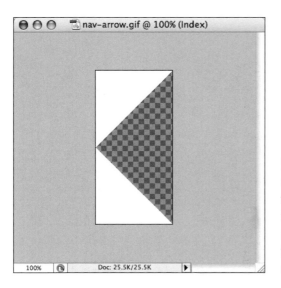

Figure 5.33 A larger-than-needed GIF image with a transparent area (to be filled by the box color) and a white area that masks the box to create the arrow shape.

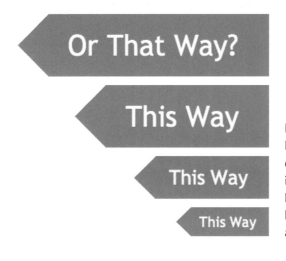

Figure 5.34 More or less of the vertically centered background image is revealed as the box changes dimensions, by text size or content amount.

The markup for the arrow could be as simple as this:

```
<h2>This Way</h2>
```

And here's the CSS that positions the image 0 50% (left, vertically centered) and creates the arrow effect:

```
h2 {
  width: 4.5em;
  padding: .5em .8em .5em 1.5em;
  font-weight: normal;
  color: #fff;
  background: #693 url(nav-arrow.gif) no-repeat 0 50%;
  }
```

Notice I'm using ems for width and padding. As the arrow's text increases or decreases, that will ensure that the proportions and spacing around the text and arrow diagonals remain consistent. You don't have to use ems of course—it just makes for a truly scalable unit.

LIMITATIONS BREED CREATIVITY

To help you understand the limitations of the box model, as well as the current state of browser support for CSS, you'll find it beneficial to experiment with ways that slightly tweak the box so that it's not *just* a box anymore. Four rounded corners too much trouble? Try something simpler (not to mention smart and flexible). Using creative techniques that combine flexibility with subtle design detail is what being bulletproof is all about. Occasional sacrifices are sometimes necessary—but that's a reality of designing for the Web.

Summary

CSS lets you create boxes that not only have rounded or nonsquare corners but that are flexible—cutting down on unnecessary code and separating the design of the box from the content that's being presented. In this chapter, I shared methods for creating fixed-width and fluid-width rounded boxes, and I hope it will encourage you to experiment with these techniques and others, creating bulletproof boxes that defy the box model of CSS.

Here are some points to remember when creating indestructible, rounded-corner boxes:

- Fixed-width, rounded-corner boxes are usually easy to create using lean markup and just two background images.

- Fluid-width, rounded-corner boxes require a little more markup in order to reference background images on all four corners. Use your best judgment on whether this extra markup is worth it.

- Combine background images and use positioning to reveal only the desired portion of the image.

- Build in extra width and height to background images, using your best judgment for deciding the maximum dimensions a box may reach. Take into account the context on the page, and what types and amounts of content may be placed inside. Then add a little more.

- Experiment with simple methods like box hinting that reduce complexity and yet lend style to an otherwise boring box.

6

No Images?
No CSS?
No Problem!

Ensure that content is still readable in the absence of images or CSS.

The first several chapters of this book have addressed flexibility from a *component design* angle and stressed the importance of allowing design to accommodate varying amounts and sizes of content. You can take additional measures to bulletproof your designs and thus provide flexibility in the many *stages* a Web page could be interpreted. When CSS is unsupported or unavailable, is the page still readable? If images are slow to load, or turned off via a user preference, is the content still visible and understood? These are important questions to answer when building any Web site.

Planning for the worst-case scenario can improve a Web site's chances of being readable and usable in a variety of situations. In this chapter, we look at two simple strategies for ensuring a bulletproof design, even if images and/or CSS aren't present.

A Common Approach

A few years ago, I received an e-mail from a faithful reader of my business site and weblog, SimpleBits (www.simplebits.com). In the e-mail, the reader explained that while he enjoys reading the site, he often browses the Web with images turned *off*, further explaining that he connects to the Internet via a slow dial-up connection and likes to read content rather than waiting for graphics to load. He's not alone—to speed up an otherwise sluggish experience, many users disable images in their browsers, allowing pages to load content and background colors only (Figure 6.1).

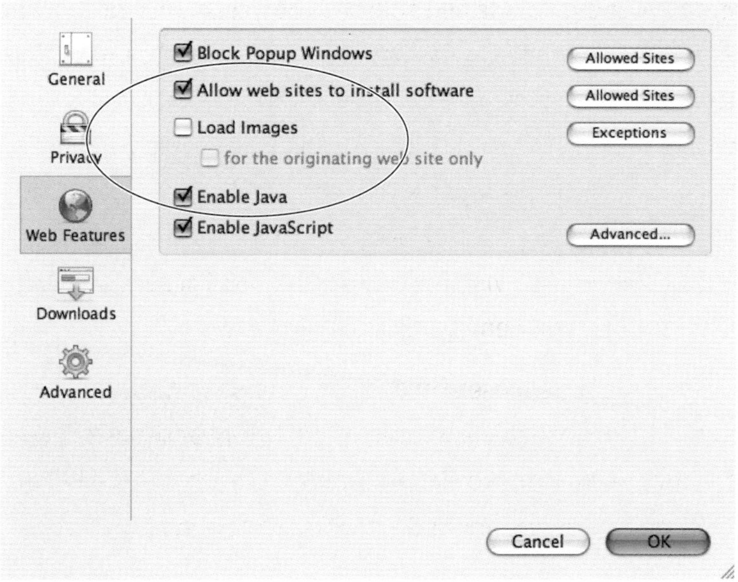

Figure 6.1 Unchecking the Load Images box in the Firefox browser disables all images.

We'll get back to why the reader was explaining the reason he browses this way in just a minute, but first, it'll be helpful to explain how a tiled image was used on SimpleBits that sat behind all of the site's content.

It's a common approach, especially when utilizing CSS and the background and/or background-image properties. An image is used behind text to add color, patterns, and so forth. At the time, the columns and decorative border on SimpleBits were achieved by using a repeating background image on the entire page. A single image controlled the side stripes, the white content area, and the light-gray sidebar (Figure 6.2).

Figure 6.2 The bg.gif image was tiled vertically on top of dark gray to create the columned background of the site.

This single image was tiled vertically from top to bottom, creating the columns and side borders that sat on top of a dark-gray background assigned to the <body> element (Figure 6.3).

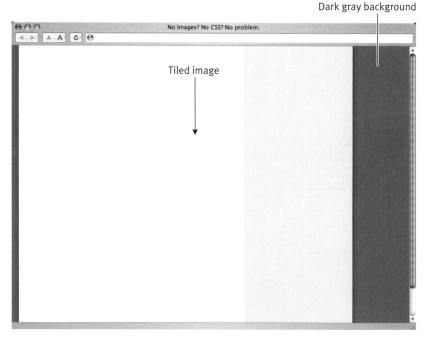

Figure 6.3 When bg.gif was tiled, it created the white and gray columns that sat behind the page's text content.

So, by declaring a dark gray for the background on the <body>, I was essentially setting a default background color for the entire page, unless overridden on any inner element.

```
body {
  background: #666;
}
```

The tiled image was assigned to an inner <div> that contained all of the pages' content; therefore, it would lay on top of the gray background behind it, creating the white and gray columns for text. This all works rather nicely. By layering a tiled image on top of a background color, we're creating space for text to be easily read when placed over the tiled image (Figure 6.4).

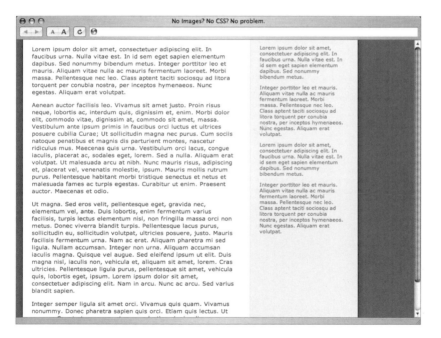

Figure 6.4 The dark-gray text sits on top of the tiled image.

The problem is when the image isn't there and the site's *unbulletproofness* (perhaps a new word that I've invented) is exposed.

Why It's Not Bulletproof

Getting back to my helpful reader's e-mail—you know, the one who wisely disables images when he browses on a slow dial-up connection—the reason for his note was to inform me that the content on my site was either hard to read or just plain *not there at all*. Oh my. I have to admit this was rather embarrassing, but let's take a look at why this happened.

Because the content's text color was two shades of gray, when the tiled image was removed (or disabled by the reader) the text was left sitting on the default background color, which was also a dark gray. The result was a semi-unreadable page; one could barely make out the text in the wider main column, and even worse, the text in the smaller right column was *invisible*. The text in this column shared the same color gray as the background, leaving the text completely hidden.

Figure 6.5 shows what happens when the tiled image is removed. There's not exactly an optimal contrast between the text in the main column and the background color, which makes it difficult to read. But even worse, the right column's text disappears completely because it's the same color as the background.

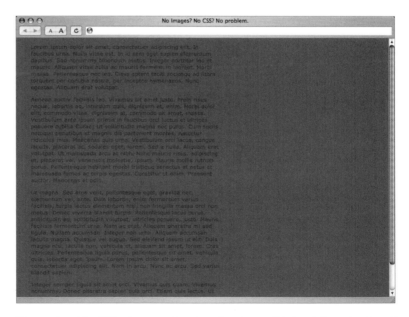

Figure 6.5 It's difficult to read and, wait, where did the right column go?

For users who browse with images turned off to conserve bandwidth, or for those on slow connections that make image loading seem to take forever, this scenario can certainly be frustrating. Text can even be unreadable, depending on your color combinations. Fortunately, there's an easy step to keep in mind to prevent this unreadable state.

A Bulletproof Approach

To ensure that your page's text is still readable, even in the absence of images, the bulletproof fix is rather simple. Remember to always provide *background color equivalents* for any background images that you may use.

For instance, looking back at our unreadable example, if I had simply added background color to content areas of the page, my helpful reader would still be able to view the text without any problems.

Since the content portion of the page sits on top of a white background, I need to add that color to the containing `<div id="content">` that wraps that column:

```
#content {
  background: #fff;
  }
```

Similarly, since the sidebar's text sits on top the light-gray background portion of the tiled image, I just need to declare that color for the `<div id="sidebar">` that wraps the right column:

```
#sidebar {
  background: #eee;
  }
```

Figure 6.6 shows the results of adding those two simple rules to the style sheet—with *images still turned off*. You'll notice that while the tiled image is gone, each text column has a background color sitting behind it, masking the dark-gray default of the entire page.

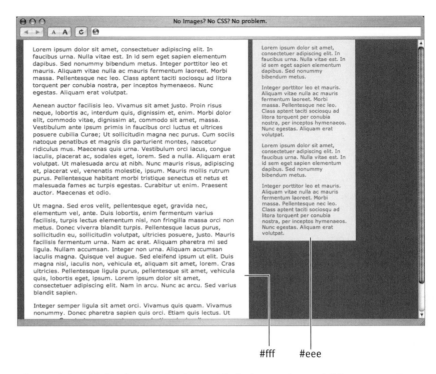

#fff   #eee

Figure 6.6 With background colors added, the text is readable once again.

Why It's Bulletproof

By taking the extra time (and we're talking seconds here) to provide equivalent background colors for any images used as backgrounds, you'll make your site one step closer to being bulletproof. Users who visit your pages with images turned off to conserve bandwidth will still be able to read them. Users who have slow connections will see the text and background color load first and be able to read the page before any images load.

Bulletproof means *being prepared for whatever is thrown at your design*. This is just one small, easy step that can help ensure your design doesn't break down when viewed without images.

To illustrate a similar example, let's look at the sidebar headings found on SimpleBits (Figure 6.7).

The "About Sections" and "Bits to Buy" headings are contained in <h3> elements (i.e., <h3>About Sections</h3>), while a subtle background fade image is placed behind the *white* text.

The CSS to achieve this for the top (green) heading looks like this:

```
#sidebar h3 {
  margin: 30px 0 12px 0;
  padding: 5px 10px;
  color: #fff;
  font-size: 120%;
  background: url(../img/sub-h-bg.gif) repeat-x top left;
  }
```

Figure 6.7 On simplebits.com, "About Sections" and "Bits to Buy" are contained in <h3> elements.

Where sub-h-bg.gif provides the green fade background, the text on top of it is white. The page's default background color is also white. I think you can see where I'm going with this.

If we were to turn off images, the headings would completely disappear (Figure 6.8).

White text on top of a white background equals magically disappearing content.

Fortunately, the simple fix that we learned earlier in the chapter applies here as well. By choosing a similar background color equivalent and declaring that along with the image, we'll achieve bulletproofness:

```
#sidebar h3 {
  margin: 30px 0 12px 0;
  padding: 5px 10px;
  color: #fff;
  font-size: 120%;
  background: #538620 url(../img/sub-h-bg.gif) repeat-x top
left;
  }
```

Figure 6.8 The magically disappearing heading text!

In this CSS, we're declaring a shade of green that's found in the background fade image along with the image itself—in one single rule. Because background images always sit *on top of* background colors, we have a safe *backup* in case the image is unavailable, turned off by the user, or loading slowly.

Additionally, if the user increases the text size of the page, the background image will stay aligned to the top of the box, while the background color will extend down as far as it needs to (Figure 6.9). This also ensures the white text of the heading will be readable, always sitting above the green background.

Solid background

Tiled image

Figure 6.9 A 3D view of the stacking order showing the white text and tiled gradient image sitting on top of the solid-green background.

Figure 6.10 shows the headings with images turned off, but this time, their background color equivalents make the white text readable once again.

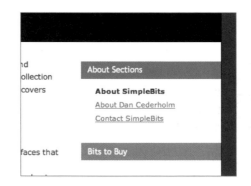

Figure 6.10 With green and orange background colors specified, the headings become readable, even in the absence of images.

Now that we've handled the absence of images, let's see what happens in the absence of *CSS*.

With or Without Style

Throughout the book so far, we've been focusing heavily on the use of CSS to help *bulletproof* designs—preparing them for a multitude of scenarios, and helping to protect the content that's there for the design to support. But what happens when the CSS is taken away? What do pages look like, and act like, when the design is tossed out and the content is left naked to stand on its own?

It's an important and simple step to take—one that I advise all Web designers to embrace when building sites that utilize lean markup and CSS for their design. By looking at a page's bare structure (don't worry, pages don't embarrass easily), it quickly becomes obvious as to how the content is going to fare in browsers and devices that *don't* support CSS. While you can lean heavily on CSS to create beautiful and compelling designs, it's important to make sure the page is still readable and functional when it's unsupported or unavailable.

So, here's another way to bulletproof your design: take that design out of the mix completely, then assess the readability of the page. Does it still work?

THE 10-SECOND USABILITY TEST

I often refer to this disabling of CSS as the "10-second usability test." To be sure, it's not a scientific method for determining the true usability of a site, something that often takes focus groups, surveys, time, and other debatably useful measurements. But by quickly taking away the design, you'll find it easier to get a handle on how the core of this page is going to be presented to the world. Most people using modern browsers will get your lovely design, but some may be delivered the raw content only, and it's helpful to keep this in mind during the design and development process.

Historically, designers have built pages using tables and presentational markup (<font> tags, image spacers, and so on) with the goal of making the page look precisely the same in every browser imaginable. And most of the time it worked. But these sites were the most inflexible, inaccessible beasts, incapable of being viewed and read in anything but a typical Web browser. As the number of different devices and software increases, as well as the broader understanding for creating Web sites that are more accessible to all types of users, it becomes critical to measure your designs against a variety of scenarios. Turning off CSS is another item on the checklist. Let's take a look at two possible results.

A COMMON APPROACH

A somewhat dangerous scenario is a site that mixes CSS to handle *certain aspects* of a site's design, with presentational markup and background images coded within the page itself (often using nested tables for its layout).

For example, Figure 6.11 shows BaseballDog.com (a fictitious example based on a real-world site, which surprisingly declined our enticing offer to expose it) with CSS turned off. The page becomes quite unreadable, with default black text and blue links sitting on top of a dark-blue tiled background image. Under normal conditions, with CSS turned on, the site looks and reads just fine.

What's happening here is a mixture of presentation and structure, where inessential graphics (such as the tiled background image) are tied directly to the *markup*. For instance, if BaseballDog.com wanted to place a tiled background image on the entire page, they would add a background attribute to the <body> element:

```
<body background="/img/tile.gif">
```

Figure 6.11 BaseballDog.com, a fictitious site that's based on a real-world example, is shown here with CSS turned off. Notice how difficult the default text color and links are to read.

But adding graphics directly to the markup like this has consequences, as we see when CSS is removed.

CSS is used to control text and positioning only, and when it's taken away, we're left with an unreadable combination. Quite obviously, BaseballDog.com hasn't yet chosen to embrace CSS and meaningful markup completely, where the separation of content and design can help a site become readable and usable under a much broader set of circumstances.

It is possible to take a transitional approach when building a site, using CSS for only a handful of elements, while using tables for the framework and layout of a page. When done well, taking away the CSS styles will leave a readable and functional site. I'm stressing the importance of testing what occurs when styles are disabled, which can leave a site unreadable (as in the case of BaseballDog.com), or ideally, unhindered by the absence of CSS. Let's take a look at one such example.

A BULLETPROOF APPROACH

Evidence of *good* page structure is almost immediately noticeable when a page is viewed without CSS. Take, for example, virus protection software maker McAfee's nicely designed site (www.mcafee.com) (Figure 6.12). When viewed sans style, the thoughtful organization and easy-to-read content are right up front, and emphasis has been placed on using markup that will work well, regardless of what browser or device is reading it (Figure 6.13).

Figure 6.12 The clean design of McAfee's home page, shown here in February 2005, is a product of good markup structure and CSS.

Figure 6.13 With CSS turned off, the skeleton of McAfee's site is revealed.

As you scroll through the entire page, it's clear that meaningful markup was used to structure link titles, descriptions, and lists of links. It's as if you've taken an *x-ray of the document*, peeking in at the bones behind its design (Figure 6.14).

If the browser or device happens to *not* support CSS, the page's design goes away, but the content and functionality remains. Think: phones, PDAs, handheld computers, small-screened devices, screen-reading software, and text-only browsers. Although *some* of these may support the use of style sheets in some capacity, many do not. By ensuring pages are readable and usable regardless of what state they may be rendered in, you'll be closer to making your site bulletproof.

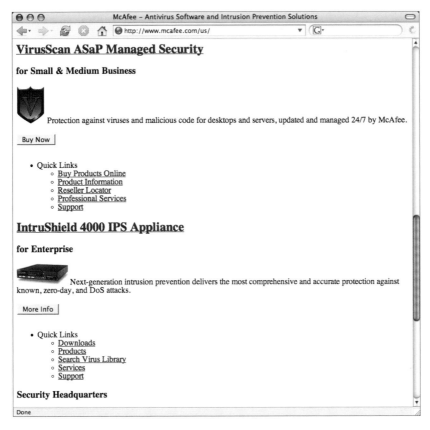

Figure 6.14 More of McAfee's structure is revealed as you scroll down the page.

The Dig Dug Test

Remember the arcade game classic Dig Dug? You controlled the character who inflated the bad guys with an air pump until they burst (Figure 6.15). It was one of my favorites, for sure. Much like the game, a quick *integrity test* of a design's bulletproofness can be easily achieved by bumping up and down the text size using the browser's controls to see how the page reacts. Does the design burst at the seams, or do things stay intact?

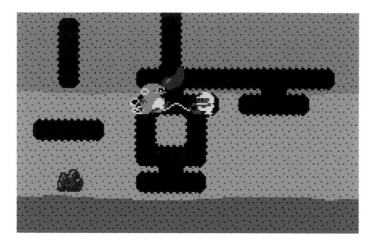

Figure 6.15 The classic '80s arcade game Dig Dug.

Enlarging text is something I do often throughout the construction of a new design, and one of the first things I check on existing ones. How do page components fare when text is ballooned up or down a few notches? The most important question to ask is whether text gets lost or hidden when the font size is increased.

I usually aim for at least two levels above the default base font-size before wanting to see things start breaking apart. Just like the Pookas and Fygars that Dig Dug strives to enlarge, *any* design is surely going to have a breaking point—it's just important that there be some breathing room and flexibility. I find that two notches is usually a good baseline—not an unreasonable demand for most designs.

In previous chapters we've explored techniques that ensure your design *scales* along with whatever is thrown in it. Just remember to easily test for the breaking point by adjusting text up and down using the browser's controls— on a Mac, often Command++ (plus) or Command+- (minus) and on a PC often Ctrl++ or Ctrl+-. Add this step to your bulletproof checklist.

Bulletproofing Tools

Fortunately, a few tools are available that make testing various states of a page's design quick and easy. Like any good tool, if it's easy to access, easy to use, and doesn't get in the way, it's a keeper. If you want to test a page's readability in the absence of images and/or CSS, you can do so using a few different methods: favelets, the Web Developer Extension toolbar for the Firefox and Mozilla browsers, or the Web Accessibility Toolbar for IE/Win.

FAVELETS

Favelets are tiny applications written in JavaScript that dynamically trigger events on a Web page. The JavaScript is contained in a bookmark or favorite that the browser can store, offering single-click access. This JavaScript is really just a long string of commands that's put into a hyperlink. Favelets can do handy things like validate the current page's HTML, toggle or disable style sheets, reset the dimensions of the browser's window to simulate different screen resolutions, and much more.

One such repository of favelets can be found at Accessify.com (www.accessify.com/tools-and-wizards/accessibility-tools/favelets/) (Figure 6.16), where a list of helpful links is available. Bookmarking these little snippets of JavaScript to your favorite browser enables quick access to various test modes.

tip

Find more favelets at these sites: http://tantek.com/favelets/ and www.andybudd.com/bookmarklets/.

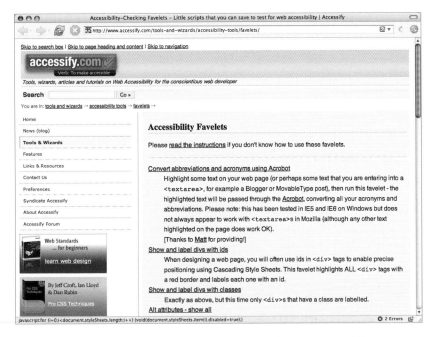

Figure 6.16 Accessify.com is a useful collection of resources and links devoted to Web site accessibility.

For instance, in Figure 6.17, I've dragged the "Disable stylesheets" favelet to my browser's bookmark bar. Now disabling CSS for any site is just a click away at any time. Applying the 10-second usability test mentioned earlier in this chapter just got a whole lot easier.

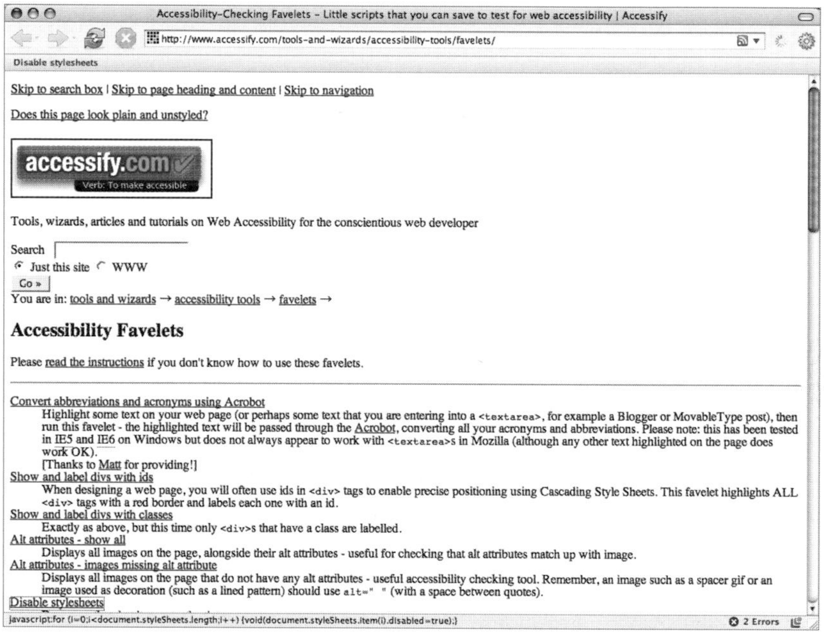

Figure 6.17 After you drag a favelet to the browser's bookmark bar, it's there and ready to disable style sheets on any site you happen to land on.

Similarly, other favelets can alter the page in additional ways. For instance, the "Show all DIVs" favelet outlines all `<div>` elements, giving you an instant view of the page structure (Figure 6.18).

Because of their unobtrusive nature, favelets can become part of your everyday design work and allow you to check your bulletproofness at any time.

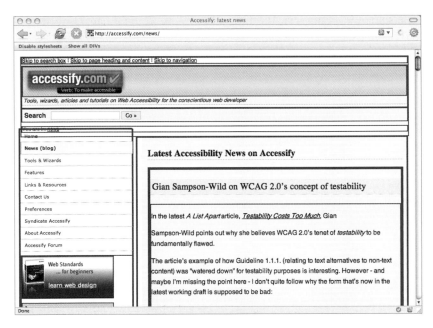

Figure 6.18 Accessify.com looks like this after you enable the "Show all DIVs" favelet, which outlines all `<div>` elements with a red border.

WEB DEVELOPER EXTENSION

If you're a Firefox (or Mozilla, Flock, or Seamonkey) browser user, I highly recommend the Web Developer Extension toolbar, written by Chris Pedrick (`http://chrispederick.com/work/web-developer/`). The toolbar is essentially a collection of actions, much like favelets, that are applied to the current page. The actions are grouped in a toolbar at the top of the browser (Figure 6.19).

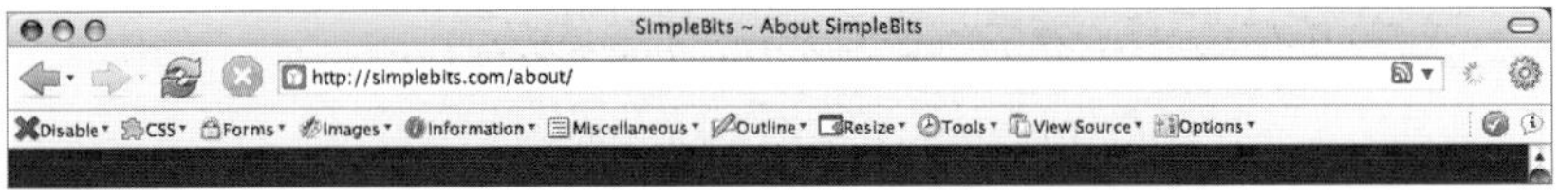

Figure 6.19 The Web Developer Extension contains dozens of actions via drop-down menus from the toolbar.

Every test imaginable is included here. For example, under the Images menu, you can quickly test the page with images turned off and make sure background colors are specified along with their related images, as described earlier in this chapter.

Figure 6.20 shows the Hide Images option applied to SimpleBits; setting this option instantly turns off images so that you can check for readability. Other options combine the best favelets (resizing the window, validating the markup and style sheets, etc.), with other options such as the ability to edit a site's CSS right within a sidebar. This is handy for quickly testing small edits.

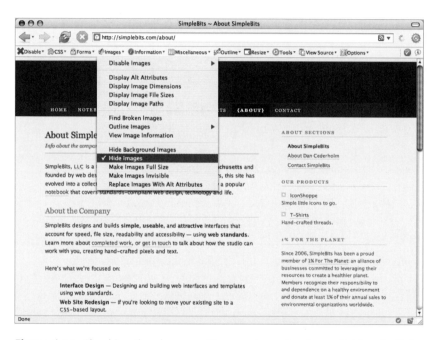

Figure 6.20 Checking the absence of images is as simple as clicking the link to instantly reveal a page's bulletproofness.

The Web Developer Extension creates a "bulletproofing dashboard" of tools, indispensable for anyone who creates pages for the Web. Testing for the absence of images, CSS, and a bevy of other scenarios is no problem.

WEB ACCESSIBILITY TOOLBAR

Much like the Web Developer Extension, the Web Accessibility Toolbar (www. visionaustralia.org.au/ais/toolbar/) offers a dashboard of helpful tools for users of IE/Win (Figure 6.21).

Figure 6.21 Check pages on their level of accessibility with the Web Accessibility Toolbar for IE/Win.

In addition to validation, window resizing, and CSS options, the toolbar includes extra accessibility diagnostics that can be instantly applied to any given Web page. This is a great option for those using Internet Explorer for Windows.

FIREBUG

Similar to the Web Developer Extension mentioned earlier, Firebug (http:// getfirebug.com) is a browser extension for Firefox that has some incredibly handy *inspection* tools made available to any page.

Navigate the document by HTML element and highlight that particular element of the design, viewing key information about its dimensions, the CSS that's applied to it, or DOM (Document Object Model) information (useful for scripting).

Firebug also allows you to modify the CSS and HTML of the current page in *real time*, helpful for debugging and quick edits or problem solving (see Figure 6.22).

Figure 6.22 Firebug, a browser extension for Firefox, gives an interface designer a magnifying glass into the HTML, CSS, and JavaScript of any page on the Web.

VALIDATION AS A TOOL

I had mentioned automatic page validation as a favelet and feature of the Web Developer Extension, but validation of markup and CSS is a tool in and of itself.

Validating a page's markup and CSS against the specifications written by the World Wide Web Consortium (W3C) ensures better, faster rendering of pages and thus gives your designs the greatest chance of being properly delivered. Think of this as you would spell-checking a paper and making sure all your *t*'s are crossed and your *i*'s are dotted.

Complete validation can sometimes be difficult, if not impossible, on large-scale sites, with large teams all working on the same documents. Further complicating matters is content management software that unintentionally spits out markup that is invalid, which makes the challenge for good-intentioned designers even harder. It's often a goal to *strive* for, but perfection is sometimes out of a single person's hands.

But what I'm stressing here is the importance of validation during *the initial design phase of a Web site*—another tool to leverage while you're striving to make your sites bulletproof. As you're building flexible, accessible designs, don't forget to validate your markup and style sheets as you go along; doing so may save you the headache of an unknown rendering error.

For example, a single unclosed `<div>` element could mean the difference between a functioning CSS-based layout and one that's aggravatingly broken. I can attest to this: I've spent hours trying to fix an error, but because I failed to validate the page, my simple omission of a closing element became the obvious root of the problem. By regularly validating your files, you're preventing an overlooked mistake from ruining your designs. And that one overlooked mistake could mean different results in different browsers. *A validated page stands a better chance at being read no matter which browser is reading it.*

How to validate

Validating your XHTML is as simple as using a DOCTYPE at the top of your pages, then running those pages through a validator to check for errors. The DOCTYPE tells the validator (and any other software that cares to know) what *rules* your page is intending to stick by. For example, the bulletproof examples used throughout this book use the XHTML 1.0 Transitional DOCTYPE, and so have the following code at the very top of their pages:

```
<!DOCTYPE html PUBLIC "-//W3C//DTD XHTML 1.0
Transitional//EN"
  "http://www.w3.org/TR/xhtml1/DTD/xhtml1-transitional.dtd">
```

You may, of course, choose to use a different DOCTYPE—it's just important to settle on one and understand the rules associated with it so that proper validation is possible.

 tip

For more on choosing DOCTYPES, see www.htmlhelp.com/tools/validator/doctype.html.

A validator is an application that parses the document and checks for errors against the W3C specification. The DOCTYPE declaration at the top of the page tells the validator which spec to use.

The W3C itself has a free Web-based markup validator (`http://validator.w3.org/`). Using it is as simple as entering the URL to check a page's validness (Figure 6.23). The aforementioned favelets and Web Developer Extension provide one-click access to this tool by sending the current page's URL directly to the W3C's validator.

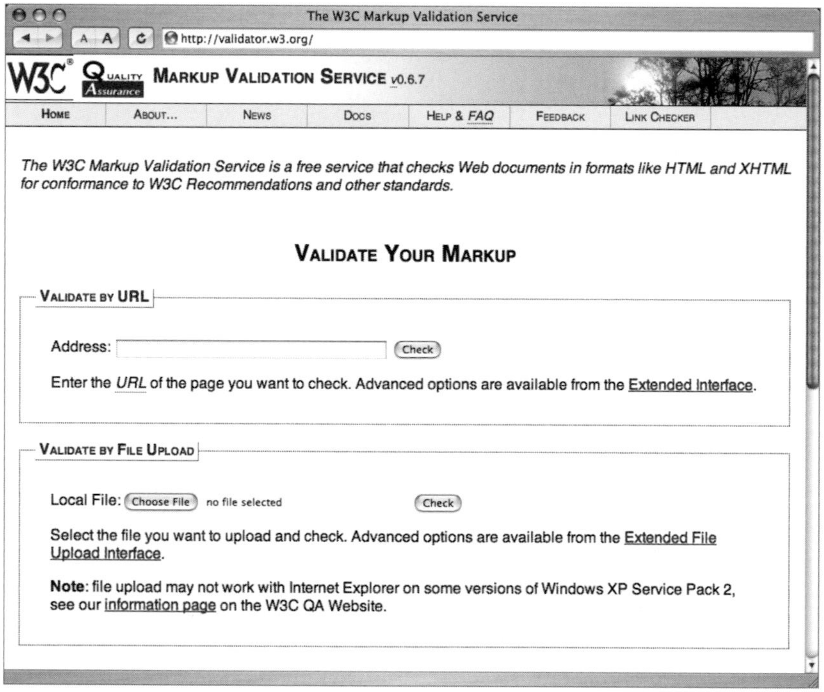

Figure 6.23 You can find the W3C's free Web-based validation tool at `http://validator.w3.org/`.

I often use the W3C's "Validate by File Upload" feature, which allows for the uploading of local files that you are working on that aren't yet available on the public Web. The validator will take your working file and validate it as it would a page out on the actual Web. Even easier is to use the "Validate Local HTML" feature in the Web Developer Extension toolbar (mentioned earlier).

Choosing this option will automatically upload a local HTML file that's currently being viewed in the browser. Again, it's that early design phase where I find it most helpful to stay on top of validating errors.

If you're a Safari user, check out the Safari Tidy plug-in (http://zappatic. net/safaritidy/). It'll automatically warn you of validation errors on the current page in the status bar of the browser, then point out *where* those errors are in the markup when viewing source (Figure 6.24).

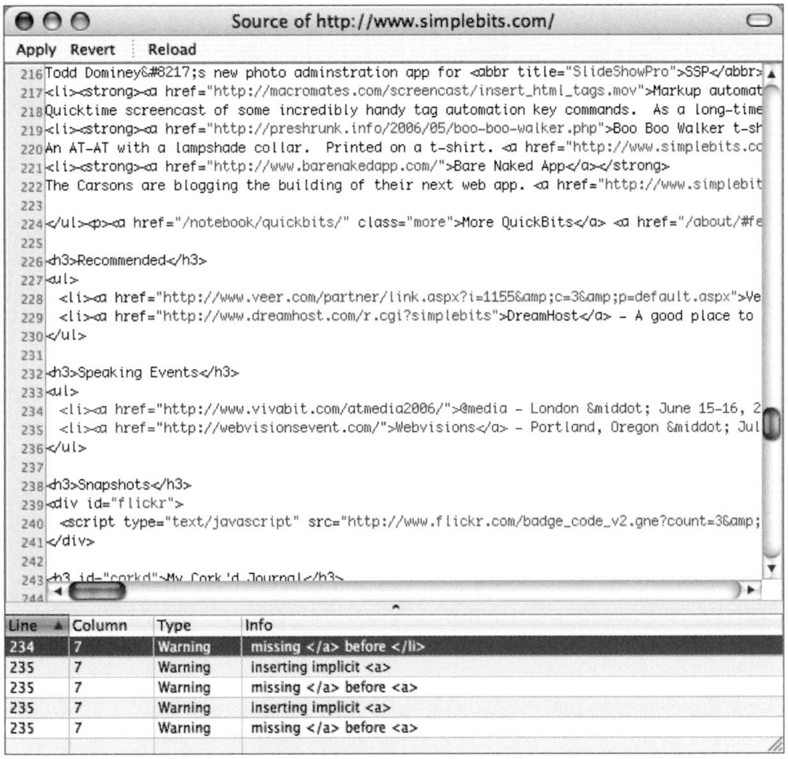

Figure 6.24 Safari Tidy highlights validation errors in the source code.

In addition to validating markup, it's just as important (and just as simple) to validate your CSS. The W3C offers its own validator (http://jigsaw. w3.org/css-validator/), which works almost identically to the markup version mentioned earlier. Via a favelet or toolbar extension, this validator's functions are also just a single click away.

Summary

As important as designing flexibility into the *visual* aspects of your Web page, ensuring the page's integrity under a variety of scenarios can help bulletproof its content. By testing your page in the absence of images and CSS, you'll make sure that its content is still readable under unanticipated circumstances.

Bulletproofing tools such as favelets, browser toolbars, and validation help ease the process of that testing and provide a nondisruptive and simple way to prepare your designs for a multitude of scenarios.

Here are a few things to keep in mind:

- Routinely use the "10-second usability test" to check your page's readability in the absence of images and/or CSS. Familiarize yourself with how your design reacts to the various states it could find itself in.

- Remember to specify background color equivalents for any background images you're including in your designs. Users who turn images off or who have slow connections will still be able to read your pages.

- Use favelets and/or browser toolbars to make the process quick and easy; include this step in your everyday workflow.

- Run the Dig Dug Test to check the integrity and scalability of your designs.

- Embrace validation during the design phase as a way to eliminate head-scratching errors from ruining your afternoon.

7

Convertible Tables

Strip the presentation from data tables, and refinish with CSS.

In many of the previous examples, we've replaced nested table designs with minimal markup and CSS. But there are times when tables are the right tool for the job—for presenting *data*. Whether it be a table of financial data, statistics, or a comparison of information, a table is in these cases necessary and appropriate.

In this chapter we address *styling* the table. Instead of dovetailing the presentation in with the table's data, we strip that presentation (the design) from the markup and move it to CSS. The result is less code, a more accessible table, and a flexible design that's easily changed or updated.

A Common Approach

Just like with the other common components we've explored, you can create stylish tables by using spacer GIF shims and additional table cells that exist solely for the purposes of the design. These extra presentational bits have nothing to do with the *data* being presented, yet they are tangled deep within the table's code. The resulting table looks great in modern browsers—but from a flexibility and accessibility view it is quite a mess.

To illustrate this commingling of data and design, let's use the message boards found at the official site for a series of popular science fiction films. To protect its identity, we'll refer to the site as "Lance Spacerunner," named for its unlikely hero (Figure 7.1).

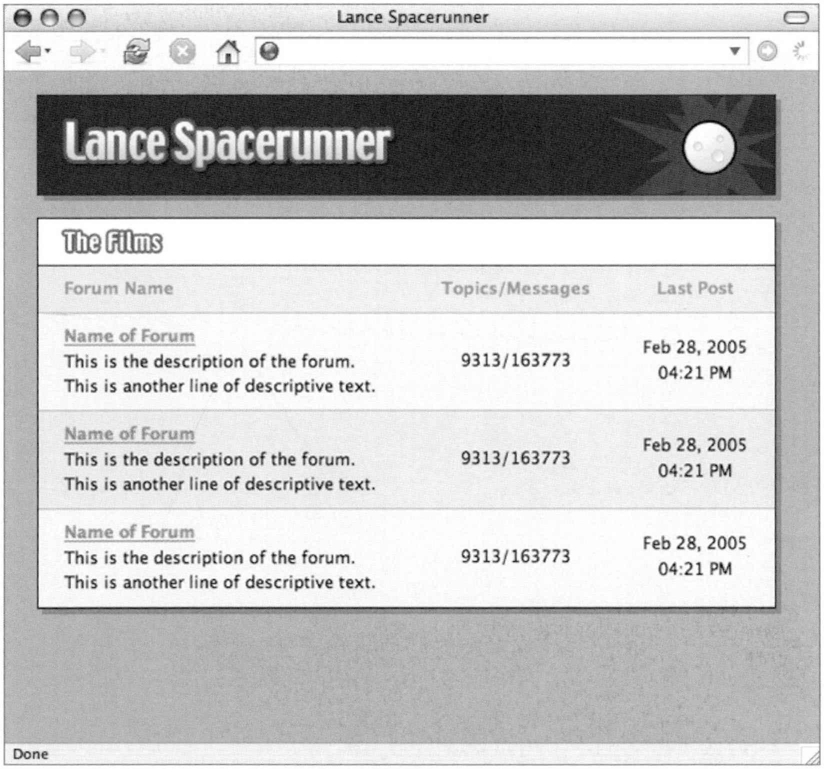

Figure 7.1 For our example, we'll use the message boards found at "Lance Spacerunner," a fictitious site that is based on a real-world example.

Each message board is really a table of data that presents the name and description of each discussion, the number of topics and messages, and the date and time of the last post. At the top sits the category name of the listing—in this case, "The Films."

Let's zoom in and inspect the design details that make this table *insert hokey sci-fi adjective here*.

Figure 7.2 shows the details of the table design that we'll want to keep in mind when we rebuild the style. The table contains a title at the top, followed by column headings, followed by alternating row colors, with a single-pixel gray line separating each row. There is also a 4-pixel drop shadow on the entire table, offset by a few pixels at the top-right and bottom-left corners, giving the table a three-dimensional effect.

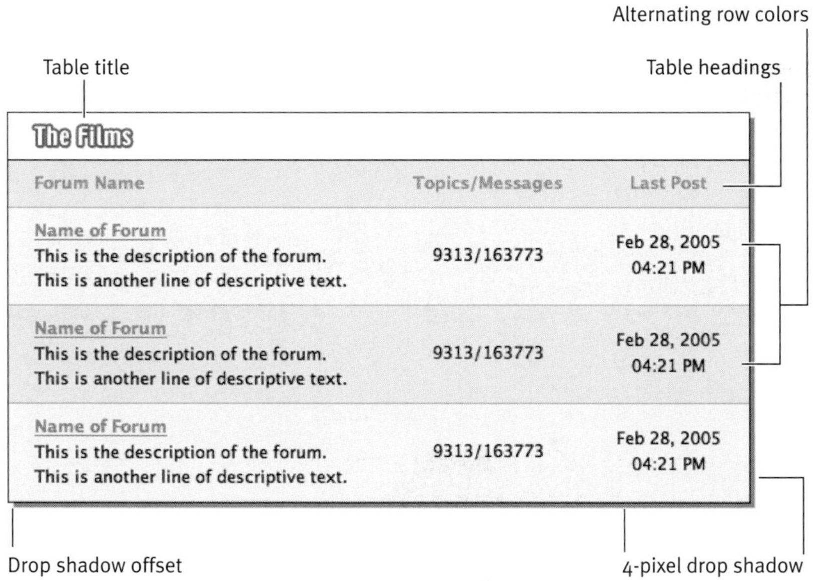

Figure 7.2 Let's examine the design details of a single table from the message boards section.

All in all, it's a nicely designed table—one that fits the intergalactic theme of the rest of the Lance Spacerunner site.

Why It's Not Bulletproof

To achieve its stylish appearance, the data table is a series of nested tables, with a galaxy of extra table cells to control such things as spacing and the one-pixel lines that border the table's elements.

Figure 7.3 shows the table that we're going to zero in on; all table cells are outlined with red lines (a feature that can be similarly replicated using the Web Developer Extension toolbar mentioned in Chapter 6, "No Images? No CSS? No Problem!"). You can see that extra cells are used to control spacing between the cells of data, to add borders and lines, and to add the drop shadow behind the table. I say "extra" because these cells have nothing to do with describing the data and everything to do with the design and appearance of the table.

The Films			
Forum Name		Topics/Messages	Last Post
Name of Forum This is the description of the forum. This is another line of descriptive text.		9313/163773	Feb 28, 2005 04:21 PM
Name of Forum This is the description of the forum. This is another line of descriptive text.		9313/163773	Feb 28, 2005 04:21 PM
Name of Forum This is the description of the forum. This is another line of descriptive text.		9313/163773	Feb 28, 2005 04:21 PM

Figure 7.3 With table cells outlined, you can only guess at the vastness of the extra amount of code that's required.

That said, one downside to this common method is the commingling of design and content. This commingling means you'll run into more difficulty when changing the design at a later date. It also means more code is required and that you'll need to use extra table cells and graphics to achieve what a few lines of CSS can do when applied to a fraction of the code.

But in addition to the bulky code and deep tangling of design and data, this table could benefit from some accessibility enhancements—markup that will make it easier for those browsing with screen readers and text browsers to understand the table's structure and the data it represents. As it stands now, the table scores very low points in terms of accessibility, with screen readers having to navigate a universe of nonessential code in order to find the real data contained within—a bit like flying a space ship through a maze of enemy fire on the surface of an unfamiliar planet. It's not impossible if you're Lance Spacerunner—but is surely difficult for the average person. And you want to present the data to the widest audience possible, with a flexible design applied by using CSS.

A Bulletproof Approach

To bulletproof this table design, let's strip away the excess presentational code from the markup, add accessibility enhancements, and then use CSS to refinish the table. Along the way we'll keep the code light and flexible and still maintain the interesting design.

To begin, let's structure the data with a single table, using the appropriate markup—and nothing more. At this point we're focusing on the correct structure for the data being presented; we'll worry about design details in a bit.

THE MARKUP STRUCTURE

Starting with a basic framework, let's mark up the table in order to show the forum name, topics/messages, and the date of the last post. Let's be sure to include each column's heading as well, putting each grouping in its own column.

```
<table>
  <tr>
    <td>Forum Name</td>
    <td>Topics/Messages</td>
    <td>Last Post</td>
  </tr>
  <tr>
    <td><a href="/forum/">Name of Forum</a> This is
the description of the forum.  This is another line of
descriptive text.</td>
    <td>9313/163773</td>
    <td>Feb 28, 2005 04:21 PM</td>
  </tr>
```

```
<tr>
  <td><a href="/forum/">Name of Forum</a> This is
the description of the forum.  This is another line of
descriptive text.</td>
  <td>9313/163773</td>
  <td>Feb 28, 2005 04:21 PM</td>
</tr>
<tr>
  <td><a href="/forum/">Name of Forum</a> This is
the description of the forum.  This is another line of
descriptive text.</td>
  <td>9313/163773</td>
  <td>Feb 28, 2005 04:21 PM</td>
</tr>
</table>
```

The previous markup (with now simplified content for the example) sets up
each row and column in the right order. Figure 7.4 shows the results.

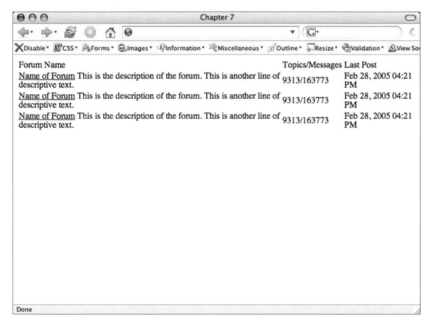

Figure 7.4 Here is the default rendering of the table, shown in the Firefox
browser.

While everything is in its right place, we can enhance the meaning of the column headers (Forum Name, Topics/Messages, Last Post) by using <th> elements. The purpose of the <th> element is to denote headers for a table's content. That extra level of clarification will help any browser or device better understand how we've organized the table. As an added bonus, this unique element allows us to style those headers differently from other cells using CSS—without the need for adding extra markup (i.e., a class).

```
<table>
  <tr>
    <th>Forum Name</th>
    <th>Topics/Messages</th>
    <th>Last Post</th>
  </tr>
  <tr>
    <td><a href="/forum/">Name of Forum</a> This is
the description of the forum.  This is another line of
descriptive text.</td>
    <td>9313/163773</td>
    <td>Feb 28, 2005 04:21 PM</td>
  </tr>
  <tr>
    <td><a href="/forum/">Name of Forum</a> This is
the description of the forum.  This is another line of
descriptive text.</td>
    <td>9313/163773</td>
    <td>Feb 28, 2005 04:21 PM</td>
  </tr>
  <tr>
    <td><a href="/forum/">Name of Forum</a> This is
the description of the forum.  This is another line of
descriptive text.</td>
    <td>9313/163773</td>
    <td>Feb 28, 2005 04:21 PM</td>
  </tr>
</table>
```

With <th> elements used for the column headers, we can see that most browsers treat them with a slightly different style—often bolding and centering the text (Figure 7.5). Remember, we can adjust these effects later using CSS, but right now we're only concerned about optimal structure. Semantically, using <th> elements for "table headers" makes the most sense here.

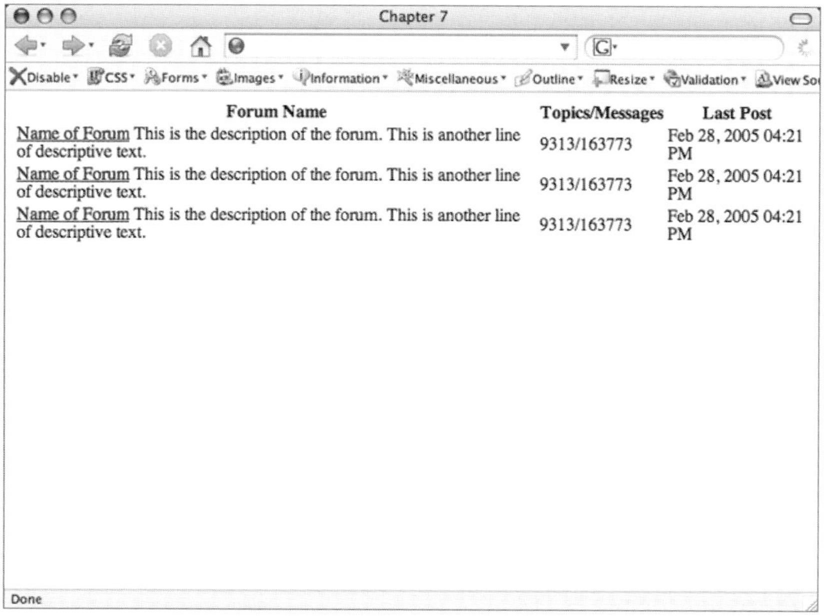

Figure 7.5 We've added <th> elements to each column's header.

Adding scope

Now that we have table headers in place, we can help users browsing with screen-reading software a bit more by adding the scope attribute. The value of the scope attribute designates which cells belong to the header. For instance, in our example, we use the value col, which specifies that the cells in the column underneath the header are associated with it.

```
<table>
  <tr>
    <th scope="col">Forum Name</th>
    <th scope="col">Topics/Messages</th>
    <th scope="col">Last Post</th>
  </tr>
```

```
  <tr>
    <td><a href="/forum/">Name of Forum</a> This is
the description of the forum.  This is another line of
descriptive text.</td>
    <td>9313/163773</td>
    <td>Feb 28, 2005 04:21 PM</td>
  </tr>
  <tr>
    <td><a href="/forum/">Name of Forum</a> This is
the description of the forum.  This is another line of
descriptive text.</td>
    <td>9313/163773</td>
    <td>Feb 28, 2005 04:21 PM</td>
  </tr>
  <tr>
    <td><a href="/forum/">Name of Forum</a> This is
the description of the forum.  This is another line of
descriptive text.</td>
    <td>9313/163773</td>
    <td>Feb 28, 2005 04:21 PM</td>
  </tr>
</table>
```

Similarly, if we'd used a horizontal layout for the table, with the header in front of each cell in a single *row*, we could use the value row for the scope attribute.

Adding the title

Looking back at Figure 7.2, you can see that we have a title above the table's columns and rows that spans across the entire width. At the Lance Spacerunner example site, this is an image of the text "The Films." We could also use an image here, if we wished, but since my futuristic spacey font collection is a bit thin, we'll just use plain ol' hyper(space?) text for our bulletproof version.

To mark up the table's title, it makes perfectly good sense to utilize the child element of <table> that was designed for the job: the <caption> element. The table's caption sits directly underneath the <table> element, and typically, browsers will center this text above the entire table width (Figure 7.6).

```
<table>
  <caption>The Films</caption>
  <tr>
    <th scope="col">Forum Name</th>
    <th scope="col">Topics/Messages</th>
    <th scope="col">Last Post</th>
  </tr>
  <tr>
    <td><a href="/forum/">Name of Forum</a> This is
the description of the forum.  This is another line of
descriptive text.</td>
    <td>9313/163773</td>
    <td>Feb 28, 2005 04:21 PM</td>
  </tr>
  <tr>
    <td><a href="/forum/">Name of Forum</a> This is
the description of the forum.  This is another line of
descriptive text.</td>
    <td>9313/163773</td>
    <td>Feb 28, 2005 04:21 PM</td>
  </tr>
  <tr>
    <td><a href="/forum/">Name of Forum</a> This is
the description of the forum.  This is another line of
descriptive text.</td>
    <td>9313/163773</td>
    <td>Feb 28, 2005 04:21 PM</td>
  </tr>
</table>
```

tip

There are additional elements we could add to our table, notably <thead>, <tfoot>, and <tbody> for grouping rows and giving context to longer table sections. Similarly, we could add <col> and <colgroup> to group columns while allowing browsers to render the table incrementally rather than waiting for the entire table to download.

I recommend reading the W3C's specification on tables (www.w3.org/TR/html401/struct/tables.html), or (perhaps easier to digest) Roger Johansson's "Bring on the tables" article (www.456bereastreet.com/archive/200410/bring_on_the_tables/) to dive into additional markup possibilities for structuring data tables.

Since our table is a short, relatively simple table, we're going to move on with the markup as is.

The Films		
Forum Name	**Topics/Messages**	**Last Post**
Name of Forum This is the description of the forum. This is another line of descriptive text.	9313/163773	Feb 28, 2005 04:21 PM
Name of Forum This is the description of the forum. This is another line of descriptive text.	9313/163773	Feb 28, 2005 04:21 PM
Name of Forum This is the description of the forum. This is another line of descriptive text.	9313/163773	Feb 28, 2005 04:21 PM

Figure 7.6 The <caption> element is often centered above the table's contents.

Cellspacing

Before we begin applying CSS, let's add one more bit of markup: the `cellspacing` attribute on the `<table>` element. By assigning the attribute a value of 0, we eliminate any gaps between cells and instead control spacing completely with CSS.

```
<table cellspacing="0">
```

Using the `cellspacing` attribute is the most surefire way to give yourself a clean slate when styling tables, but it's not the only way. The CSS property `border-collapse` exists to essentially achieve the same results that `cellspacing="0"` does. By specifying

```
table {
  border-collapse: collapse;
  }
```

you can keep the `<table>` element free of attributes. But browser support then becomes a problem. Most browsers support the `border-collapse` property, but not all (for example, IE/Mac). For this particular example, I don't think it causes much harm to add the `cellspacing` attribute, so we'll do just that, and move on to adding style.

APPLYING STYLE

With our lean table markup complete, we can now start applying CSS in order to fold in the design. We've already cut in half the amount of markup by removing the extra table cells and keeping only what's needed to structure the data.

To set up the whole page, let's first add a background color and default font and link colors (I'll omit repeating these rules as we move along).

```
body {
  margin: 0;
  padding: 30px;
  font-family: "Lucida Grande", Arial, sans-serif;
  font-size: small;
  background: #b5b5b5;
  }
a { color: #77985C; }
```

Border and background

Next, we'll set a one-pixel black border around the table, and a background color of white. We'll also set the width of the table to 100%, so that it will expand as far as it can. In our example, it'll expand to the width of the browser window (minus the 30 pixels of padding we've previously declared on all sides of the <body> element). In the case of the Lance Spacerunner site, it would expand as wide as the container that it sits in (the main content column of the page).

```
table {
  width: 100%;
  border: 1px solid #000;
  background: #fff;
  }
```

Figure 7.7 reveals our progress thus far.

note

Specifying a width of 100% for the table results in a horizontal scrollbar in IE5/Mac. Setting a width that is less than 100% will fix this, or depending on the overall container width that the table will eventually sit inside, omitting a width altogether may be a possibility as well—just letting the table expand as far as it can on its own. The IE5/Mac scrollbar issue is just something to be aware of, but certainly nothing to lose sleep over, especially if you're not concerned with an absolute rendering of perfection in an increasingly outdated browser. In other words, if your site statistics tell you that IE/Mac's slice of the pie is miniscule and continuing to drop, then certainly take that into consideration for any minor inconsistencies you encounter. Let *your* particular site's stats dictate how much you should bend over backward for a particular browser!

![Browser window titled "Chapter 7" displaying a table titled "The Films" with columns Forum Name, Topics/Messages, and Last Post. Three rows each show "Name of Forum This is the description of the forum. This is another line of descriptive text." with 9313/163773 and Feb 28, 2005 04:21 PM.]

Figure 7.7 Notice how the <caption> appears outside the table's borders, even though the element is inside.

note

I could've written this declaration by just stating th, td, as these elements are always contained within a <table> element. But for CSS code organization, often I'll use explicit selectors—it's not necessary to specify "cells within table elements," but it's a simple way of visually grouping declarations in your style sheets.

Padding and dividing line

Next, we'll add padding within each <th> and <td> element, and create the single-pixel gray line that divides each row:

```
table {
  width: 100%;
  border: 1px solid #000;
  background: #fff;
}
table th, table td {
  margin: 0;
  padding: 8px 20px;
  text-align: center;
  border-bottom: 1px solid #b5b5b5;
}
```

Figure 7.8 shows the added 8-pixel padding on top and bottom, the 20-pixel padding on both sides, as well as the gray lines separating the rows that span across the entire table. By adding a border-bottom to each cell, we achieve a continuous straight line. This works only when cellspacing is zeroed out (as we've done) or if border-collapse: collapse; is specified for the <table> element. We've also centered text within all cells—something we'll want to override for the "Forum Name" column only. 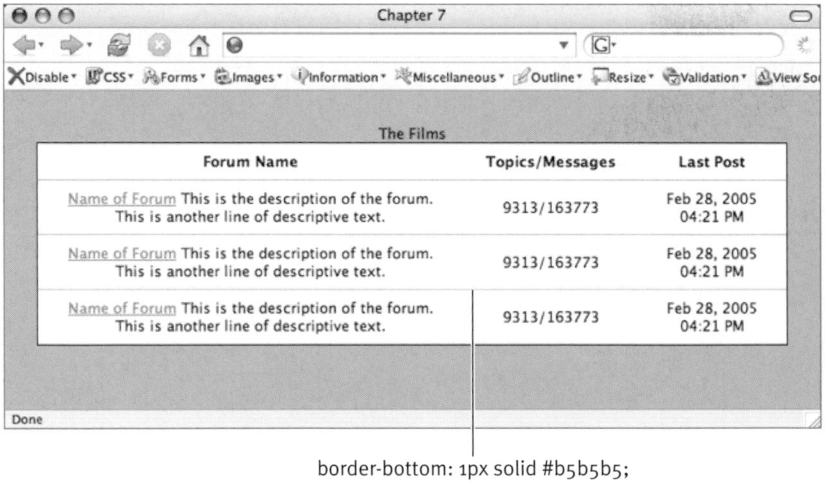

border-bottom: 1px solid #b5b5b5;

Figure 7.8 Because we've removed cellspacing, a consistent line can be achieved by assigning borders to the cells.

Custom alignment

To left-align the text for only the "Forum Name" header and the column underneath, let's create a class that we can attach to those elements that overrides the text-align: center; previously declared.

```
table {
  width: 100%;
  border: 1px solid #000;
  background: #fff;
  }
table th, table td {
  margin: 0;
  padding: 8px 20px;
  text-align: center;
  border-bottom: 1px solid #b5b5b5;
  }
table .name {
  text-align: left;
  }
```

Once we've created a generic name class, we can attach it to the appropriate spots in the markup:

```
 <table cellspacing="0">
  <caption>The Films</caption>
  <tr>
    <th scope="col" class="name">Forum Name</th>
    <th scope="col">Topics/Messages</th>
    <th scope="col">Last Post</th>
  </tr>
  <tr>
    <td class="name"><a href="/forum/">Name of Forum</a>
This is the description of the forum.  This is another line
of descriptive text.</td>
    <td>9313/163773</td>
    <td>Feb 28, 2005 04:21 PM</td>
  </tr>
  <tr>
    <td class="name"><a href="/forum/">Name of Forum</a>
This is the description of the forum.  This is another line
of descriptive text.</td>
```

```
    <td>9313/163773</td>
    <td>Feb 28, 2005 04:21 PM</td>
  </tr>
  <tr>
    <td class="name"><a href="/forum/">Name of Forum</a>
This is the description of the forum.  This is another line
of descriptive text.</td>
    <td>9313/163773</td>
    <td>Feb 28, 2005 04:21 PM</td>
  </tr>
</table>
```

Figure 7.9 shows the results. The text and heading for the "Forum Name" column are left-aligned but the other two columns are centered.

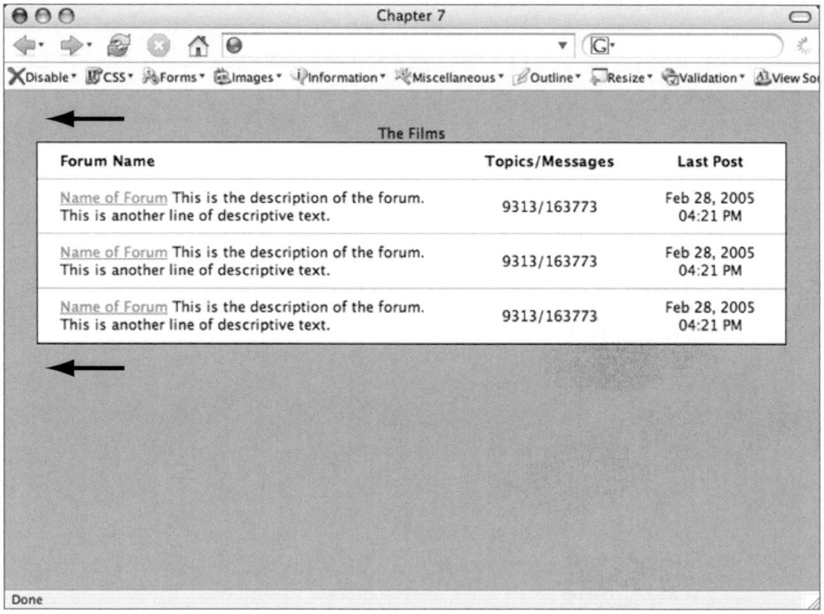

Figure 7.9 Since the "Forum Name" column is the exception, we left-aligned these cells by adding a class.

Alternating row colors

A little extra markup is also necessary to handle the alternating row colors from the original Lance Spacerunner design (unless you don't mind using a bit of JavaScript to dynamically handle this; see "Zebra Tables," www.alistapart.com/articles/zebratables/). We want to denote the alternate row color by adding a class to the desired <tr> elements.

I like to use the value alt for these situations, staying away from values named gray or dark or any other visual description. This keeps the class name generic enough to be used wherever desired. If the alternate color is gray today, it doesn't mean that color won't change in the future to green (or anything else) and thus result in a confusing class name.

```
<table cellspacing="0">
  <caption>The Films</caption>
  <tr>
    <th scope="col" class="name">Forum Name</th>
    <th scope="col">Topics/Messages</th>
    <th scope="col">Last Post</th>
  </tr>
  <tr class="alt">
    <td class="name"><a href="/forum/">Name of Forum</a>
This is the description of the forum.  This is another line
of descriptive text.</td>
    <td>9313/163773</td>
    <td>Feb 28, 2005 04:21 PM</td>
  </tr>
  <tr>
    <td class="name"><a href="/forum/">Name of Forum</a>
This is the description of the forum.  This is another line
of descriptive text.</td>
    <td>9313/163773</td>
    <td>Feb 28, 2005 04:21 PM</td>
  </tr>
  <tr class="alt">
    <td class="name"><a href="/forum/">Name of Forum</a>
This is the description of the forum.  This is another line
of descriptive text.</td>
    <td>9313/163773</td>
    <td>Feb 28, 2005 04:21 PM</td>
  </tr>
</table>
```

We first define a default row color of gray for all `<tr>` elements; then we override that value with a lighter shade for alternating rows marked with the `alt` class:

```css
table {
  width: 100%;
  border: 1px solid #000;
  background: #fff;
  }
table th, table td {
  margin: 0;
  padding: 8px 20px;
  text-align: center;
  border-bottom: 1px solid #b5b5b5;
  }
table .name {
  text-align: left;
  }
table tr {
  background: #e6e6e6;
  }
table tr.alt {
  background: #f1f1f1;
  }
```

Figure 7.10 shows the alternating row colors, and as you can see things are starting to look rather nice.

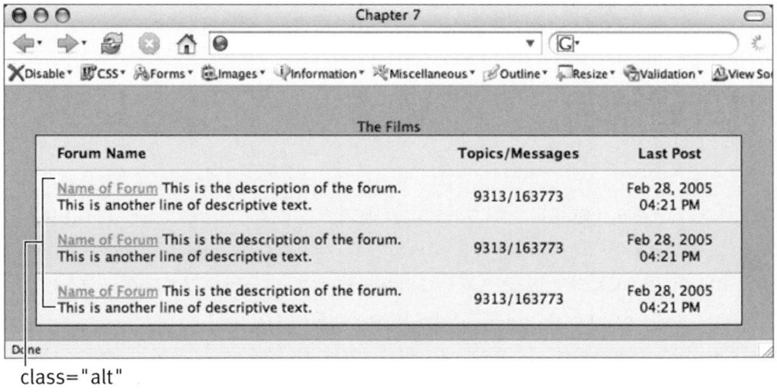

class="alt"

Figure 7.10 Instead of `alt` we could've used a color or other description, but keeping it generic is always a good idea in case color or appearance changes later on.

New line without the

To get each forum name and description on its own line rather than drop in a <br /> element, we could specify links within <td> elements of our table to use the display: block; property. This way, we force the description that comes after it to start on the line below—with no extra markup needed. While we're at it, let's make those links bold as well:

```
table {
  width: 100%;
  border: 1px solid #000;
  background: #fff;
  }
table th, table td {
  margin: 0;
  padding: 8px 20px;
  text-align: center;
  border-bottom: 1px solid #b5b5b5;
  }
table .name {
  text-align: left;
  }
table tr {
  background: #e6e6e6;
  }
table tr.alt {
  background: #f1f1f1;
  }
table td a {
  display: block;
  font-weight: bold;
  }
```

As Figure 7.11 shows, each link is now bold and on its own line as a result of the added declaration. Using the display: block; rule to force items onto separate line without using a <br /> is a nice trick—but *only* if the content still makes sense when CSS is taken away. In this particular case, I think devices that don't support CSS will understand the link and description that follows just fine.

note 📖

Setting display: block; on a link, as we've just done, extends the clickable area of that link to the entire width of its parent container. In other words, the entire line (whether the text extends all the way or not) is clickable—not just the text itself. This could be seen as a usability improvement, giving the user a larger area to click on (see http://1976design.com/ blog/archive/2004/09/07/ link-presentation-fitts-law/ for more on how a larger, clickable area can improve hyperlinks). Whether or not it's useful could be debated, but it's something that's worthy of pointing out, should you decide to use this method for forcing text onto its own line when links are involved.

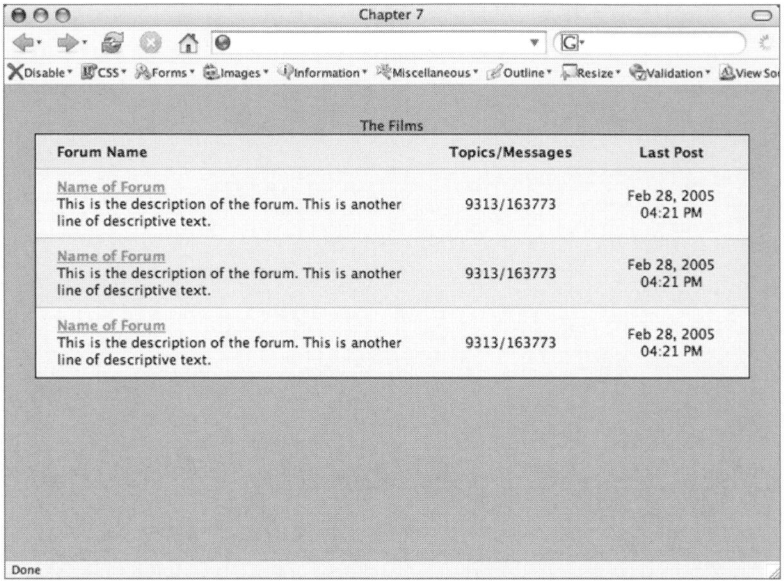

Figure 7.11 Using display: block; on the link works here, as long as there are no other links within the same cell, since those would be forced onto their own lines as well.

Header color

As mentioned earlier, one of the side benefits of using table headers (<th>) properly is that doing so gives you control over these elements in terms of style—without the need for extra markup in the way of classes.

For instance, in the Lance Spacerunner example, table headers are a lighter shade of gray than the rest of the table's text—and we can easily match that by adding a simple rule to turn all <th> elements the color we wish:

```
table {
  width: 100%;
  border: 1px solid #000;
  background: #fff;
  }
table th, table td {
  margin: 0;
  padding: 8px 20px;
  text-align: center;
```

```
  border-bottom: 1px solid #b5b5b5;
  }
table th {
  color: #999;
  }
table .name {
  text-align: left;
  }
table tr {
  background: #e6e6e6;
  }
table tr.alt {
  background: #f1f1f1;
  }
table td a {
  display: block;
  font-weight: bold;
  }
```

Figure 7.12 shows the results of adding the declaration. The table headers are now gray, as opposed to the default black.

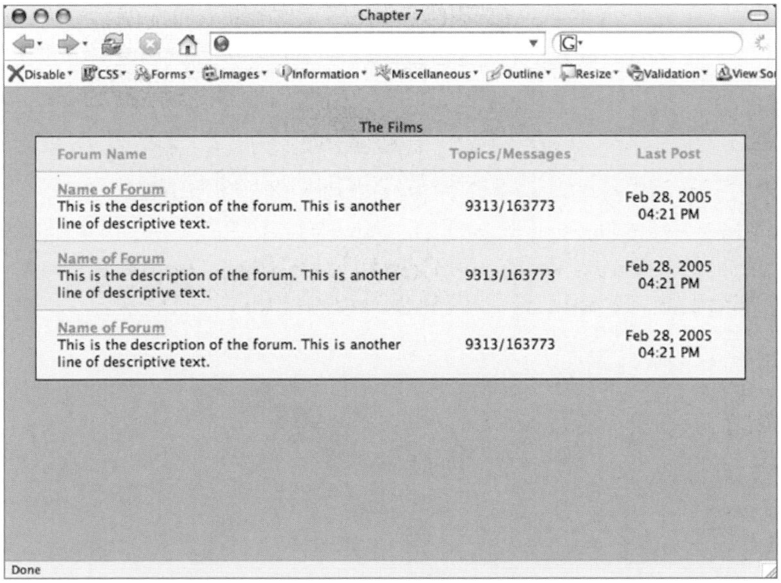

Figure 7.12 We needed to turn the column headers a different color, and it was painless because we used proper <th> elements to structure them.

Styling <caption>

Next, let's style the <caption> element, giving it a white background and adding a border on three sides (omitting the bottom border, since that's already part of the <table>).

We originally chose to use the <caption> element for the title of the table for semantic reasons. It's the markup choice that makes the most sense. Safari and IE/Mac treat the styling of <caption> differently than other browsers; you may get mixed results depending on the styles you choose to apply. For instance, in our example the <caption> appears to be several pixels less wide than the <table> itself, even though <caption> is contained *within* the <table> element. This could be the result of odd behavior, or a different interpretation of the specification. Either way, use your judgment when choosing to use either the <caption> (the optimal choice) or another element (i.e., a heading element).

```css
table {
  width: 100%;
  border: 1px solid #000;
  background: #fff;
  }
table caption {
  margin: 0;
  padding: 8px 20px;
  text-align: left;
  border: 1px solid #000;
  border-bottom: none;
  background: #fff;
  }
table th, table td {
  margin: 0;
  padding: 8px 20px;
  text-align: center;
  border-bottom: 1px solid #b5b5b5;
  }
table th {
  color: #999;
  }
```

```
table .name {
  text-align: left;
  }
table tr {
  background: #e6e6e6;
  }
table tr.alt {
  background: #f1f1f1;
  }
table td a {
  display: block;
  font-weight: bold;
  }
```

By default, a table's caption is centered, so in addition to some padding, background, and border on all sides but the bottom, we're left-aligning the text (Figure 7.13). Again, the Lance Spacerunner example featured a graphic for the words "The Films" that could also be located within the <caption> element in place of the plain text that we're using.

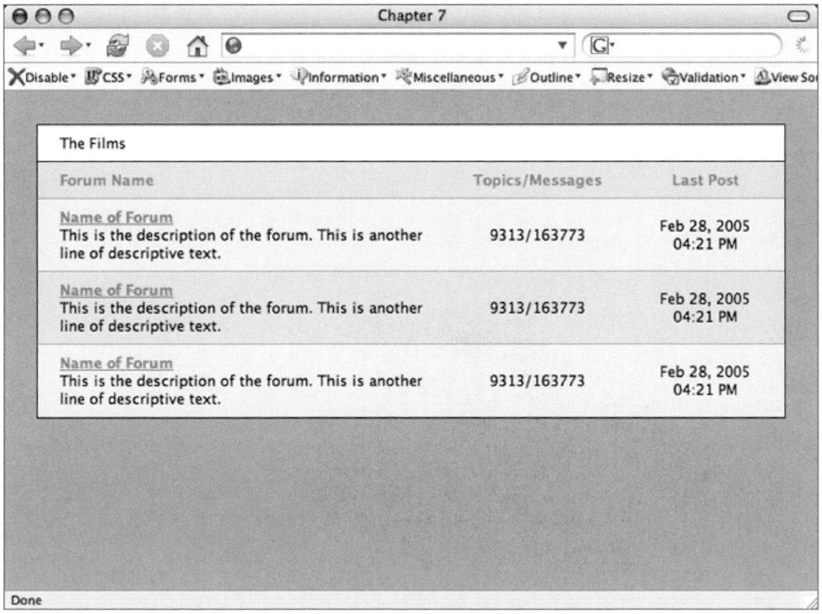

Figure 7.13 The caption is styled nicely in the Firefox browser.

The offset shadow

For the offset drop shadow on the entire table, Lance Spacerunner added an extra column and row, placing graphics in those cells to create the shadow effect (Figure 7.14). We're going to achieve the same result—without adding unnecessary cells and using *no* graphics at all.

We will, however need to add a containing `<div>` around the table, one that will fill in the shadow color as a background. We'll then bump the table out of the container's edges by 4 pixels, using a little positioning.

So, our markup will change slightly with the addition of a `<div>` wrapped around the table. Let's begin by defining a class for this wrapper that we can reuse for additional tables on the page:

```
<div class="forums">
  <table cellspacing="0">
  . . .
  </table>
</div>
```

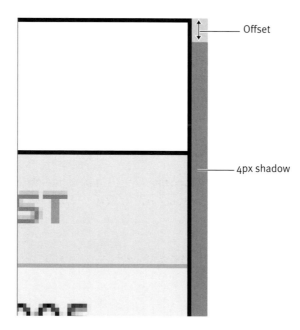

Offset

4px shadow

Figure 7.14 The offset effect that's essential for drop shadows is possible by using an additional outer element around the table.

We'll assign the shadow color as a background for the entire containing
`<div>`. However, with the table sitting *inside* this container, the background
color will be completely obscured. To reveal that background behind the
table on the right and bottom edges, as well as achieve the offset on the top-
right and bottom-left corners, we need to use a little *negative* positioning to
nudge the table (Figure 7.15).

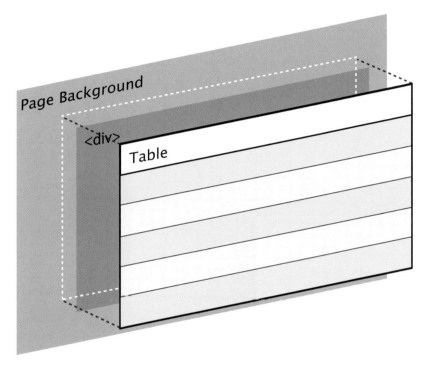

Figure 7.15 Using negative positioning to nudge the table up and to the left
by a few pixels, the containing `<div>`'s background will be revealed on the
bottom and right sides.

So first, we add the background color (a dark gray) that we'd like the shadow
to be on the containing `<div>` in a new declaration:

```
.forums {
  background: #919191;
  }
```

Next, we'll add the negative positioning to the main <table> declaration, nudging the entire table exactly 4 pixels up and to the left:

```
.forums {
  background: #919191;
  }
table {
  position: relative;
  top: -4px;
  left: -4px;
  width: 100%;
  border: 1px solid #000;
  background: #fff;
  }
table caption {
  margin: 0;
  padding: 8px 20px;
  text-align: left;
  border: 1px solid #000;
  border-bottom: none;
  background: #fff;
  }
table th, table td {
  margin: 0;
  padding: 8px 20px;
  text-align: center;
  border-bottom: 1px solid #b5b5b5;
  }
table th {
  color: #999;
  }
table .name {
  text-align: left;
  }
table tr {
  background: #e6e6e6;
  }
table tr.alt {
  background: #f1f1f1;
  }
```

```
table td a {
  display: block;
  font-weight: bold;
  }
```

By using position: relative here, we'll adjust the position of the table from the spot on the page where it already lies, as opposed to position: absolute, which would position the table in terms of the coordinates of its *parent* container.

Using a negative value here will "nudge" the table out from the <div> that wraps it, revealing 4 pixels of its background on the right and bottom, as well as the offset that creates the shadow effect (Figure 7.16).

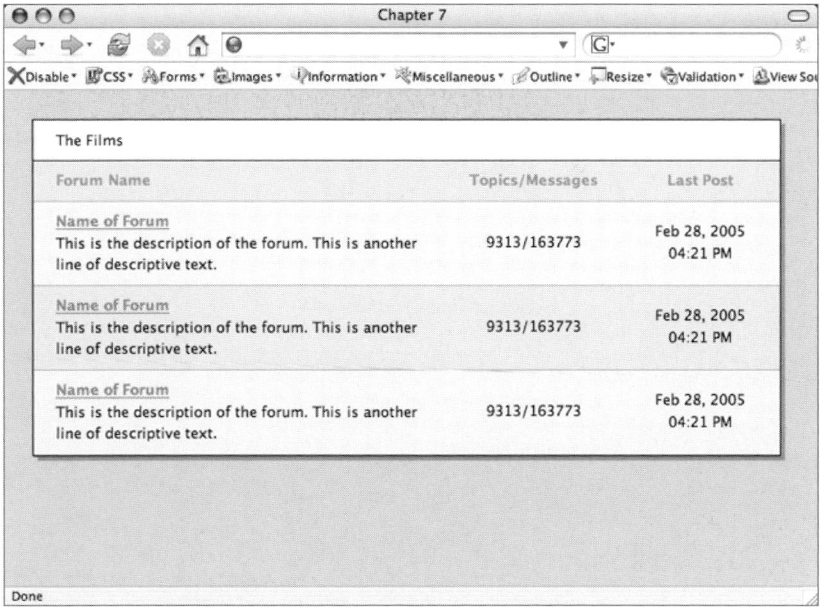

Figure 7.16 The completed design features a graphic-free drop shadow.

Why It's Bulletproof

By stripping the example down to a core, semantic structure, we rebuilt the table using only the essential elements. Along the way, we increased the accessibility of the table while trimming the code down by a gigantic amount.

In addition, we were able to re-create the table's stylish appearance using no images whatsoever, untangling the design from the markup and moving it over to CSS. Future updates to the design and/or data will be easier, and we won't have to wade through dozens and dozens of extra table cells—cells that exist solely for the purpose of stylizing the table.

The table itself is also flexible from a height and width point of view. We've refrained from specifying a pixel dimension on anything, and since no images are used, this design could be dropped inside any container and will stretch to fit (Figure 7.17).

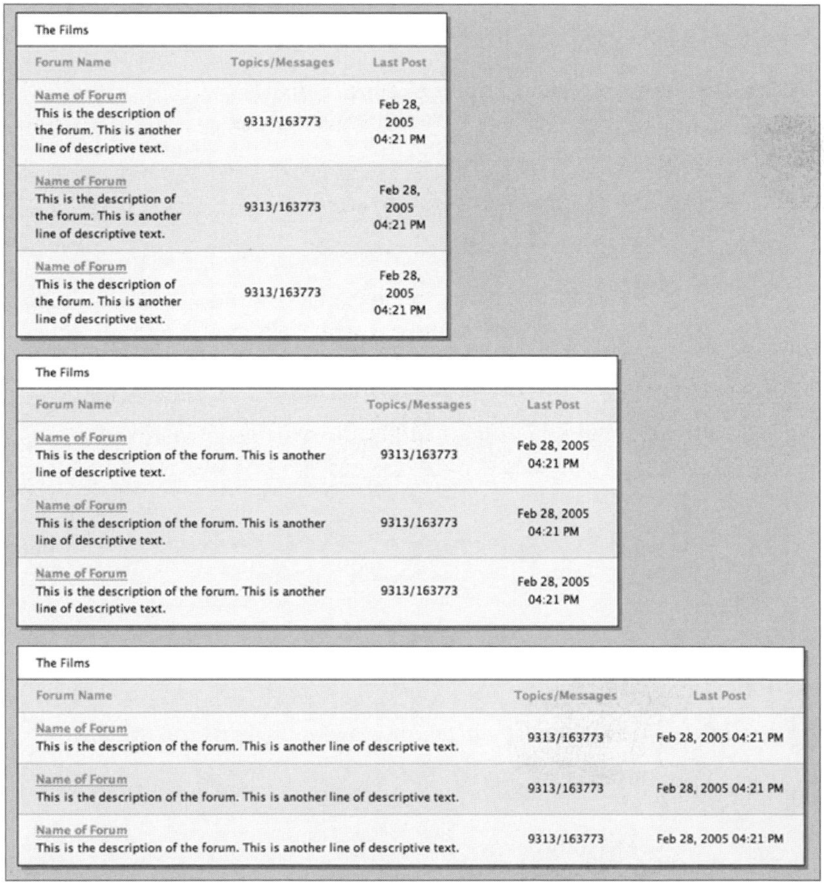

Figure 7.17 Widening or shrinking the container of the table won't hinder this design, with its ability to expand and contract flawlessly.

Summary

When you're creating stylish data tables, it's important not to abuse the markup structure by attaching extra, unnecessary cells for the sole purpose of the design. By building a meaningful structure for the table first—using only the necessary elements to support the data—you'll cut down on code and be able to later style the table however you'd like using CSS.

Borders, backgrounds, and colors can all be kept in the style sheet, which leaves the markup clean and lean and highly accessible to whatever device happens to read it.

Here are a few things to keep in mind when styling tables:

- Collapse the table using `<table cellspacing="0">` (or the `border-collapse` property), and move all other borders, background, and spacing to the style sheet.

- Use the `<caption>` element to properly assign a title to the table. Be aware that Safari and IE/Mac render styled `<caption>`s differently.

- Use `<th>` elements to properly denote the table's headers, thus providing better structure and a way to uniquely style those cells with CSS.

- Create grid lines by adding borders to the `<th>` and/or `<td>` elements.

- Add background colors to rows by styling the `<tr>` elements. Alternate background row colors by adding a `class` to the desired `<tr>`.

8

Fluid and Elastic Layouts

Experiment with page layouts that expand and contract.

It's only natural to talk about how an *entire page* can embrace flexibility as well as the components contained within it. We've gone over several components in previous chapters of the book, but now let's explore page layouts in general—how CSS can be utilized to create columned pages that expand and contract regardless of screen, window, or text size.

Before we begin, I should mention that I'm not going to fuel the debate over whether a fluid or elastic layout is *better* than a fixed-width layout (or vice versa). I believe that each has its own place, and deciding to use a fluid, elastic, or fixed-width layout hinges on many variables—factors that are unique to each project and its requirements. Choosing fluid versus elastic versus fixed isn't a religious choice but rather an option dependent on the site at hand.

That said, this chapter *will* cover strategies for creating fluid and elastic layouts—additional tools for the bulletproof arsenal. Knowing how to comfortably execute them will only add to your toolbox of flexible options.

Fluid (sometimes also called *liquid*) layouts are not exclusive to CSS; in fact, you could create a fluid layout using tables. But you can derive other benefits from keeping layout details in style sheets, as you'll discover in this chapter.

Elastic layouts involve column widths designated in em units. Like a few of the previous em-based examples in this book, em-based *layouts* will expand or contract along with the current font size, giving your entire design a "zoomable" quality.

A Common Approach

As I just mentioned, multicolumn layouts are not exclusive to CSS. Additionally, fluid layouts, which expand and contract along with whatever width the browser window happens to occupy, can also be achieved using tables. Traditionally, a designer may think in columns, forming each using a series of table cells.

Figure 8.1 shows a commonly used layout structure, with a header that spans across the top, then two columns for content, followed by a footer that spans across the bottom.

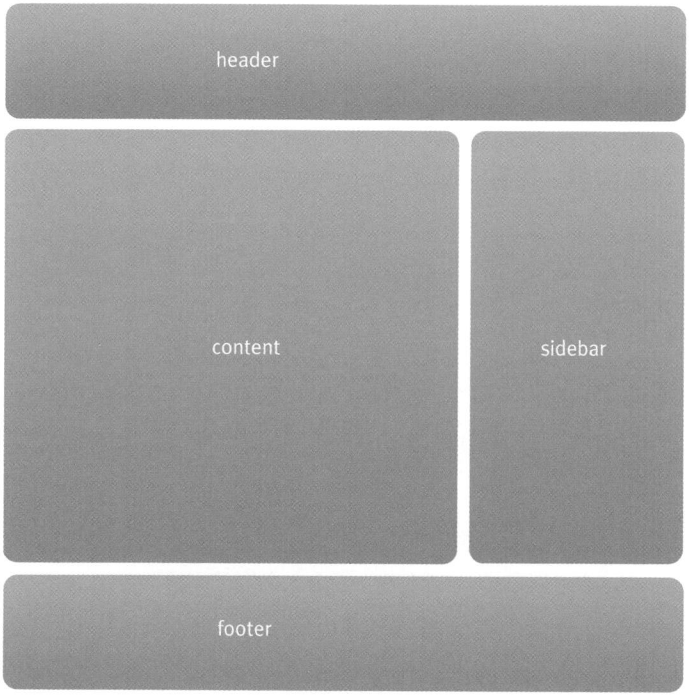

Figure 8.1 You often see a two-column layout structure like this.

Historically, a table seemed like a natural way to mark up this structure, using the `colspan` attribute to span the header and footer across multiple content columns. A rough approximation of that markup would look something like this:

```
<table>
  <tr>
    <td colspan="2">header</td>
  </tr>
  <tr>
    <td>content</td>
    <td>sidebar</td>
  </tr>
  <tr>
    <td colspan="2">footer</td>
  </tr>
</table>
```

But most designers and developers didn't stop there. Once they constructed a basic shell, they could nest additional tables inside each cell to create borders and pixel-precise spacing for the layout. In the end, an enormous amount of markup was used to create both the framework for the layout as well as the visual style of the page.

To achieve fluidity, it's possible to set table cell widths as percentages, which allows the layout to fully expand regardless of browser window size:

```
<table width="100%">
  <tr>
    <td colspan="2">header</td>
  </tr>
  <tr>
    <td width="70%">content</td>
    <td width="30%">sidebar</td>
  </tr>
  <tr>
    <td colspan="2">footer</td>
  </tr>
</table>
```

The entire table gets a width of 100%, while the columns get broken down into whatever widths are desired—in this case, a larger content column to the left of a narrower sidebar. Expanding or contracting the browser window will resize the layout and proportionately render the columns.

So, it's proven that tables *can* work for creating layouts, and it's also proven that tables *can* be used to achieve fluid layouts that stretch along with the browser window. But there's an easier way—a better way. Let's talk about why the table method is *unbulletproof*.

Why It's Not Bulletproof

One of the main problems that table layouts suffer from is a tangling of content and design. In other words, borders, spacer GIFs, and graphics are embedded right in the markup along with the important content. This means only typical desktop browsers will be able to read the page with any great success. Users of screen-reading software, text browsers, or other small-screened devices are likely to have difficulty.

AN ABUNDANCE OF CODE

This tangling can also mean *lots of code*. The amount of markup necessary to design compelling layouts with nested tables can, at times, be staggering. Unnecessary table cells are used to create *gutters* (space between columns of text), borders, and other visual characteristics of a page. By using CSS, the markup can be stripped down to its bare essentials, and presentational instructions can be moved to the style sheets. This immediately improves readability on nontraditional devices and software, not to mention being far friendlier to search engines (an additional, free benefit).

A MAINTENANCE NIGHTMARE

All that code and the tangling I've mentioned (I do seem to like that word *tangling*, don't I?) only add to the maintenance nightmare caused by nested table layouts. Changing the look and feel of a table-based design requires much heavy lifting—navigating through table cells and extra markup to change a page's design. It can be maddening, if not at times pointless, with the best option often just to start from scratch.

NONOPTIMAL CONTENT ORDERING

Another downside to creating table-based layouts is the order in which the contents are presented in text browsers and screen readers. For instance, taking a three-column layout, we know that order in the markup will always be left column, middle column, and then right column (Figure 8.2). This is the way tables operate.

Figure 8.2 The (sometimes) nonoptimal ordering of table-based content is left column, middle column, and then right column.

Those viewing with a text browser or screen reader will always digest the content in that order only. But the real meat of the document might not be contained within that first left column. Typically, the important information is held within the *middle* column, which would be buried further down the page. When using tables for layout, it is impossible to source-order the layout, an arrangement that allows the important content to be read first in alternate browsers and software. There is one order for all devices, which forces text and screen readers to wade through less important content before getting to the good stuff.

Fortunately, CSS-based layouts *do* allow for that reordering, enabling your document's source to be marked up in an optimal order but presented in another. In addition, far less code is required, as well as a simple separation of content from presentation. Let's move on to start building fluid, multicolumn layouts using CSS.

A Bulletproof Approach

While it makes perfect sense to create flexible, fluid layouts for the bulletproof example of this chapter, it's important to note that fixed-width CSS-based layouts also share many of the advantages that their non-width-restrictive siblings have. The main difference here is that fluid layouts can expand and contract along with the browser window, giving the reader some additional control.

We'll be walking through the necessary steps to create fluid layouts with CSS, gathering up the reasons for doing so along the way. Let's get to it, starting with a simple two-column design—with a header and footer.

THE MARKUP STRUCTURE

Instead of using table cells to lay out the page's column structure, we'll use simple <div>s to divide the content into chunks. We'll also keep in mind an optimal content order while doing so (this will become more important when we talk about three-column designs later on).

At its most basic, a simple two-column layout could be marked up easily like this:

```
<div id="wrap">
  <div id="header">
    <h1>Header Goes Here</h1>
  </div>

  <div id="content">
    ... content goes here ...
  </div>

  <div id="sidebar">
    ... sidebar goes here ...
  </div>

  <div id="footer">
    ... footer goes here ...
  </div>
</div> <!-- end #wrap -->
```

tip

It is possible to utilize a JavaScript solution that will clear absolutely positioned elements. See "Absolutely Positive" (www.shauninman.com/plete/2004/07/absolutely-positive) for an example and code by Shaun Inman.

That's it. You can't get much simpler than that. Order-wise, this makes the most sense: header, content, sidebar, footer. We're thinking in terms of how this page will flow *without* CSS applied. So far, so good.

I've added a wrapper <div> that surrounds the entire layout. This can often come in handy for various design purposes (as we'll discover further on). So, any time I'm building a CSS-based layout, I often start with a containing <div>, right off the bat.

CREATING COLUMNS: FLOAT VS. POSITIONING

One method for creating columns with CSS involves *absolute positioning*—that is, using pixel coordinates on the screen to place elements in very specific locations. The biggest downside when using absolute positioning is the inability to have a footer clear the bottom of all columns.

For instance, at its most basic, two columns (content and sidebar) might be created with positioning by giving the content <div> a left or right margin—enough space to accommodate the sidebar. Using positioning, we could drop in the sidebar, giving it a width roughly equal to the content's margin, positioning it top and right (Figure 8.3).

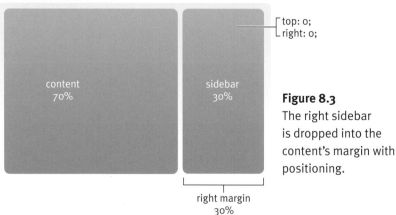

browser window

content 70%

sidebar 30%

top: 0;
right: 0;

right margin 30%

Figure 8.3
The right sidebar is dropped into the content's margin with positioning.

For example, we could write a few CSS rules to handle this:

```
#content {
  width: 70%;
  margin-right: 30%;
  }
```

```
#sidebar {
  position: absolute;
  top: 0;
  right: 0;
  width: 30%;
  }
```

This code creates a margin that equals the width for the sidebar and places that element using `position: absolute;`. This approach makes sense and is easy to grasp—especially for those just beginning with CSS-based layouts. But there is an important flaw when using this method: being unable to *clear* positioned elements.

In other words, if the sidebar happens to be longer than the content column, then it would overlap any subsequent elements on the page (e.g., the footer in our markup example) (Figure 8.4).

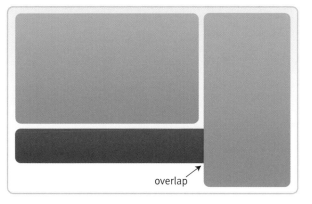

Figure 8.4
If the absolutely positioned column is longer than its neighbor, over-lapping can occur.

This happens because when `position: absolute;` is used on an element, it's taken out of the *normal flow of the document*. Other elements around it can't and won't be affected by its size or location on the page. For properly clearing footers that sit below multiple columns, this is a bummer.

This lack of flexibility often steers CSS-savvy designers toward using the `float` property when building multicolumn layouts. Because floated elements can be *cleared* (as we explored in Chapter 4, "Creative Floating"), they are the best tool we have for taking control of columnar layouts.

APPLYING STYLE

With floats chosen as the method for creating the columns, we want to divide up the two areas: content and sidebar using *percentages*. For this example, let's go with a 70/30 split (70% content and 30% sidebar).

Our first step is to add a few background colors to the header, sidebar, and footer. This makes it a bit easier to distinguish the components as we go along.

```
#header {
   background: #369;
   }
#sidebar {
   background: #9c3;
   }
#footer {
   background: #cc9;
   }
```

Figure 8.5 shows the results, with the header, sidebar, and footer containers defined by their background colors.

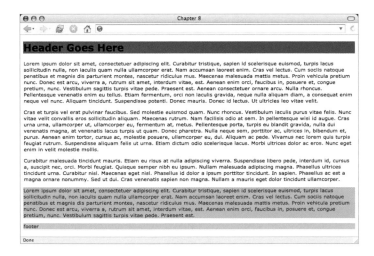

Figure 8.5 The layout looks like this before we float each column.

Next, let's do two things. First, we assign a width of 70% for the content column and 30% for the sidebar. We then float the content left while floating the sidebar right. This positions the two columns opposite each other.

```
#header {
  background: #369;
  }
#content {
  float: left;
  width: 70%;
  }
#sidebar {
  float: right;
  width: 30%;
  background: #9c3;
  }
#footer {
  background: #cc9;
  }
```

Figure 8.6 shows what happens here, with the content and sidebar columns successfully forming—but notice the footer getting all caught up in the floats the precede it. Because the footer follows the sidebar in the markup, it's placed there. Additionally, the footer doesn't have a width specified; therefore, its background attempts to take over the entire width of the container.

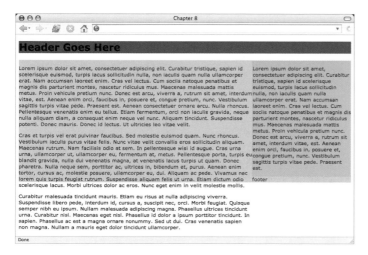

Figure 8.6 The footer gets tangled up in the floats that precede it.

To fix this, we want to clear the footer from the floats that precede it in both directions. This ensures that the footer will always sit below the two columns—regardless of the length of either column. This is bulletproofing.

```
#header {
  background: #369;
  }
#content {
  float: left;
  width: 70%;
  }
#sidebar {
  float: right;
  width: 30%;
  background: #9c3;
  }
#footer {
  clear: both;
  background: #cc9;
  }
```

And you can see in Figure 8.7, with the clear rule added, things are starting to look as they should.

Figure 8.7 Because it clears both directions, the footer will always sit below the two columns.

Already we have a flexible CSS-based layout. It may not look spectacular, but the foundation is there. If we expand or contract the window, the column widths will resize, always keeping the 70/30 proportion intact (Figure 8.8).

Figure 8.8 The floated layout, shown here at three different window widths, always keeps the 70/30 proportion intact.

Both columns will grow or shrink, depending on the browser's window size. This is what a flexible CSS-based layout is all about: fluidity, giving the reader the power to control the layout's dimensions.

Now that we have a solid base, let's move on to talk about the trickier aspects of fluid layouts.

GUTTERS

The term *gutter* has been around for ages, and refers to the spacing between columns of text (Figure 8.9). Gutters become significantly more difficult when dealing with fluid column widths. In a *fixed-width* design, we're dealing with predictable widths in pixels, which makes it easier to calculate gutter widths along with columns.

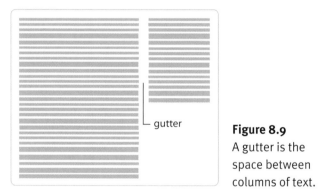

Figure 8.9
A gutter is the space between columns of text.

But with fluid columns, we have two options: use a *percentage* value for the gutter width as well as the column width, or add extra <div> elements to apply margins and padding *separate* from the column widths. The latter approach is certainly less optimal from a markup standpoint, yet it does provide an additional level of control that may be necessary for complex designs. More on this in a bit.

An example of setting a percentage value gutter between our content and sidebar is to assign a right margin to the content, then subtract that value from the content's width. We always need the total percentage to equal 100% (Figure 8.10).

```
#header {
  background: #369;
  }
```

```
#content {
  float: left;
  width: 65%;
  margin-right: 5%;
  }
#sidebar {
  float: right;
  width: 30%;
  background: #9c3;
  }
#footer {
  clear: both;
  background: #cc9;
  }
```

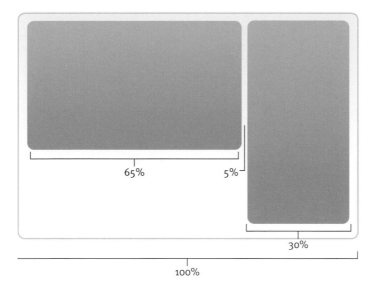
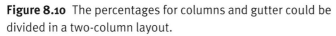

Figure 8.10 The percentages for columns and gutter could be divided in a two-column layout.

In the preceding rules, we've decreased the width of the content by 5%, and added that same amount as a right margin to set the gutter between columns. Figure 8.11 shows the results, with some additional white space between the content and sidebar.

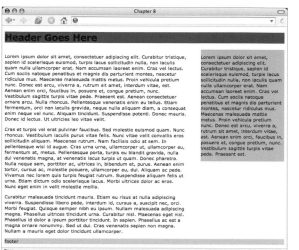

Figure 8.11 The space between columns will vary as the window width changes.

Keep in mind when using percentage value gutters that the space between columns will vary, depending on the window width. It will be smaller at narrow widths and larger at wider widths. This could be a problem, depending on the design requirements—for instance, if specific borders or background styles are attached to the columns that require a fixed space between them. For those instances, adding a second level of container <div>s might be the best option, which we explore a little further on in this chapter. But if simplicity is what you're after, using percentage margin values is the easiest option.

COLUMN PADDING

A similar issue arises when you're setting padding on columns that have been specified with percentage widths. Because of the way padding is calculated (added to the width declared on the element, or in the case of IE5/Win, *subtracted;* see www.tantek.com/CSS/Examples/boxmodelhack.html) if you use anything but a percentage value for padding on the columns, the total width has a good chance of being over or under what you intend. This can throw off float layouts rather easily.

For example, let's add 20 pixels of padding to the sidebar, to give it a chance to breathe a bit more:

```
#header {
  background: #369;
  }
```

```
#content {
  float: left;
  width: 65%;
  margin-right: 5%;
  }
#sidebar {
  float: right;
  width: 30%;
  padding: 20px;
  background: #9c3;
  }
#footer {
  clear: both;
  background: #cc9;
  }
```

In a fixed-width layout, we can easily subtract those 20 pixels of padding on both sides of the column from the declared width. But in fluid-width layouts, we're using a percentage, and there's no way to specify a width of 30% minus 40 pixels. The box becomes larger than 30%, too large to sit opposite the content <div>, thus forcing it to sit *below* the content (Figure 8.12). Not so good.

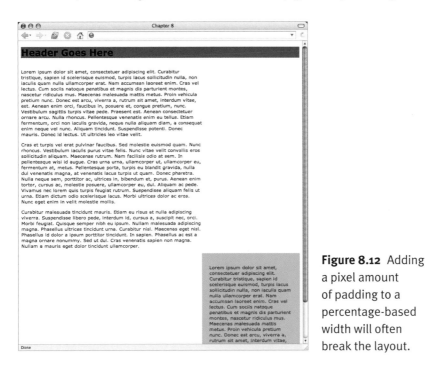

Figure 8.12 Adding a pixel amount of padding to a percentage-based width will often break the layout.

What are your options in a case like this?

- Use a percentage for padding as well, and subtract that value from the declared width of the column (like we did when creating the 5% gutter between columns earlier).

- Apply padding to elements *inside* the sidebar only.

- Add an additional <div> to separately assign padding using any value you wish.

Apply padding to inside elements

One option is to apply padding to common block-level elements that you anticipate will live in the sidebar. For example, if paragraphs and lists are known to exist there, assign left and right padding to those elements:

```
#sidebar p, #sidebar ul, #sidebar ol, #sidebar dl {
  padding-left: 20px;
  padding-right: 20px;
  }
```

This padding will not affect the width of the sidebar itself, but the caveat here is that unforeseen elements could be added to the sidebar at a later date, and you as the designer would need to make sure this "catchall" declaration included them to ensure proper padding.

This method can work for simple, predetermined content. But something a bit more bulletproof, with a tad more extra markup, would probably be a better choice.

The extra <div> method

For the "set it and forget it" mentality inside all of us, an extra <div> ensures that anything stuffed in the sidebar will have the proper padding without affecting the overall width of the column.

For example, if in the markup we add a second <div> that sits just inside the sidebar:

```
<div id="sidebar">
  <div>
    ... sidebar goes here ...
  </div>
</div>
```

we could then apply padding to that inner <div>, while keeping the width of 30% set on the outer one:

```
#header {
  background: #369;
  }
#content {
  float: left;
  width: 65%;
  margin-right: 5%;
  }
#sidebar {
  float: right;
  width: 30%;
  background: #9c3;
  }
#sidebar div {
  padding: 20px;
  }
#footer {
  clear: both;
  background: #cc9;
  }
```

Applying padding to the inner <div> won't affect the declared width of its parent wrapper. Now we can apply any value of padding we wish, and that padding will remain constant regardless of window width.

Similarly, if we wanted a fixed-width *gutter* in between columns, we could also add an inner <div> to the content and assign right padding of any pixel amount we wished:

```
<div id="content">
  <div>
    ... content goes here ...
  </div>
</div>
```

So with the extra <div> in place, let's add 40 pixels of padding on the right to create a fixed gutter:

```
#header {
  background: #369;
```

```
  }
#content {
  float: left;
  width: 70%;
  }
#content div {
  padding-right: 40px;
  }
#sidebar {
  float: right;
  width: 30%;
  background: #9c3;
  }
#sidebar div {
  padding: 20px;
  }
#footer {
  clear: both;
  background: #cc9;
  }
```

Figure 8.13 shows the results. At various window sizes, the padding on the sidebar as well as the 40-pixel gutter in between the columns remains intact as the column widths themselves expand and contract.

The downside to fixed-width gutters and padding is the additional, meaningless `<div>` in the markup. It's a trade-off to consider—do you need fixed padding or margins in your layout? Then it's probably worth the extra markup. If you're aiming for pure simplicity, then experiment with percentage values.

note

For the rest of this chapter, I'm going to stick with the extra `<div>` method in order to demonstrate some additional tricks when dealing with fluid layouts.

SETTING MIN AND MAX WIDTH

One of the hurdles that designers face when building fluid layouts is *line length*. Giving readers the ability to stretch the layout as wide as they'd like is beneficial, but there comes a point when the line length of any given column can be so long that the text becomes difficult to read or so narrow that it breaks other aspects of the page's design.

This is where the `max-width` and `min-width` CSS properties come into play. Setting a maximum or minimum width on a fluid layout will stop the columns from stretching or collapsing past a specified point. Unfortunately,

Figure 8.13 We've assigned padding separately from column width.

they are *unsupported* in Internet Explorer versions 5 and 6. Ouch. But these are enhancements that are quick and easy to add for browsers that *do* support them.

For example, in our test case, if we set a `max-width` on the `<div id="wrap">` that contains the entire layout, we can ensure that the columns won't get unbearably wide:

```
#wrap {
  max-width: 1200px;
  }
```

Figure 8.14 shows our example with the `max-width` rule added. The layout is flexible, yet will stop at 1200 pixels—even if the window is stretched beyond that point.

You could choose to apply the `max-width` property on individual columns as well. For instance, to stop the content column at 600 pixels but allow the layout as a whole to expand further (Figure 8.15), use this:

```
#content {
  max-width: 600px;
  }
```

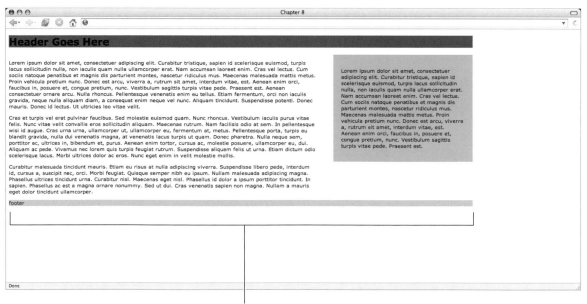

1200px

Figure 8.14 If the window width is increased past 1200 pixels, the layout will stop expanding.

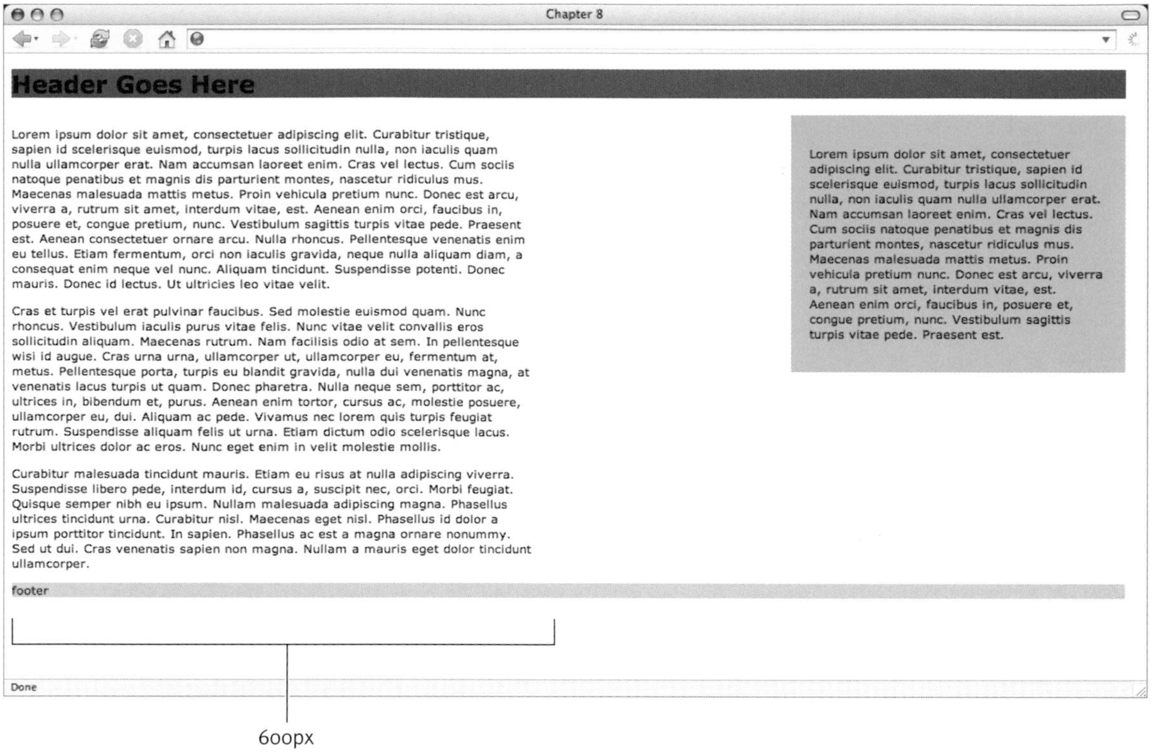

Figure 8.15 If the content column is stretched beyond 600 pixels, the content will stop.

Conversely, we could also set a min-width on the entire layout (or individual columns) to prevent the design from compressing to an unreadable width:

```
#wrap {
  max-width: 1200px;
  min-width: 600px;
}
```

Figure 8.16 shows the layout with the min-width rule added, *locking* the layout at 600 pixels when the window is sized below that value. Horizontal scroll bars will appear when the browser window is decreased below this amount.

Figure 8.16 If the layout is decreased below 600 pixels, horizontal scroll bars will appear.

This behavior can be handy when a fixed-width object is contained within the column (such as an image) that would otherwise "poke out" when its column shrinks narrower than the object's width.

For example, if we drop a 500-pixel-wide image into the content column but resize the window so that the content column is *less* than 500 pixels wide, we get some overlap with the sidebar (Figure 8.17)—or worse, in some browsers this may break the layout entirely.

tip

It's possible to use CSS to cleverly resize or crop images that live inside fluid layouts. See Richard Rutter's "Experiments with wide images" (www.clagnut.com/ sandbox/imagetest/) for some interesting examples.

500px

Figure 8.17 Overlapping occurs when we drop in an image that is 500 pixels wide but resize the window so that the content column is less than 500 pixels wide.

By experimenting with min-width on the containing <div> (just as we had with max-width), you'll prevent any overlap or layout damage. Um... at least in most browsers *other* than IE/Win. Again, these are simple additions that won't *harm* IE/Win, but will be highly beneficial for other browsers—and crucial for managing fluid layouts.

```
#wrap {
  max-width: 1200px;
  min-width: 750px;
}
```

SLIDING FAUX COLUMNS

If we look again at the example two-column layout we've been working with thus far throughout the chapter, you'll notice that while we've set a green background color on the sidebar, that background only extends as far as it has to. So, depending on the amount of content contained within that column, the column will appear to be a different length than the content column.

Often, the appearance of equal-height columns is desired, with solid backgrounds and/or borders that define them. When using fluid layouts, there is no way to *force* a column height to match another.

I wrote about one solution to this problem at *A List Apart*, in an article titled "Faux Columns" (www.alistapart.com/articles/fauxcolumns/, Figure 8.18). In the article, I describe a technique for faking equal-height columns for CSS-based layouts, using a tiled background image.

With this technique, the tiled image sits behind the columns and creates the illusion that the columns are the same height. This allows background colors, patterns, and borders to sit behind the layout and always reach the bottom of the page at the same place. However, this technique only works in fixed-width layouts—where column widths are predetermined and built into the tiled image.

Douglas Bowman (www.stopdesign.com/log/2004/09/03/liquid -bleach.html) and Eric Meyer (www.meyerweb.com/eric/thoughts/ 2004/09/03/sliding-faux-columns/) took this idea a step further, developing the "Sliding Faux Columns" approach, where the tiled image can *slide* around behind fluid-width columns, thus creating the equal-height effect while remaining flexible. Let's see how it works.

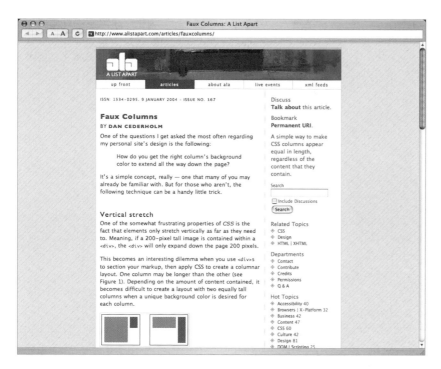

Figure 8.18 The "Faux Columns" article, as seen at *A List Apart*, describes a technique for faking equal-height columns for CSS-based layouts, using a tiled background image.

Creating the background image

When creating the background image that will tile vertically, we want to make it wide enough to accommodate large screens (for those viewers who will expand the layout on their 200-foot-wide displays). Using a nice round number like 2000 pixels will work, and will make the math required to position the image easier.

What we're looking to accomplish is a green background and border that will tile behind the sidebar all to the way down to the footer. We know that the sidebar's width is 30%, so if we take 30% of 2000 pixels, we get 600 pixels.

Next, let's add a 600-pixel-wide green area to a white canvas of 2000 pixels wide by 100 pixels tall (Figure 8.19). The height here is irrelevant, since we'll tile this image vertically.

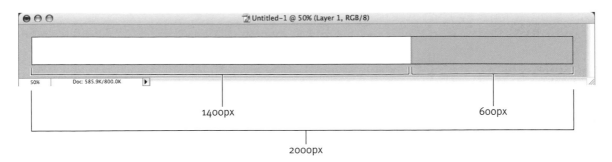

Figure 8.19 This GIF image will be used to create the "faux columns."

To this green area, we add a darker single-pixel border and a slight shadow on the left side (Figure 8.20).

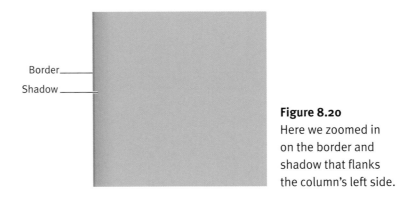

Figure 8.20
Here we zoomed in on the border and shadow that flanks the column's left side.

Positioning the image

Now, the magic happens when we position this background image on the `<div id="wrap">` that contains the entire layout. By setting it to tile vertically, 70% from the left, we ensure that the green background will always stay aligned behind the sidebar. More or less of this image will be shown depending on the window width.

```
#wrap {
   max-width: 1200px;
   background: url(img/twocol-bg.gif) repeat-y 70% 0;
   }
```

Figure 8.21 shows the results, with the green sidebar extending to the footer, as well as expanding and contracting along with the varying window width.

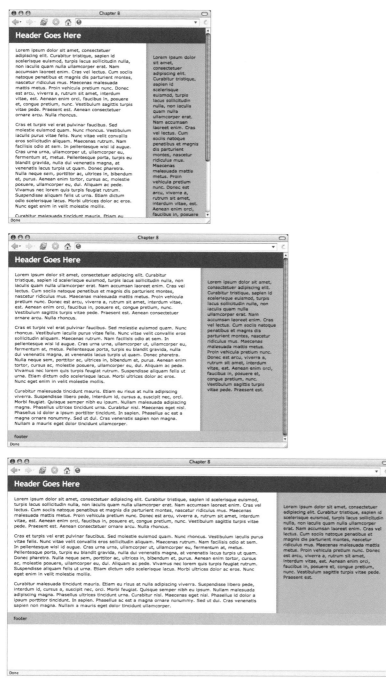

Figure 8.21 Sliding Faux Columns in action.

To better illustrate why this works, Figure 8.22 shows the window's "viewport" (the viewable area), with the invisible, unused portions of the 2000-pixel-wide background image sticking out each side. More or less of this image will be revealed as the window expands and contracts. Giving the image a "catchall" width of 2000 pixels is important here, because it ensures that even gigantic monitors will still be able to view the design as you intended.

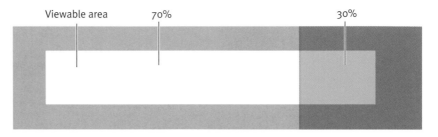
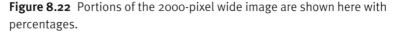

Figure 8.22 Portions of the 2000-pixel wide image are shown here with percentages.

THREE-COLUMN LAYOUTS

So far, we've focused on two-column layouts. They're a bit easier to start with in order to grasp the important concepts. But let's move on now to discuss three-column layouts. Many of the same principles apply, with just a slightly more complex way of initially setting up the columns. Let's start with the slightly altered markup structure.

The markup structure

When creating three-columns layouts, we still want to take advantage of source ordering—that is, putting the main content *first* in the markup for the benefit of those with text browsers or screen readers. To do that, and to also ensure we can have a footer that clears all three columns at the bottom of the page, we'll use the float method as we did for the two-column layout.

But in order to put the content first in the markup, we just need an extra containing <div> that wraps the content and left-hand sidebar only. The reasoning will become clear (ahem) in a minute.

```
<div id="wrap">
 <div id="header">
   <h1>Header Goes Here</h1>
 </div>

 <div id="main-body">
   <div id="content">
     ... content goes here ...
   </div>

   <div id="sidebar">
     ... left sidebar goes here ...
   </div>
 </div> <!-- end #main-body -->

 <div id="sidebar-2">
   ... right sidebar goes here ...
 </div>

 <div id="footer">
   ... footer goes here ...
 </div>
</div> <!-- end #wrap -->
```

In order to achieve three columns here, let's break this down into two stages. First, we create two columns by floating #main-body and #sidebar-2 against each other. This is exactly what we did earlier for the two-column layout using #content and #sidebar.

Next, we float #content to the right and #sidebar to the left. These two <div>s will make up the two columns that are both already floating to the left of #sidebar-2. Voilà! Now we have three columns, with the main content first in the markup.

Figure 8.23 shows how the `<div>`s are set up, with the arrow illustrating the direction of the float. Notice that `#main-body` is floating left, while `#content` and `#sidebar` are opposing floats *within* it.

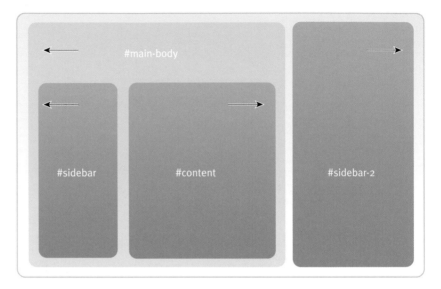

Figure 8.23 Each `<div>` is floated in order to preserve the optimal content ordering.

It's this structure and float order that allows us to optimally control the order of the markup, while still being able to clear the columns with a full-width footer.

Applying style

With the markup in place, it's now just a matter of setting the floats and percentage widths for the individual columns. First, we assign a 70% width to `#main-body` (the left sidebar and content combined) and float it left, and assign 30% to `#sidebar-2` and float it right. This will give us two columns to start with:

```
#header {
  background: #369;
  }
#main-body {
  float: left;
  width: 70%;
  }
```

```
#sidebar {
  background: #9c3;
  }
#sidebar-2 {
  float: right;
  width: 30%;
  background: #df9f20;
  }
#footer {
  clear: both;
  background: #cc9;
  }
```

I've also assigned some background colors so that we can see where the pieces are ending up. Figure 8.24 shows #sidebar-2 in orange, while #sidebar (in green) sits below the main content.

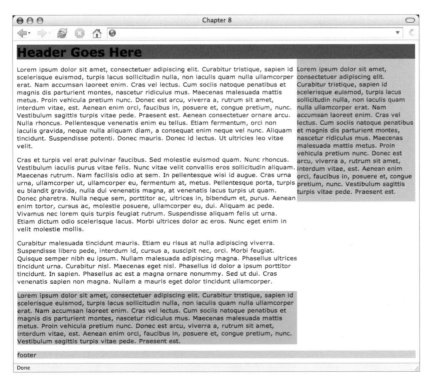

Figure 8.24 The right sidebar is floated against the content and left sidebar combined.

With two of the three columns in place, we can now float #content right and #sidebar left to finish the basic structure. We assign percentages to these columns as well, which are actually contained within 70% of the page's total width (in #main-body).

```css
#header {
    background: #369;
    }
#main-body {
    float: left;
    width: 70%;
    }
#content {
    float: right;
    width: 60%;
    }
#sidebar {
    float: left;
    width: 40%;
    background: #9c3;
    }
#sidebar-2 {
    float: right;
    width: 30%;
    background: #df9f20;
    }
#footer {
    clear: both;
    background: #cc9;
    }
```

Figure 8.25 shows the results, with the three columns now in place.

Gutters and padding

Now, you'll notice that we'll run into the same issues regarding gutters and padding that we talked about earlier. The tips that we discussed for two-column layouts apply to their three-column siblings as well. You can either divvy up the percentages between width and margins, or add extra wrapper <div>s to each column and specify padding separately from width. Use your best judgment here, taking into account the design requirements.

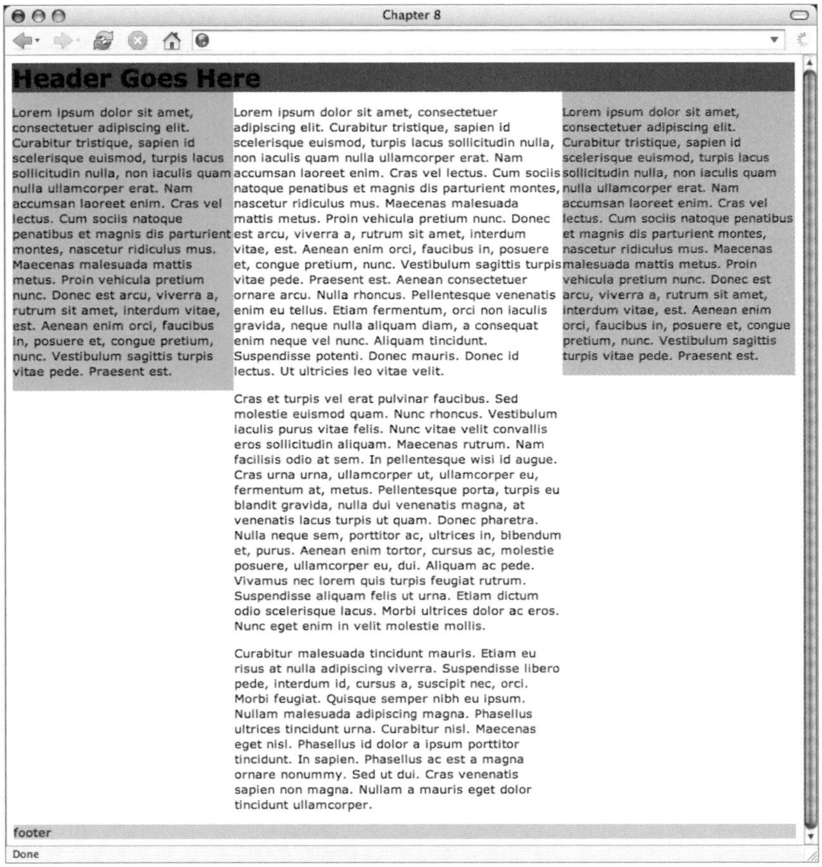

Figure 8.25 With floating complete, the three columns take their places.

Sliding Faux Columns for three

Faking equal-height columns (as we did using the Sliding Faux Columns technique earlier) becomes a little more complex when dealing with three flexible columns rather than two—it's not impossible, but it requires an extra wrapper <div> around the entire layout and *two* background images.

So, first we add that extra all-encompassing <div> just inside the already existing <div id="wrap"> around the layout—this will allow us to reference the two background images needed to backdrop the two outer, flexible columns:

```
<div id="wrap">
 <div id="wrap-inner">
```

```
… rest of layout goes here …
</div> <!-- end #wrap-inner -->
</div> <!-- end #wrap -->
```

Next, we create two background images, based on the same principles that the two-column version used. Each image will be 2000 pixels wide to accommodate large screens. Since the right column is 30% wide, we know we'll need to make the background area for that column 600 pixels wide (30% of 2000). We call this image `threecol-r.gif` (Figure 8.26).

Figure 8.26 This GIF image is used to sit behind the right sidebar.

For the left column, its width is actually 40% of the 70% that the sidebar and content take up, combined. A little math tells us that 40% of 70% equals 28% of the total width. So for the left sidebar's background area, we'll use 28% of 2000, which equals 560 pixels. We'll also make the rest of this image transparent, so that when we stack this background image on top of the other, it won't obscure the right sidebar's background underneath it (Figure 8.27).

With the images completed, we're now ready to position them behind the two wrapper <div>s we have in the markup:

```
#wrap {
    max-width: 1200px;
    background: url(img/threecol-r.gif) repeat-y 70% 0;
    }
#wrap-inner {
    background: url(img/threecol-l.gif) repeat-y 28% 0;
    }
```

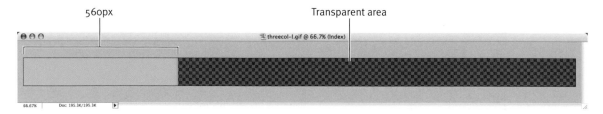

Figure 8.27 When we stack our background image on top of the other, it won't obscure the right sidebar's background underneath it.

You'll notice that we've placed the orange background image 70% from the left (just as we'd done with the two-column version earlier in the chapter) on the main #wrap, then placed the partially transparent image over that on the #wrap-inner at 28% from left (equaling the width of that left column).

With the images in place, we now have a flexible, three-column layout, with "faked" equal-height, colored sidebars. Each column expands and contracts along with whatever size the browser window happens to be (Figure 8.28).

note

In Figure 8.28, I've also used the extra <div> method for creating padding on all three columns.

Figure 8.28
Sliding Faux Columns in action on a three-column layout.

Why It's Bulletproof

For the very same reasons that table-based layouts *aren't* bulletproof, let's remind ourselves why flexible CSS-based layouts *are*.

The first reason: *less code*. Instead of tying borders, background, and spacing to the markup using nested tables, you can easily structure them in a multicolumn layout using just a few simple <div>s rather than using CSS for the position and style of each column. Even with the extra (but necessary) <div>s added for static-width gutters and/or Sliding Faux Columns (in three-column layouts), there is still far less markup than the nested table approach.

Second, you have a more easily maintainable codebase. Because the design details are held in the style sheet, the markup becomes easier to read, and making changes to the appearance of the layout is as easy as updating a few style rules.

Using the float property in CSS, you're also able to stack the content in a more optimal order when dealing with multicolumn layouts and put the important content first in the markup. This is benefit for those browsing with screen readers, text browsers, and other devices that do not support CSS.

And finally, you're giving the user an additional facet of control when you deliver a flexible, fluid layout. Readers will be able to widen the layout if they wish, or shrink the width of the window if they're viewing on a small screen. This extra level of control is yet another way to bulletproof your design and make it adaptable to as many environments as possible.

Em-Based Layouts

Em-based layouts offer a different flavor of flexibility. Dubbed *elastic layouts* by Patrick Griffiths in an article for *A List Apart* (http://www.alistapart.com/articles/elastic), em-based layouts describe column widths using em units (rather than pixels or percentages). The width of the layout and its columns is determined by the current base font size, and so adjusting the text also grows or shrinks the entire design along with it.

Although elastic layouts are a fixed width to begin with, they require a flexible mind-set when designing—that the layout itself could be a variety of widths depending on the size of text on the page.

Previously in this book, we've taken a few examples and applied em units to see how the entire component scales with text size. Let's now apply that concept to a two-column structure to see what happens.

AN ELASTIC EXAMPLE

Take, for instance, the experimental social network for wig-wearers, ToupeePal (`http://toupeepal.com`). The site utilizes a two-column structure using ems. As the text size increases, so too does the layout, enabling the entire design to scale in proportion (Figure 8.29).

tip

See the "Elastic Lawn" entry at the CSS Zen Garden (`http://www.csszengarden. com/?cssfile=/063/063. css`) for another great example of an em-based layout that scales flawlessly with text size.

Figure 8.29
ToupeePal is constructed with an em-based layout and will scale along with the text size if adjusted.

This scaling of the design requires a shift in thinking about what happens not only to the layout but to its contents as well. However, applying the bulletproof concepts we've been exploring throughout this book will assist in creating successful, em-based designs. At the core, it's about planning for expansion and contraction throughout the *entire* page—and truly letting go of pixel precision.

Let's tackle the assembly of a simple, two-column layout using ems (Figure 8.30).

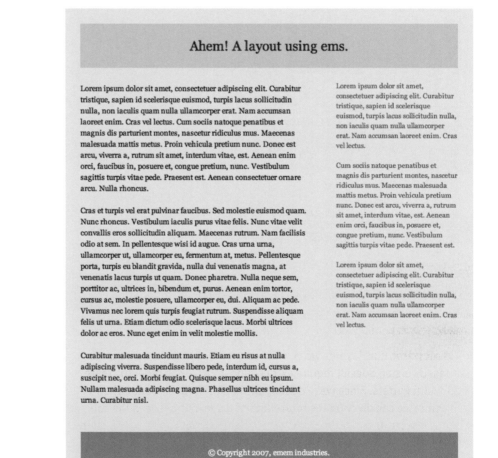

Figure 8.30 A simple, two-column layout example that we'll build using ems.

THE MARKUP

Like any CSS-based layout (including the fluid versions covered earlier in this chapter), an em-based layout's XHTML structure will look familiar. We'll continue to use floats to position content and sidebar `<div>`s, keeping the markup order optimal, flanked by a header and footer.

```
<div id="wrap">

<div id="header">
  <h1>Ahem!  A layout using ems.</h1>
</div>

<div id="content">
  <p>Lorem ipsum dolor ... </p>
</div>

<div id="sidebar">
  <p>Lorem ipsum dolor ... </p>
</div>

<div id="footer">
  <p>&copy; Copyright 2007, emem industries.</p>
</div>

</div> <!-- end #wrap -->
```

A main #wrap `<div>` contains everything inside and sets the width of the entire layout, with a single `<div>` for each component of the page: header, content, sidebar, and footer. Very straightforward.

Now, unlike the fluid layouts we've created previously in this chapter, this em-based version doesn't require extra wrapper `<div>`s in order to create fixed-width gutters. Since we're dealing with finite width amounts when using ems, we can divvy up the total width of the layout between the columns and margins or padding in between them to create gutters. The math becomes simpler!

For example, if you look at Figure 8.31, you can see that after setting an overall width of 50em on the main containing `<div>`, we can set specific widths that add up to that total on the two columns and a gutter in between (30em + 2em + 18em = 50em).

So, building a multicolumn layout using ems is similar to setting widths in pixels—we're just using a different unit, and one that will vary depending on the current font size. For instance, 50em might equal 700px at a medium base text size, but it might also equal *900px* when text is bumped up a size. Similarly, the slight variation in how a particular browser displays font sizes will also correlate to slight variations in widths specified with ems. This is OK! It requires an understanding that things won't match to exact pixels, but that understanding is healthy and very much a positive characteristic of the creating for the *Web*.

Figure 8.31 A 50em-wide layout broken down into two columns with a gutter.

THE CSS

Let's apply the basic styles to our markup structure that create the two-column, elastic layout. The important parts are as follows:

```
#header {
  margin: 0;
  padding: 2em;
  text-align: center;
  background: #baccd8;
  }
```

```css
#header h1 {
  margin: 0;
  padding: 0;
  font-size: 180%;
  line-height: 1em;
  font-weight: normal;
  color: #333;
  }
#wrap {
  width: 50em;
  margin: 0 auto;
  padding: 2em;
  background: #dae3e9;
  }
#content {
  float: left;
  width: 30em;
  padding: 2em 0;
  }
#sidebar {
  float: right;
  width: 18em;
  padding: 2em 0;
  }
#footer {
  clear: both;
  padding: 1em 2em;
  text-align: center;
  color: #fff;
  background: #8194a1;
  }
```

We've assigned an overall width of 50em to the #wrap container. Then, inside that, we've styled the #header as well as the <h1> within it. Also, we've given the #content <div> a width of 30em and floated it left, while floating the #sidebar right with a width of 18em (leaving an extra 2em as the gutter in between the two columns). The footer clears the two floats that precede it, just as we did in the previous fluid examples.

You could carve out columns and overall layout widths however you'd like. Add margins or padding directly to column elements to create specific gutter widths in between them—with ems, the math is simple and there's no need to add extra markup as we had to when combining percentage-based columns with fixed-width gutters.

So there we have a simple, two-column layout using ems. The entire layout will scale along with whatever the current font size is (Figure 8.32).

Figure 8.32
Boosting the browser's default text size will scale the entire em-based layout proportionately.

CONSISTENCY IS IDEAL

With the main layout set in ems, ideally you'd use em units on the *internal* portions of the design as well (spacing between elements, line height, etc.). That way, not only does the layout itself scale proportionately but the components within it do as well. This isn't always easy—especially when you're dealing with fixed, pixel-width elements such as advertisements or images. But if you strive toward making your work as bulletproof as possible, as we've done throughout the examples in this book, then switching from fixed-width, fluid-width, or elastic layout could be an easy decision that won't require too much heavy lifting.

BEWARE OF SCROLLBARS

One important point to mention when talking about elastic layouts is that, because the entire layout will expand along with text size, an unfortunate drawback is the appearance of a horizontal scrollbar when the layout's width exceeds the browser's viewport (Figure 8.33). For layouts that are extra-wide to begin with, this could be a factor to be aware of. For narrower designs, the issue isn't usually a concern.

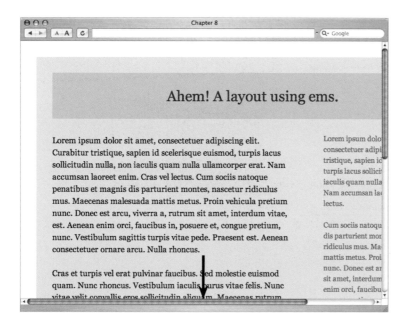

Figure 8.33 Our em-based layout, with text sized boosted to the point where a horizontal scrollbar is necessary to view the entire page.

Summary

Fixed-width? Fluid-width? Elastic? Is one approach superior to the other? The important thing to remember when deciding what type of layout to use is that *each* has its appropriate place. It helps to experiment with each to get a handle on how they operate, and to learn the pros and cons of each solution.

I'm going to stress again that I chose to cover fluid and elastic layouts in this chapter not because I think they are *always* superior to fixed-width versions. Rather, each has its appropriate place, and depending on the design requirements, it's not always a decision that Web designers should make solely by themselves.

That said, if fluidity or elasticity is a characteristic you *can* add to your designs, then enjoy the benefits that your readers will gain from it.

Here are some things to keep in mind when building flexible layouts:

- Use the `float` property in order to build multicolumn layouts that can be cleared with a full-width footer.

- Subtract a percentage from column widths for gutters, or add an extra wrapper `<div>` to set padding separate from column width when building fluid layouts.

- Set `min-width` and `max-width` on fluid layouts to prevent extreme dimensions in both directions. Try to ignore the fact that this is unsupported in IE/Win versions 5 and 6.

- Experiment with the Sliding Faux Columns approach to create the appearance of equal-height (but flexible) columns with borders and backgrounds that meet the footer.

- Em-based layouts can offer a different type of flexibility; just keep in mind that adjusting text up a few notches can put portions of the design out of the viewport and require horizontal scrolling.

Now that we've covered the basics of building a flexible, fluid, CSS-based layout, let's pull together all the pieces that have been covered in the book thus far to create a complete, one-page *bulletproofed* design. The final chapter awaits.

9

Putting It All Together

Apply bulletproof concepts to an entire page design.

To close out the book, I'd like to pull together many of the guidelines and techniques for being bulletproof into a single full-page design. By walking through an entire example, we'll be able to see how these flexible strategies work simultaneously within a *complete* page.

I've created the fictitious "Bulletproof Pretzel Company" for us to use as an example. The content is irrelevant (although I've long thought that if this Web thing didn't work out, perhaps I could make pretzels); what's important is how the various concepts woven throughout this book can work *together* to create a flexible design. This example is not intended to be the best design ever created in the history of the Web, or the most perfectly bulletproof page. Rather, it's a chance to refresh your memory about what you can do to apply bulletproof concepts and guidelines to real pages that contain a variety of components.

We'll start by looking at our goal—the finished product—and then tackle the markup needed to create a fluid, two-column layout. Then we'll go step by step through the various components of the page, reminding ourselves along the way of the bulletproof techniques featured in previous chapters.

The Goal

Figure 9.1 shows the goal we'll be striving toward throughout the chapter. The Bulletproof Pretzel Company Web site is designed to be a simple, informative vehicle for the company, but most important it is constructed to utilize several of the concepts described previously in this book.

Figure 9.1 Over the course of this chapter, we'll piece together this design.

The two-column layout used in this design should look familiar to you, as it's commonly found throughout the Web. It features a header that includes the company name (in text) followed by a "promotional row" below it—a space for calling out the message of the day. In the content column, we have a page title and text, with an image/title/description combination dropped in midpage. Over in the sidebar at the right are a series of boxes that separate various small bits of content, each with two rounded corners at both the top left and bottom right. The footer stretches across both columns at the bottom of the page, with a slight "sheen" added to the background color that sits behind it.

Why It's Bulletproof

So, all in all, we have an attractive (and yes, I suppose I'm speaking for myself here) one-page design that, when deconstructed, will reveal its *bulletproof-ness*. We'll be going step by step through the evolution of this design, but first let's talk about why it *is* bulletproof.

FLUID LAYOUT

Using the CSS techniques explained in Chapter 8, "Fluid and Elastic Layouts," this two-column design achieves a fluid, flexible layout. Expanding or contracting the browser window will, in turn, modify the layout to fit whatever screen width the user desires (Figure 9.2).

Figure 9.2 With a fluid layout, the columns and everything within them can expand and contract as necessary.

As you know, choosing between a fixed-width, fluid-width, or elastic layout can be difficult. Although each style has its pros and cons, a fluid layout is a great way to give your reader that extra bit of control—not to mention, it prepares your layout design for a multitude of screen resolutions. To reiterate, each layout type can be appropriate depending on a number of variables, including design requirements, audience, site statistics, and so forth. While we've chosen to use fluid for this final example, a fixed-width or elastic layout could also be applied to this particular design.

You'll notice in Figure 9.2 that design elements remain intact on the page even when the user expands or contracts the browser window. For example, the box design in the sidebar stretches and/or contracts as necessary, all the while maintaining the original design details. I'll explain in depth how this is done a bit further along in the chapter.

FLEXIBLE TEXT

This design also applies what you learned in Chapter 1, "Flexible Text"; as you can see in Figure 9.3, increasing the text size (which is set using the `font-size: small;` keyword as a base) a few notches does nothing to hinder the design. The page components expand with ease, while the design details throughout remain intact. For instance, the header and promotional message rows *expand*, allowing larger text or additional content to live within those rows. Also, the half-rounded boxes in the sidebar retain their shape.

Figure 9.3
Increased text size does nothing to hinder the design of each component within the design.

Most important, though, is that the page *allows* readers to adjust the size of text on the page as they see fit. Those with low vision are able to bump up the font size to increase its readability, regardless of the browser or device they are using.

NO IMAGES? NO CSS? NO PROBLEM

Making sure the design of the page holds up in as many scenarios as possible, we can also test for the absence of images and CSS, as discussed in Chapter 6 (which shares this section's title). Figure 9.4 shows the page with images turned *off*. Readers who visit the page over slow connections can still view the content immediately while images load. Should the reader disable images purposefully to save bandwidth and speed up downloading, the page still operates perfectly and remains readable thanks to the background color equivalents specified behind any background images.

Figure 9.4 With images turned off, the entire page is still readable due to the background color equivalents we specified.

Similarly, if we *disable* CSS, we can get a quick glance at the underlying structure of the page with the "10-second usability test," also described in Chapter 6. Text browsers, assistive software (like a screen reader), or any device that doesn't support CSS will interpret the page this way. As Figure 9.5 shows, even without styles applied the page remains very readable and logically structured.

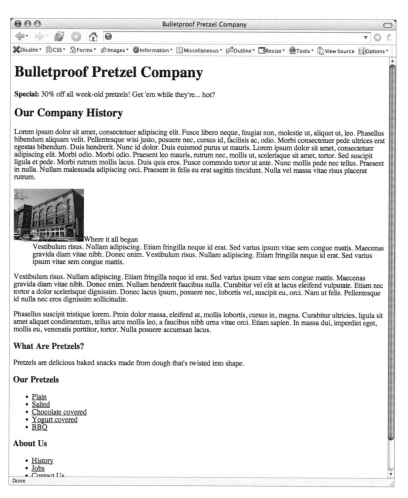

Figure 9.5 The "10-second usability test" reveals a well-structured page, suitable for a wide range of devices.

Take away CSS and/or images, and our Bulletproof Pretzel Company is ready for it—all the while remaining readable, functional, unflappable, and arguably delicious.

INTERNATIONALIZATION

Another important and positive by-product of a bulletproof design is how well it helps in terms of internationalization issues. For instance, Figure 9.6 shows a translated version of the Bulletproof Pretzel Company in German (of course), where the English text is easily replaced by its German equivalents.

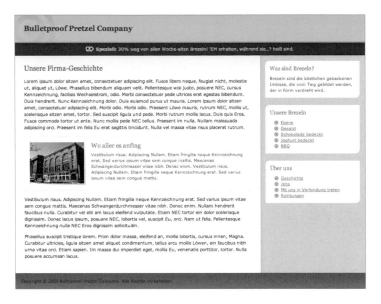

Figure 9.6 The Bulletproof Pretzel Company design, translated into German using Google's Translate tool: `http://translate.google.com`.

By designing with flexibility in mind, you ensure that an internationalized version of your page stands a better chance of gracefully handling words and content that varies in length. Short words or phrases in English may become long, unbroken strings in another language (or vice versa). Content may be shuffled around to make more sense in another part of the world. Bulletproofing your design can certainly assist here, and it's yet another example of planning for the unknown.

The Construction

Now that we've outlined the ways in which this one-page design is bullet-proof, let's walk through the construction of the design. I'll note the necessary steps it took to ensure flexibility without compromising attractive visuals.

We'll begin where we left off in Chapter 8, "Fluid and Elastic Layouts," by first applying a flexible, two-column layout to a lean markup structure. Then we'll go through each component of the page piece by piece, refreshing our memory from previous chapters on how best to bulletproof these areas.

THE MARKUP STRUCTURE

Let's start by thinking about the very basic structure that we'll need in terms of markup to create the fluid, two-column layout. We'll employ the "Sliding Faux Columns" technique here that we described in Chapter 8 and use a tiled background image to create the illusion of a full-length sidebar.

Our markup structure for the header, promotional row, two columns, and footer looks like this:

```
<div id="wrap">

<div id="header">
  <h1>Bulletproof Pretzel Company</h1>
</div>

<p id="message">
  <strong>Special:</strong> 30% off all week-old pretzels!
Get 'em while they're... hot?
</p>

<div id="content">
  ... content goes here ...
</div>

<div id="sidebar">
  ... sidebar goes here ...
</div>

<div id="footer">
  <p>Copyright &copy; 2005 Bulletproof Pretzel Company.  All
rights reserved.</p>
</div>

</div> <!-- end #wrap -->
```

The markup choices I've made here—using an <h1> for the site title and a simple paragraph for the message row—are (I think) the most appropriate elements for the task at hand. Below that are <div>s separating what will be two columns, followed by the footer at the bottom of the page.

Right off the bat, I know that I want that extra level of control on the content and sidebar's gutters—applying a fixed amount in each column. Because of that, I'm going to add that extra <div> wrapper inside both columns for future use:

```
<div id="wrap">

<div id="header">
  <h1>Bulletproof Pretzel Company</h1>
</div>

<p id="message">
  <strong>Special:</strong> 30% off all week-old pretzels!
Get 'em while they're... hot?.
</p>

<div id="content">
  <div class="gutter">
    ... content goes here ...
  </div>
</div>

<div id="sidebar">
  <div class="gutter">
    ... sidebar goes here ...
  </div>
</div>

<div id="footer">
  <p>Copyright &copy; 2005 Bulletproof Pretzel Company.  All
rights reserved.</p>
</div>

</div> <!-- end #wrap -->
```

You'll notice that I've added a class="gutter" to these two extra <div>s so that later on, I can style these consistently as a pair, in a single declaration if I so choose. We'll talk more about that in just a bit.

BASIC STYLES

With the core markup structure in place, let's next add some basic styles to get the CSS off and running. We'll start by adding a declaration for the main <body> element, zeroing margins and padding for the entire page, and adding base font information:

```
body {
  margin: 0;
  padding: 0;
  font-family: Verdana, sans-serif;
  font-size: small;
  background: #fff;
  }
```

By applying the technique described in Chapter 1, we're assigning a base font-size with a keyword of small. Later, we'll adjust sizes from that keyword by using percentages in either direction.

LAYOUT STRUCTURE

Next, let's add the necessary rules that set up the two-column layout by floating the content and sidebar against each other and clearing the footer below:

```
/* layout structure */

#content {
  float: left;
  width: 70%;
  }
#sidebar {
  float: right;
  width: 30%;
  }
#footer {
  clear: both;
  background: #828377;
  }
```

We're floating the content column left and giving it a width of 70%, while the sidebar is floated right with the remaining width of 30%. Below the columns sits the footer, which clears both columns and gets a background color (Figure 9.7).

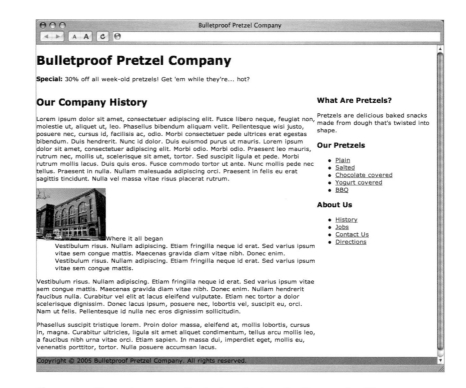

Figure 9.7 The columns are floated against each other, each with a percentage specified for width.

You'll notice that thus far, we haven't specified any spacing within or between the columns. We'll save that for the extra `<div class="gutter">` that we added inside each column. That will give us further precision in defining the gutters in between and allow us to use pixel values along with the percentages that we've just specified for the actual column widths.

SIDEBAR BACKGROUND

We'll use the same technique described in Chapter 8 to achieve the "Sliding Faux Columns"—specifically the khaki background that sits behind the sidebar.

Since we've specified the sidebar to be 30% in width, we'll create a 2000-pixel-wide image (wrap-bg.gif) that has a 600-pixel-wide area on the right with the sidebar's background color and shadowed edge (Figure 9.8). This will allow us to position this image 70% from the left, enabling it to slide behind the column to show only the amount of sidebar background necessary.

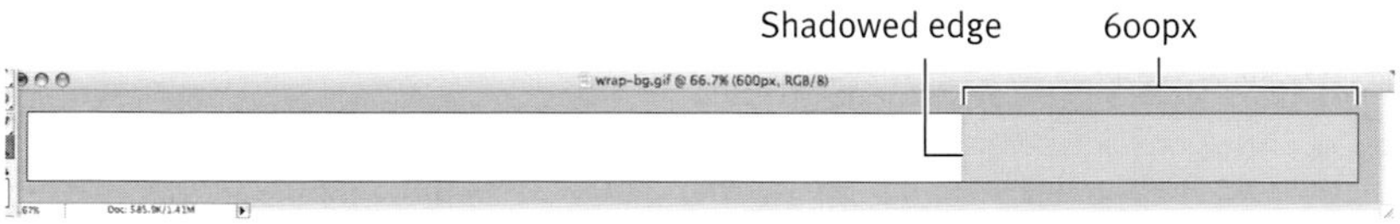

Figure 9.8 The image wrap-bg.gif is 2000 pixels wide and will be tiled vertically behind the columns.

Let's now add the styles necessary to position wrap-bg.gif as a background of the <div id="wrap"> that surrounds the entire layout of the page:

```
/* layout structure */

#wrap {
  min-width: 500px;
  max-width: 1400px;
  background: url(img/wrap-bg.gif) repeat-y 70% 0;
  }
#content {
  float: left;
  width: 70%;
  font-size: 95%;
  line-height: 1.5em;
  color: #333;
  }
#sidebar {
  float: right;
  width: 30%;
  }
#footer {
  clear: both;
  background: #828377;
  }
```

We've added a #wrap declaration that positions wrap-bg.gif 70% from the left, repeating it vertically from the top. You'll also notice that I've added min and max-width rules for the browsers that recognize those rules. Remember that these values give a fluid layout "extreme parameters" in which to expand and contract. Users of browsers *other* than Internet Explorer 5 and 6 will benefit from these.

Also included are some basic font styles for the content column; we're shaving off a little size from the base keyword previously specified on the <body> element and adding some increased space between lines as well as a dark gray color.

Figure 9.9 shows the results of adding those rules to our style sheet, with the tiled background image now properly tiled on the sidebar.

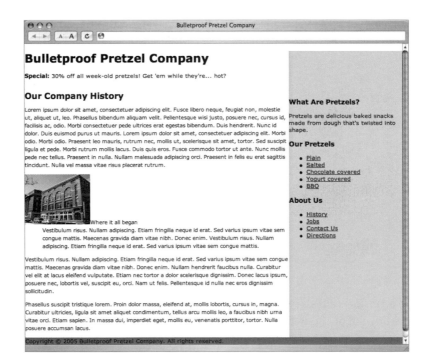

Figure 9.9 The correct amount of khaki is revealed when the tiled image is positioned 70% from the left.

THE HEADER

Starting from the top down, we'll apply styles to each component of the page, beginning with the header. We're going to keep "Bulletproof Pretzel Company" in text enabling the reader to adjust its size at will without breaking the design of this particular piece. It will also allow extra long titles to be placed in this row, with the design details always remaining intact.

We'll need two small images for this component: the bull's-eye that sits behind and to the left of the site title, as well as a tillable gradient fade that adds the "sheen" to the row.

Figure 9.10 shows header-bg.gif, the image that will tile horizontally across the header row, a gradient fade into a solid green. That solid green has been knocked out in favor of transparency (shown by the checkerboard pattern in Photoshop). This transparent area will be filled in by a background color in the CSS. Aligning this image at the top will allow the solid color to grow or shrink depending on the size of the text within the header.

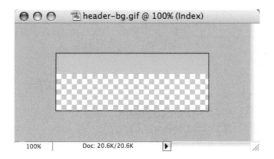

Figure 9.10 The image header-bg.gif contains a gradient fade into a solid green, where the green has been "knocked out" for transparency.

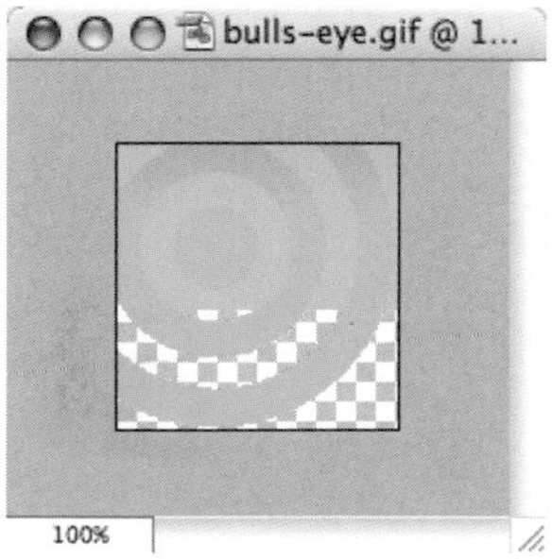

Figure 9.11 shows bulls-eye.gif, the image that will sit to the left and behind the site title but on top of the header's tiled image and background color. I've created this image to be larger than I think I need it to be, with more or less of the bull's-eye artistically cropped by varying text size.

You'll notice that part of the image is transparent as well. The upper portion duplicates the gradient fade found in header-bg.gif so that when the images are stacked on top of each other, they will blend properly.

With images created, let's now add the CSS necessary to make it all work together:

Figure 9.11 The image bulls-eye.gif includes the gradient in the upper portion, then fades into transparency, which will be filled in later by a background color.

```
/* header */

#header {
  border-bottom: 3px solid #87B825;
  background: #B4E637 url(img/header-bg.gif) repeat-x top
left;
  }
#header h1 {
  margin: 0;
  padding: 25px;
  font-family: Georgia, serif;
  font-size: 150%;
  color: #374C0E;
  background: url(img/bulls-eye.gif) no-repeat top left;
  }
```

We've added a three-pixel solid border to the bottom of the entire row, thus ensuring that the border will always sit at the very bottom regardless of the size or amount of text that's above it. Also, we've added the solid background color and the horizontally tiled image (header-bg.gif) that will add the gradient fade to the row.

As for the <h1> that sits inside <div id="header">, we've adjusted its margins and padding, changed its typeface to the serif Georgia, and increased its size from the base by a percentage. We've also positioned the bull's-eye background behind it. Giving that padding of 25 pixels all the way around the heading will ensure that enough of the bull's-eye image is revealed on the left (Figure 9.12).

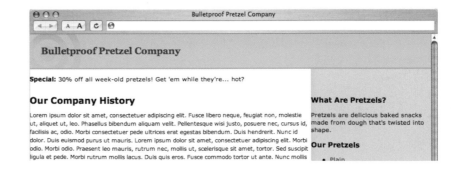

Figure 9.12 In the finished header, the bull's-eye is layered on top of the header's gradient and green background color.

As a quick test, let's bump up the text size a few notches. As you can see in Figure 9.13, more of the bull's-eye is revealed and the overall background of the header row remains perfect.

Figure 9.13 Increasing the text size pushes the three-pixel border down and reveals more of the bull's-eye image that was previously cropped higher.

THE MESSAGE ROW

Moving on down the page, let's next tackle the message row that sits just below the header that we just finished. The message row is simply a paragraph element that we've uniquely identified:

```
<p id="message">
  <strong>Special:</strong> 30% off all week-old pretzels!
Get 'em while they're... hot?.
</p>
```

We'll need just one small image that will tile across the top of the row, which blends into the background color that we'll also specify behind it in the CSS (Figure 9.14). This image consists of one-pixel vertical lines that fade into the dark-green background.

Figure 9.14 We've zoomed in to show the detail of the "comb" pattern that spans across the message row.

Figure 9.15 shows a zoomed-in message-bg.gif. The image tiles horizontally, and a solid color fills in its transparent areas.

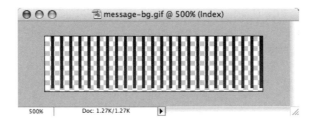

Figure 9.15 The message-bg.gif image will tile horizontally, and the transparent areas will be filled in by a background color in the CSS.

Let's next add the CSS necessary to style the row: assigning padding around the text, changing its color and size, as well as tiling the background image on top of the dark-green background color.

```
/* message row */

#message {
  margin: 0;
  padding: 10px;
  font-size: 90%;
  color: #cc9;
  text-align: center;
  background: #404530 url(img/message-bg.gif) repeat-x top
left;
  }
```

We also want to attach the small pretzel icon to the left of the text. We can take advantage of the <strong> element that wraps around the first word "Special" and add the pretzel as a background image by adding left padding to the text.

```
#message strong {
  padding: 0 0 0 28px;
  background: url(img/pretzel.gif) no-repeat 0 50%;
  }
```

So the <strong> element within the message row gets 28 pixels of padding on the left—just enough to accommodate the pretzel icon, which is centered vertically as a background image.

Figure 9.16 shows the results of styling the message row completely. The figure also demonstrates that when a larger-sized text (or a greater amount of text) is placed within the row, the row will expand without any problems. Because we chose a repeating pattern that sits flush to the top of the row and *blends* vertically into the background, we ensure that the design details will remain intact regardless of what's contained inside the row.

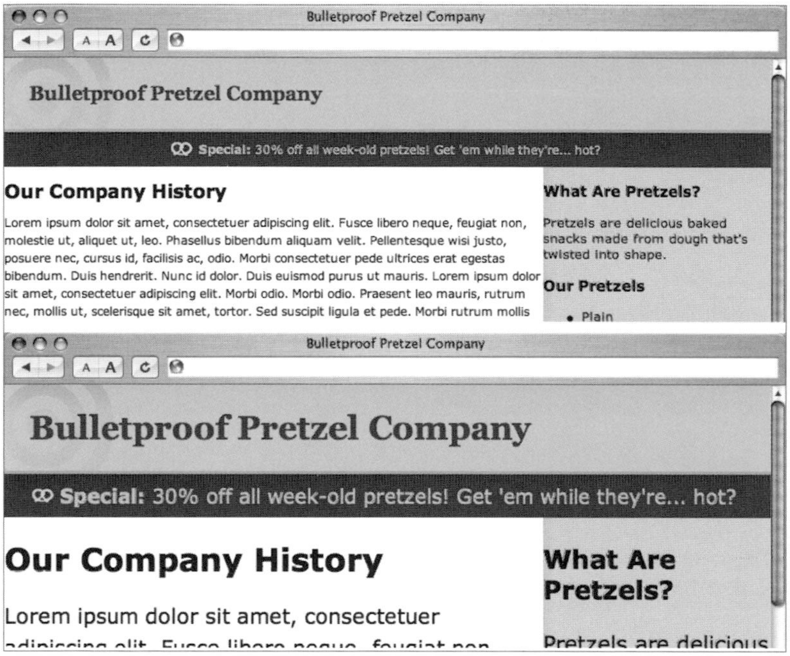

Figure 9.16 In the completed message row, an increase in text size does nothing to harm the "comb" pattern and background.

> **tip**
>
> This is a nice example of how you can creatively make bulletproofing components easier—by creating graphics that have a start point but that fade into a solid color. We allow that solid color to expand or contract, while the graphic portion stays anchored. It's the mixture of CSS-generated visuals (background colors and borders) with graphics that enable us to present adaptable designs.

GUTTERS

In order to give the content and sidebar columns a fixed amount of padding on all sides, let's next add styles for the `<div class="gutter">` that we added inside both columns:

```
/* gutters */

#content .gutter {
  padding: 25px;
```

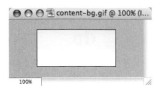

Figure 9.17 The image content-bg.gif will tile horizontally across the top of the content column.

```
    background: url(img/content-bg.gif) repeat-x top left;
  }
#sidebar .gutter {
  padding: 15px;
  }
```

To give the content and sidebar columns different values in terms of padding, we've added two declarations here. On the content column, we've added 25 pixels of padding all the way around, while in the sidebar column we've added 15 pixels of padding. We've also added that yellow gradient fade that repeats horizontally across the top, above "Our Company History." Figure 9.17 shows the image, which, when tiled, fills out the entire top of the content column.

Figure 9.18 shows our progress thus far, with the columns now sporting room to breathe between them—a *fixed* amount, regardless of screen width.

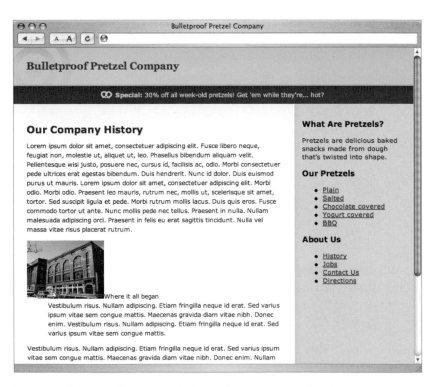

Figure 9.18 The gutters now add breathing room to each column.

CONTENT COLUMN

For the content column, we'll style the image/title/description combination that sits in the middle of the page, but first, let's add a declaration for the "Our Company History" heading that lives at the top.

Since we're using an `<h1>` for the site's title already, for the page's title we'll use the next heading level in line:

`<h2>Our Company History</h2>`

And then we'll add the simple and straightforward CSS that styles the heading:

```
/* content */

#content h2 {
  margin: 0 0 1em 0;
  padding: 0;
  font-family: Georgia, serif;
  font-size: 150%;
  font-weight: normal;
  color: #663;  }
```

In the previous declaration, we've specified styles for any `<h2>` elements that live within the content column. These headings will have only a bottom margin of 1em (or the height of one character at whatever text size the heading happens to be). Zeroing the top margin that headings have by default will tighten up the top of the content area, ensuring an even 25 pixels of padding on all sides (as we declared on the extra `<div>` used for gutters earlier).

For more interesting examples that utilize ems for sizing images or even complete layouts, see Patrick Griffiths's "Elastic Design Demonstration" (www. htmldog.com/articles/elasticdesign/demo/).

In addition, we've changed the typeface to Georgia, increased it to 150% of the base size, and assigned it an olive-green color. By default, heading elements are bold, and we've reversed that by specifying `font-weight: normal;` (because I happen to think it looks best this way on screen for this particular font).

Figure 9.19 shows the results of that simple declaration, with the title of the content column styled nicely.

 tip

I often like to use ems for margins and padding on text elements that stack on top of each other (headings, paragraphs, lists, etc. in body sections of a page), where the margins and padding will increase proportionately along with the element's text size. Unlike a pixel unit, that would remain constant regardless of text size, ems are relative units that correspond to the element's current font size. For instance, as the text size of the page is increased, our bottom margin of 1em on the `<h2>` will increase proportionately as well.

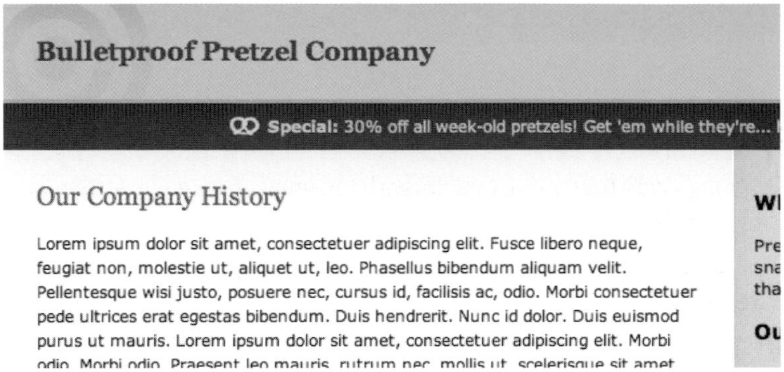

Figure 9.19 The title of the page is now styled in Georgia in a lovely shade of olive green.

With the heading now styled, let's turn our attention to the image/title/description further down the page. Recall how we handled this back in Chapter 4, "Creative Floating"; instead of using a table to lay these elements out in a grid-like fashion, we'll use a simple definition list and utilize the float property in CSS to position things as we'd like.

Remember that in the example in Chapter 4, we used the "Opposing Floats" method for positioning the title to the right of the image, while keeping the markup in an optimal order. In that example, we were dealing with a fixed-width container, which made it a bit easier to apply margins and widths to the elements to ensure they'd line up properly. This time around, since we're working with a fluid-width layout, we don't have that luxury. Instead, we'll place the image *before* the title in the markup, thus trading optimal markup order for flexibility.

So, in our markup (within the <div class="gutter"> of the content column) we'll stick the image just before the title within the <dt> element like this:

```
<dl class="feature">
  <dt><img src="img/bldg.jpg" width="150" height="113"
alt="building" />Where it all began</dt>
  <dd>Vestibulum risus. Nullam adipiscing. Etiam frin-
gilla...</dd>
</dl>
```

In a moment, we'll position that image using the `float` property to sit to the left of both the title and description. The image is just sort of jammed in there, and it may seem odd for it to be placed this way. As I mentioned before, the placement in the markup is somewhat of a trade-off because of the fluid-width layout that we're working with. Looking back at Figure 9.5, unstyled, things look pretty reasonable, with the image not really getting in the way of the title and description.

Let's start adding the styles for this component, beginning with a general declaration for the `<dl>` element itself, adding dotted lines on the top and bottom, as well as margins and padding:

```
dl.feature {
  margin: 15px 0;
  padding: 15px;
  border-top: 1px dotted #ccc;
  border-bottom: 1px dotted #ccc;
  }
```

Figure 9.20 shows the results of that single declaration. We'll tackle the positioning of the image next.

Figure 9.20 We're using a dotted border on the top and bottom, with margins and padding set for the `<dl>`.

Now we want to float the image to the left, and also give a left margin to the <dd> element, so that regardless of the amount of text, the description won't wrap around the image:

```css
dl.feature {
  margin: 15px 0;
  padding: 15px;
  border-top: 1px dotted #ccc;
  border-bottom: 1px dotted #ccc;
  }
dl.feature dt img {
  float: left;
  margin: 0 15px 0 0;
  padding: 0 4px 4px 0;
  background: url(img/photo-frame.gif) no-repeat bottom
right;
  }
dl.feature dd {
  margin-left: 169px;
  font-size: 90%;
  line-height: 1.5em;
  color: #666;
  }
```

In addition to floating the image, we've added a small shadow to the bottom-right corner of the image that acts as a subtle frame (Figure 9.21). We've added the appropriate amount of padding around that portion of the image so that it will be visible. Because this image fades to white, it could be reused on a variety of image sizes.

Figure 9.21 The image photo-frame.gif will sit to the bottom right of the image, giving it a shadow effect.

Figure 9.22 shows the results so far, where you'll notice that because we applied a left margin to the <dd> element, the text won't wrap around the image should it become longer than the image is tall. This maintains the column-like effect of the two objects sitting side by side.

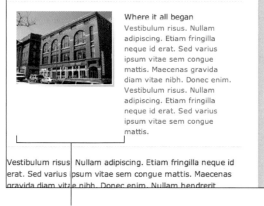

Margin

Figure 9.22 With a left margin greater than the width of the image, the two elements will stay in their respective "columns."

Next, let's style the `<dt>` element and give the title text a different font, size, and color:

```
dl.feature {
  margin: 15px 0;
  padding: 15px;
  border-top: 1px dotted #ccc;
  border-bottom: 1px dotted #ccc;
  }
dl.feature dt {
  margin: 0 0 .5em 0;
  font-family: Georgia, serif;
  font-size: 140%;
  color: #693;
  }
dl.feature dt img {
  float: left;
  margin: 0 15px 0 0;
  padding: 0 4px 4px 0;
  background: url(img/photo-frame.gif) no-repeat bottom
right;
  }
dl.feature dd {
  margin-left: 169px;
  font-size: 90%;
  line-height: 1.5em;
  color: #666;
  }
```

Figure 9.23 shows the results of turning the `<dt>` larger and bright green, with a small margin underneath to set a little spacing between it and the description.

Figure 9.23 Styling the title is made simple by adding
a few rules for the `<dt>` element.

Self-clearing

Without clearing the floated image, we run the risk of it getting in the way of
text that follows. For instance, notice in Figure 9.24 that stretching the layout
wide reduces the number of description lines and bumps the image down
into the rest of the page. We discussed several float clearing methods back in
Chapter 4. For instance, the "Float to Fix" method—that is, also floating the
container that the holds the floating image within—works especially well for
fixed-width layouts, where a predictable width can be assigned to that outer
container. In this case, however, we're utilizing a fluid-width layout, where
the description's length can vary drastically depending on the width of the
browser window.

Figure 9.24 With description text that is shorter than the floated image,
overlap occurs.

I'm going to use the "Clearing a Float Container Without Structural Markup" (a.k.a. the "Easy Clearing") method described in Chapter 4 and at Position Is Everything (http://positioniseverything.net/easyclearing.html).

You'll recall that the technique involves using the :after pseudo-class to insert (but also hide) a character after the container that clears any previous floats. Remember that the :after pseudo-class is unsupported by Internet Explorer, so we'll need to add a fix for those browsers, which we'll do later on.

So to add the self-clearing CSS to our existing image/title/description, insert the following:

```
dl.feature {
  margin: 15px 0;
  padding: 15px;
  border-top: 1px dotted #ccc;
  border-bottom: 1px dotted #ccc;
  }
dl.feature:after {
  content: ".";
  display: block;
  height: 0;
  clear: both;
  visibility: hidden;
  }
dl.feature dt {
  margin: 0 0 .5em 0;
  font-family: Georgia, serif;
  font-size: 140%;
  color: #693;
  }
dl.feature dt img {
  float: left;
  margin: 0 15px 0 0;
  padding: 0 4px 4px 0;
  background: url(img/photo-frame.gif) no-repeat bottom right;
  }
```

```
dl.feature dd {
  margin-left: 169px;
  font-size: 90%;
  line-height: 1.5em;
  color: #666;
}
```

You'll notice that the declaration inserts a period after the `<dl>` element that clears all floats that precede it but that is subsequently hidden from view. It's a neat little trick. Again, later, we'll want to address IE in a different way—and we'll do so later on in the chapter.

Figure 9.25 shows the results of the self-clearing fix, where you can see that even though the description is shorter than the image, the entire `<dl>` is cleared for the text that follows it.

Figure 9.25 With the "self-clearing" fix in place, any overlap is avoided.

SIDEBAR COLUMN

With the styling of the content column complete, let's move on to the sidebar, where we want to customize the text and lists that live there. As with the "indestructible boxes" from Chapter 5, we'll attach the rounded corners that appear on the top left and bottom right of each box (Figure 9.26). I've made it a bit easier for myself by only rounding *two* of the four corners, but I like the design effect here as well.

First, let's talk about how each box will be marked up. As we did with the example in Chapter 5, we'll use a single `<div>` to wrap the headings, lists, and paragraphs into separate, independent chunks. This will also give us just enough elements to complete the design of the boxes.

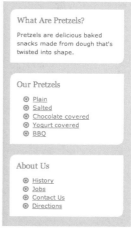

Figure 9.26 We'll create these sidebar styles that include rounded-corner boxes.

```
<div id="sidebar">
  <div class="gutter">
    <div class="box">
      <h3>What Are Pretzels?</h3>
      <p>Pretzels are delicious baked snacks made from dough
that's twisted into shape.</p>
    </div>
    <div class="box">
      <h3>Our Pretzels</h3>
      <ul>
        <li><a href="#">Plain</a></li>
        <li><a href="#">Salted</a></li>
        <li><a href="#">Chocolate covered</a></li>
        <li><a href="#">Yogurt covered</a></li>
        <li><a href="#">BBQ</a></li>
      </ul>
    </div>
    <div class="box">
      <h3>About Us</h3>
      <ul>
        <li><a href="#">History</a></li>
        <li><a href="#">Jobs</a></li>
        <li><a href="#">Contact Us</a></li>
        <li><a href="#">Directions</a></li>
      </ul>
    </div>
  </div> <!-- end .gutter -->
</div> <!-- end #sidebar -->
```

As you can see, the structure is rather straightforward, with a `<div class="box">` wrapping each segment. Heading level 3 elements are used for each box's title, followed by a paragraph or list of links.

We need just two, tiny images to achieve the rounded effect on each box. The image is the rounded portion only of the top-left and bottom-right corners. Each image is transparent with the sidebar's background around it.

Figure 9.27 shows the two rounded-corner images, zoomed in so that we can see the detail. The transparent areas of the images will be filled in by the white background color of each box.

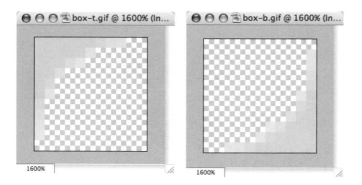

Figure 9.27 The images box-t.gif and box-b.gif will be aligned
to the top-left and bottom-right corners of each box.

Now we're ready to start adding CSS to complete the sidebar's design. First,
let's adjust margins and padding on the box itself, decreasing the text size
and adding a white background. Let's also style the <h3> elements within
each box; we'll give them even padding, and change their font, size, weight,
and color.

```
/* sidebars */

.box {
  margin: 0 0 20px 0;
  padding: 0 0 12px 0;
  font-size: 85%;
  line-height: 1.5em;
  color: #666;
  background: #fff;
  }
.box h3 {
  margin: 0;
  padding: 12px;
  font-family: Georgia, serif;
  font-size: 140%;
  font-weight: normal;
  color: #693;
  }
```

Figure 9.28 shows the results of the previous two declarations.

Figure 9.28 Giving the <div>s a white background and styling each <h3> element gives the boxes some shape.

Next, let's add the rounded-corner images in, by assigning one as a background of the box itself (bottom-right corner) and the other as a background of the heading that always sits on top (top-left corner). By attaching the two images to these two elements, we can ensure that they'll remain in their correct positions, regardless of how the box is expanded or contracted by either window width or text size adjustment.

```
/* sidebars */

.box {
  margin: 0 0 20px 0;
  padding: 0 0 12px 0;
  font-size: 85%;
  line-height: 1.5em;
```

```
  color: #666;
  background: #fff url(img/box-b.gif) no-repeat bottom right;
  }
.box h3 {
  margin: 0;
  padding: 12px;
  font-family: Georgia, serif;
  font-size: 140%;
  font-weight: normal;
  color: #693;
  background: url(img/box-t.gif) no-repeat top left;
  }
```

Figure 9.29 shows the two rounded corners in place now, with just some minor spacing issues to resolve involving the contents of the boxes.

To finish the design of the boxes, I'll add a declaration that assigns even padding on both sides of any paragraph or list items contained within, as well as a custom bullet that I've created—a mini bull's-eye:

```
/* sidebars */

.box {
  margin: 0 0 20px 0;
  padding: 0 0 12px 0;
  font-size: 85%;
  line-height: 1.5em;
  color: #666;
  background: #fff url(img/box-b.gif) no-repeat bottom right;
  }
.box h3 {
  margin: 0;
  padding: 12px;
  font-family: Georgia, serif;
  font-size: 140%;
  font-weight: normal;
  color: #693;
  background: url(img/box-t.gif) no-repeat top left;
  }
```

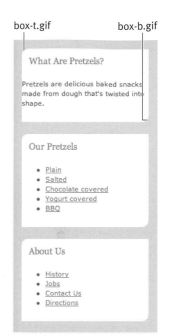

Figure 9.29 The two small corner graphics are now in place, anchored regardless of box size.

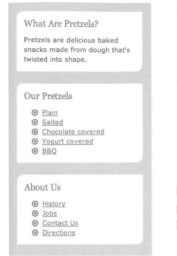

```
.box p, .box ul {
  margin: 0;
  padding: 0 12px;
  }
.box ul li {
  margin: 0 0 0 12px;
  padding: 0 0 0 18px;
  list-style: none;
  background: url(img/li-bullet.gif) no-repeat 0 3px;
  }
```

Figure 9.30 shows the completed sidebar with the left and right padding we've placed on paragraphs and lists in the sidebar, as well as the mini bull's-eye bullet that we've added as a background image to the left of each list item.

Figure 9.30 The completed sidebar has everything in place.

FOOTER

Finding ourselves now at the very bottom of the page, we just have a few simple adjustments to the footer to make. First, we'll add a tiling gradient fade that blends vertically into the solid background color. This is exactly what we've done in the header and message row areas as well. Second, we'll add padding and text styles to the paragraph that sits inside the footer to complete this portion of the page.

```
#footer {
  clear: both;
  background: #828377 url(img/footer-bg.gif) repeat-x top
left;
  }
#footer p {
  margin: 0;
  padding: 15px;
  font-size: 85%;
  color: #333;
  }
```

Figure 9.31 shows a close-up of the footer, with the text now styled with room to breathe, as well as the subtle gradient fade that tiles horizontally across the top.

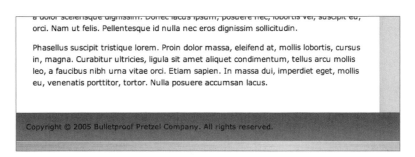

Figure 9.31 The finished footer features padding and a shadow fade across the top tiling extends horizontally; gradient fade goes from top to bottom.

Just as with the header and message row, because that gradient fades into a solid color that we've specified in the CSS, the entire footer area's background will scale gracefully as the text grows larger or more content is added (Figure 9.32).

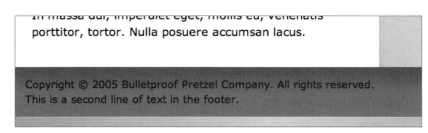

Figure 9.32 Both the increased text size and additional line of text do nothing to harm the footer's appearance.

CSS Adjustments for IE

For this particular page design, we need to address a few quirks in order for users of Internet Explorer to see things the way other, more standards-aware browsers do. For instance, if you look at our design in IE6/Win, you'll notice that the footer has a hard time properly clearing the two columns, with its background extending up into the content and sidebar (Figure 9.33).

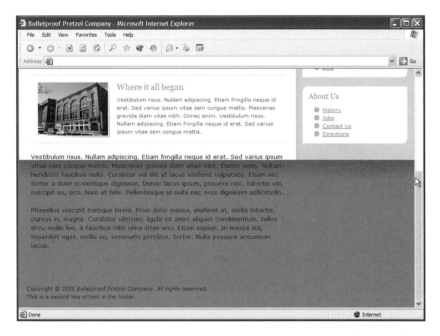

Figure 9.33 The footer renders poorly in IE6/Win and thus calls for a small CSS fix.

Before we fix this problem, it's a perfect time to talk about hack management—that is, keeping your CSS hacks separate from your clean, hack-free CSS that fully standards-aware browsers can enjoy.

HACK MANAGEMENT

There are several ways to keep things separate, and I highly recommend reading Molly Holzschlag's article, "Strategies for Long-Term CSS Hack Management" (www.informit.com/articles/article.asp?p=170511).

In her article, Molly describes utilizing various CSS filters to send hacks to appropriate browsers only, by separating the hacks into different CSS files. These filtered files are downloaded only by the browsers they are intended for, thereby saving a small amount of bandwidth (which varies depending on the amount of hacks used) for browsers that *don't* need the hacks.

Another advantage here is that just as support for older browsers can be trimmed off, so too can the CSS hacks that support them. In other words, when the time is right for a site to stop catering to IE5/Win, for example, the designer can simply delete the CSS file that contains all the hacks specific to that browser, while the hack-free CSS file remains untouched. Future-proofing is at work here.

Another big plus in keeping your primary CSS files hack-free is that they are easier to wade though. When debugging and maintaining the style sheets in the future, the hacks stay out of the way in separate files, making the hack-free CSS easier for us humans to read.

Quarantine your hacks

That said, at the very simplest, you could also quarantine all your IE CSS hacks to the *end* of the main style sheet—which makes it convenient to trim them off at a later date—rather than commingling the hacks in with the pure standards-based CSS. Or, similarly, you can put all hacks in a separate file that is referenced *after* the hack-free CSS. You won't gain the aforementioned bandwidth savings that *filtering* the separate hack files can bring, but this is usually a tiny amount.

So, hack management options are surely a good thing to investigate to keep your CSS nice and clean for the future. Regardless of where you put your hacks, let's now address the specific fixes we'll need for the Bulletproof Pretzel Company, starting with the footer.

FOOTER FIX

The simple fix for the clearing footer problem in IE/Win is the "Holly Hack," named for Holly Bergevin, who discovered it. Entire books could be filled with the explanations of CSS hacks and their related fixes, so quite simply, I'll just state that the following hack fixes the footer problem, where IE/Win needs the clearing element to have a *specified dimension*. The dimension is irrelevant, since IE/Win will always (wrongly) expand elements to fit whatever is inside them anyway, so we use `height: 1%;` to make IE/Win play nicely with

tip

Conditional comments also offer an alternate way to filter and quarantine your hacks specifically for Internet Explorer by using proprietary syntax in the <head> of the document. This syntax can be used to hide or show multiple linked style sheets to various versions of the browser, depending on its version. Because this code is contained in the markup of the document, I personally tend to avoid using conditional comments. But they do provide a powerful way of serving CSS to specific versions of IE without the need for hacking a selector (e.g., * html). Conditional comments instead allow you to set up separate CSS files for each targeted browser. For more information on conditional comments, check out this informative article by Peter-Paul Koch: http://www.quirksmode.org/css/condcom.html.

our footer. We also want to hide this rule from IE5/Mac, because it implements the height value properly, where IE/Win does not.

```
#footer { height: 1%; }
```

Next, we hide this declaration from IE5/Mac by inserting a backslash prior to the end comment before the rule:

```
/* Hide from IE5/Mac \*/
#footer { height: 1%; }
/* End hide from IE5/Mac */
```

Then we target this declaration to IE/Win only, using the star HTML hack:
```
/* Hide from IE5/Mac \*/
* html #footer { height: 1%; }
/* End hide from IE5/Mac */
```

Finally, we add a comment at the end to make sure IE5/Mac is back on track with anything that follows this declaration.

As I mentioned earlier, entire books could be devoted to explaining hacks, but this one is so common, it's certainly worth mentioning here since it relates to our working example.

SELF-CLEARING FIX

You'll recall that the "self-clearing" method for clearing the floated image in the image/title/description block does not work in IE, as we explained back in Chapter 4. Because IE doesn't support the `:after` pseudo-class, we need an alternate way of handling self-clearing floats for those browsers. Because we're keeping IE fixes and hacks separate from our clean CSS that we've previously written, it makes sense to add the fix here.

Let's add the necessary fixes to allow IE 5, 6, and 7 to self-clear any floats that happen in `<dl class="feature">`, just as we had discussed in Chapter 4:

```
* html dl.feature { height: 1%; } /* for IE5+6 */
*:first-child+html dl.feature { min-height: 1px; } /* for
IE7 /
```

When all is said and done, any floats within `<dl class="feature">` will be auto-cleared in all modern browsers. Again, this mystical voodoo might seem complex at first, but as you start reusing a few of these hacks for common purposes, they become second nature. By quarantining these fixes into their section of the style sheet or a separate file altogether, you can later easily remove them and leave clean, standards-compliant CSS intact.

Conclusion

The goal for this final chapter was to pull all the pieces that we've talked about earlier into a single example. By showing how all the various techniques work together, we hope it's clear that being bulletproof is about thinking *ahead*—planning for the unexpected. It's an ongoing process, and one that that's never 100% complete. It's never a single choice, but a series of decisions and trade-offs that, in the end, can improve a Web site's integrity and ensure that you reach the widest audience possible while still maintaining a compelling design.

The tools (XHTML and CSS) are here and ready to be used. New techniques are constantly being invented. It's an exciting time for Web designers; we can create compelling visuals that at the same time have the flexibility to convey information in as many environments and scenarios as possible.

So, I hope that you will take the guidelines and techniques explained in this book and create your own—extending the flexibility even further.

Thanks for reading!

Index

Safari.
Books Online

Get free online access to this book!

And sign up for a free trial to Safari Books Online to get access to thousands more!

With the purchase of this book you have instant online, searchable access to it on Safari Books Online! And while you're there, be sure to check out the Safari on-demand digital library and its Free Trial Offer (a separate sign-up process)—where you can access thousands of technical and inspirational books, instructional videos, and articles from the world's leading creative professionals with a Safari Books Online subscription.

Simply visit www.peachpit.com/safarienabled and enter code UXQXTYG to try it today.